Doing Business in America: A Jewish History

The Jewish Role in American Life

An Annual Review of the Casden Institute for the Study of the Jewish Role in American Life

Doing Business in America:
A Jewish History

The Jewish Role in American Life

An Annual Review of the Casden Institute for the Study of the Jewish Role in American Life

Volume 16

Steven J. Ross, *Editor*
Hasia R. Diner, *Guest Editor*
Lisa Ansell, *Associate Editor*

Published by the Purdue University Press for
the USC Casden Institute for the Study of the
Jewish Role in American Life

© 2018
University of Southern California
Casden Institute for the
Study of the Jewish Role in American Life.
All rights reserved.

Production Editor, Marilyn Lundberg

Cover photo supplied by Library of Congress Prints and Photographs Division. New York World-Telegram and the Sun Newspaper Photograph Collection. http://hdl.loc.gov/loc.pnp/cph.3c18470.
Men pulling racks of clothing on busy sidewalk in Garment District, New York City. World Telegram & Sun photo by Al Ravenna.

Cloth ISBN: 978-1-55753-836-9
ePDF ISBN: 978-1-61249-559-0
ePUB ISBN: 978-1-61249-560-6

Published by Purdue University Press
West Lafayette, Indiana
www.press.purdue.edu
pupress@purdue.edu

Printed in the United States of America.

For subscription information,
call 1-800-247-6553

Contents

Foreword

How have Jews, especially American Jews, conducted business over the past several centuries? How has their Judaism affected the ways in which they did business? These are two of the main questions explored in Volume 10 of the Casden Annual Review. Examining the history of American Jewish business at both the "street level" and across the transatlantic, our guest editor Hasia Diner has compiled a series of essays that investigate the ways in which Jews, often in concert with Christian partners, shaped a variety of business practices in the United States and Europe. Taken collectively, these essays, as Diner explains, help us understand "the deep bond between the business of Jews and the business of Jewish life."

Cutting across several centuries, volume contributors explore a wide range of topics: Jewish-Christian partnerships in the eighteenth-century transatlantic trade; the interactions of Jewish merchants and Jewish customers on Jewish streets of Baltimore, Chicago, Boston, Atlanta, New York, and a variety of twentieth-century American cities; how Jews transformed real estate and financial markets between 1870 and 1914, and how they changed popular music in the United States between the 1890s and 1945. Turning to the traumatic years of the 1930s and 1940s, our essayists describe how Jewish retailers in the United States and Europe responded to the refugee crisis between 1933 and 1945, and how one Austrian Jew fleeing Hitler's Europe drew on his Judaism to transform the textile business in Greenville, South Carolina, and later, while serving as mayor, the city itself.

A key denominator among the essays is the way in which they reveal how a commitment to Judaism and Jewish values shaped business practices across several centuries. Whether it was fulfilling a communal sense of obligation (hachnassat orchim) or a commitment to healing the world (tikkun olam), being a Jew in business contained a number of traditional expectations guided by the Torah and by longstanding ethical and religious values. This was especially true in the case of Eli Black, whose early training as a rabbi guided his subsequent efforts as a CEO to transform United Fruit into a more socially responsible business.

I wish to thank our guest editor Hasia Diner, the Paul S. and Sylvia Steinberg Professor of American Jewish History at New York University, for her stellar work. I also wish to thank Marilyn Lundberg Melzian for her tireless and superb work as our volume's copy-editor. Finally, I wish to dedicate this volume to both Stanley Gold and Bruce Ramer, two pillars of the Los Angeles Jewish business community who continue to demonstrate how the commitment to hard work and philanthropy can truly make this world a better place.

Steven J. Ross
Myron and Marian Casden Director
Professor of History

Editorial Introduction

by Hasia R. Diner

The often misquoted sentence, offered by President Calvin Coolidge in 1925, offers a way to introduce the topic of this volume, the role of Jews in the business life of America. Coolidge supposedly said, "the business of America is business," and that too would have been a fine segue into this complex and enormous topic. But in reality, in the speech he gave to the Society of American Newspaper Editors on January 17, he declared, in support of the role of the press in America's free market economy, "the chief business of the American people is business." That works even better.

Most Americans, across the centuries and the geographic breadth of the nation, met Jews in the realm of business. Regardless of race, class, or geography Americans encountered Jews, whether immigrants or those with longer roots in the nation, as the people from whom they bought goods of one kind or another. Jewish peddlers and shopkeepers, operators of urban pushcarts, the proprietors of modest dry goods stores and princes of large palatial department stores peopled the American landscape and essentially provided the human links between Jews and their non-Jewish neighbors. Through the realm of commerce, Jews made an impress on American life. In most cases their distinctively Jewish last names appeared on the windows and awnings of the stores which lined so many Main Streets and which sprang up in poor and middle class shopping districts.

Commerce also underlay the web of relationships which held Jewish communities together. Jews for the most part not only prayed with other Jews, recreated with them, married them, and were buried with them, but they also bought and sold to each other and Jewish business districts gave Jewish neighborhoods their visible and distinctive characteristics. Stores of one kind or another in which Jews encountered each other as buyers and sellers of goods helped shape community relations and those who made money from business, of whatever kind, served as the patrons of Jewish communal institutions, often assuming that they could dictate policy by virtue of their financial largesse to the *kahal,* the community.

Business as such both positioned Jews outward as they faced the larger society and inward as it shaped much of the tone of communal life. How and why did these kinds of encounters take place in America? What did it mean for Jews and for Americans? What role did America's orientation to business, embodied in the Coolidge quote, serve to draw Jewish immigrants to the United States and how did it in turn structure the kinds of relationships which developed between the small Jewish minority—which never constituted more than four or five percent of the nation—and the many Americans whom they did business? How did Jewish enclaves pivot around the world of ethnic business?

The essays which follow expose a mere sliver of this enormous topic. The larger detailed history of Jews and American business remains to be written. The historian Derek Penslar in his *Shylock's Children: Economics and Jewish Identity in Modern Europe* of 2001 challenged historians of the Jews to not shy away from contemplating the historic significance of the nexus between Jews and commerce in their research. Acknowledging that critics of the Jews, those who spewed forth anti-Jewish rhetoric, often cited the Jews' proclivity to business as evidence of their degeneracy, using it as a way to stir up hatred against the Jews, Penslar asked scholars to not worry about the sensitivity of the topic. Rather he told them to pursue it.

While this landmark book focused on Europe, America may be an equally, or maybe more, appropriate setting to uncover this history. After all, much of the Jewish migration to America, from the eighteenth century onward, a migration of millions from Europe and also the Ottoman Empire, followed the flowering of business opportunities. It more than anyplace else offered the lure of business to Jews in search of new places of residence, free from restrictions on movement and the ability to earn a comfortable living. In a provocative book, *Jewish Immigrant Entrepreneurship in New York and London,* a book which received relatively little notice, the British historian Andrew Godley noted also in 2001, that east European Jews who went to London did less well economically and moved into self-employment less often than their peers who opted for America's largest city. Godley attributed the disparity to the nature of the New York, and the American, economy, one which took root in a culture which supported, stimulated, and valorized business as the work of the nation.

So, too, a set of essays, edited by Rebecca Kobrin, aptly entitled, *Chosen Capital,* explores the many ways Jews encountered American capitalism and how many of them took as their subject the role of business in that.

The handful of snapshots that appear in the pages that follow span American and American Jewish history, extending from the eighteenth century into the late twentieth. They focus on such diverse fields of business as international shipping, rock-and-roll music, community-level banking, textile manufacturing, and more. They look at the work business did in structuring relationships between Jews and others, and the way it cemented interactions within the Jewish community.

The larger history of Jews and American business waits to be written. Indeed a whole subfield within American Jewish history which takes business seriously deserves to come into being and perhaps this volume might stimulate scholars to turn their attention to the world of commerce. Similarly historians of American business have paid scant attention to the role of Jews in the shaping of the business world, which the laconic president, Calvin Coolidge, opined constituted, "the chief business of the American people." It would certainly be worth their attention to think about the ways Jews carved out a particular niche for themselves in the American economy and how the businesses they created played a role in the economic life of the nation. This book may play a role in fostering such scholarly explorations.

JEWS AND BUSINESS: A DIASPORA STORY

This book takes America as its canvass, but the history of Jews and business in American forms only one, though important, chapter in a longer history which extends back centuries and involves much of the experience of the Jewish people in their many diaspora homes. The dispersion of the Jews from their ancient homeland at the beginning of the Common Era provides a crucial underpinning to the deep and widely practiced connection between Jews and commerce.

That history has pivoted around the centrality of trade as their métier. While in the ancient world, in their homeland, they had cultivated fields, grown crops, tended vineyards, and grazed flocks, details so vividly described in the pages of the Hebrew Bible, in their vast and long diaspora existence, they rarely engaged in these occupations. Commerce, the buying and selling of things, consumed most of their energies, although many also made a living as artisans. Those artisans, however, variously worked for Jewish merchants who sold their goods, or the craftspeople doubled as business people who also made a profit from the things they made.

Whether they sold produce grown by non-Jews who lived nearby, dealt in lumber, fur, or minerals, or if they traded in goods produced in far-off corners of the world, mattered less than the fact that wherever they went they relied on global Jewish networks for credit and goods. Whether they operated at the top echelons of these networks as wealthy importers or at the very bottom, as financiers or as on-the-road peddlers, horse traders, or sellers of old clothes, their commercial histories cannot be disassociated from diasporic ties and experiences. The Jews' ability to activate intra-communal networks facilitated their decisions, undertaken across time and space, to pick up, leave for someplace else where they would essentially do the same kind of work, albeit selling to new customers who spoke different languages, yet who still had need of the Jews' commercial skills, their human capital.[1]

Jewish life, on multiple continents lived in a plethora of languages, fostered a commitment to trade, and conversely, trade underlay the basic patterns of how and where Jews lived. The two, trade and the Jews, cannot be disentangled, or as put by the Polish Jewish historian Simon Dubnov in 1928, the two have always been "so entwined . . . they cannot be divided." Unlike the histories of "other European peoples, Jewish economic history involves not only 3,000 years," but took place across the canvas of "the whole world" (180–83).

The riddle of Jewish trade, of all kinds, whether peddling or in a fixed place, the question why so many of them gravitated to trade has puzzled scholars and commentators, both detractors and defender of the Jews, for centuries. Did, they have asked, Jews trade because they suffered disabilities all over the world, which barred them from engaging in that most fundamental and normal activity by which most human beings "earned their bread," namely agriculture? Did, particularly starting in the medieval period, the exclusion of Jews from the guilds relegate them to commerce, either commerce in fixed shops or commerce plied on the roads, with Jewish merchants carrying their misery and goods on their backs?[2]

Additionally, the long history of Jewish forced migrations which, commencing even before the onset of the Common Era, has been enlisted as an explanation of the fact that wherever and whenever they lived, Jews turned to trade in one form or another. As perpetual outsiders, always strangers and different than the autarkic people of the places where they resided, they could not assume that they would be able to remain in place, unchallenged in their right of residence. After all, they had once lived and even thrived in Spain, the Rhine Valley, the south of France, and England, four places from which they experienced painful expulsions. Those expulsions as well as others less famous conditioned them to cast their lot with trade, investing in assets that they could carry with them to wherever they went next and to hone skills transferrable from one place to another.

Even if not actually expelled, they endured sporadic waves of violence, massacres like those which convulsed Europe at the time of the Crusades and in the middle of the seventeenth century, and this too pushed Jews to seek new places that seemed to offer both greater security and enhanced prospects for making a living. Intuiting that they might have to pick up and leave a place quickly, the logic runs, conditioned Jews to turn to trade, something they could do anyplace. It constituted their movable asset.

These negative explanations of the Jewish proclivity towards trade assume that Jews would have, if circumstances or the law had allowed, become farmers and lived like all the majority of the world's population, tilling the soil and building a life that took its basic structure from the needs and rhythm of the agricultural life. But other more positive explanations have been enlisted to puzzle out the origins of the Jewish encounter with trade. These positive explanations, and not positive in the sense of good or correct, have rather asserted that something about the Jews themselves facilitated their embrace of trade. The Jews, according to this way of thinking, had a nose for business.

Some commentators, many of whom can be considered anti-Semites, presented biological or instinctive explanations. The innate Jewish character included a compulsion to trade, and with that a proclivity to cheat, and to do anything for profit. Their greed and materialism inspired their economic activities, from the peddler trudging the road to the financiers who controlled the world economy, as presented so graphically and grotesquely in the *Protocols of the Elders of Zion*. This racialized analysis in its extreme culminated in the writings of scientific racists of the late nineteenth century, which in turn received their most elaborate and horrific embodiments in Nazi rhetoric and policy.

Even if not categorically racist, many of the foundational figures of the field of sociology and political economy saw the Jew as fundamentally business-obsessed whether because of his religion, which allowed him to treat non-Jews differently than his own people, or his basic nature, which some writers attributed to his more highly developed intellect, a factor which facilitated business transactions. Karl Marx, the most complicated of these, in his "The

Jewish Question" of 1844 suggested, "Let us look at the actual. . . Jew of our time . . . the Jew of everyday life. What is the Jew's foundation in our world? Material necessity, private advantage. What is the object of the Jew's worship in this world? Usury/huckstering. What is his worldly god? Money . . . Money is the zealous god of Israel." As to peddlers, Marx did not ignore them. The Jewish peddler with "his goods and his counter on his back," thought only of making money . . . the bill of exchange is the real god of the Jews" (quoted in Arkin). With a bit more subtlety, Werner Sombart in 1911, in *The Jews and Modern Capitalism*, reiterated how Judaism as a religious system, undergirded by its canonical texts of Torah and Talmud, enabled the Jew, "*homo Judaeus*" to transform himself into "*homo capitalisticus.*"[3]

The history of Jews and trade could be perhaps better understood in terms of their long history as a migratory people. Millennia of global migrations liberated the Jews from the limitations and rigors of farming and allowed them to trade. Not tied down to fields and vineyards, they could see and seize new opportunities which allowed them to move. This point constitutes the starting point for historian Yuri Slezkine's 2004, *The Jewish Century*, in which he labels the Jews, their engagement with commerce, its portability, and the ease with which they migrated, as "mercurians," as the world's best migrants. To Slezkine, the synergy between business, migrations, and the Jews, made them the standard bearers of modernity.

Those migrations created vast Jewish networks across continents rendering the Jews a world-wide people whose communal contacts made it possible for them to secure credit and gain access to goods, through Jewish channels, regardless of where the individual Jewish trader may have lived. That transnational Jewish world, embedded in religious practice, undergirded by education and literacy, linked by the idea of collective responsibility, and the ties of trade in turn stimulated linguistic flexibility, which also shaped Jewish economic history (Muller; Karp; Israel; Botticini and Eckstein).

Because of their centuries' long immersion in world trade, Jews stood poised to take advantage, and indeed help shape, modernity and the emergence of capitalism. Business demanded of them a need to be aware of new markets, new products, and new tastes which all had to come together to inspire women and men to want to consume items they had never had before. Whether luxury goods, textiles, jewelry, furs, hides, watches, eye glasses, coffee, among others, Jewish traders depended on the expansion of markets and the accumulation of capital. Freed from a commitment to any land—England, France, Westphalia, Podolia—or any plot of land within some political jurisdiction, not chained to landowners like the serfs, then peasants, they had much to gain by following their hunches that told them that some new place offered opportunities for a better future, a better field of operation for them to do what they had long been doing, buying and selling. For many scholars, this long history helps not only contextualize the deep history of Jews and trade, but goes a long way to understanding their relationship to capitalism in the modern period (Chazan).

Counter to the notion that Jews turned to trade because anti-Jewish restrictions prevented them from doing anything else, it in fact liberated them from agriculture, from its unpredictability and its rootedness in a single and fixed place. Likewise, in numerous times and places, trade actually protected the Jews. Jews brought goods to towns, regions, principalities, and nations, enriching the coffers of the state, and extending credit and this in most places ensured that the Jews would be allowed to stay, even if they had no formal rights. Jews as merchants often played a crucial role in mediating between the poor agriculturalists who did the basic work of the society and the landowners. Jewish peddlers exchanged goods for agricultural products and engineered the transactions between fields and marketplaces, relying on a chain of Jewish middle-men who facilitated each rung of the operation. This too, while at many times inspiring hatred and resentment against the Jews or the particular Jewish business person, made possible the basic operation of the local economy. The Jew who brought the wheat or flax to market, who negotiated the sale price and provided the peasant farmers with goods, occupied a crucial niche in maintaining the status quo. The Emperor Franz in 1795, the august ruler of the Austro-Hungarian Empire who issued an edict of toleration towards his Jewish subjects, lauded in particular the very humble Jewish peddlers, the lowest on the ladder of Jewish business endowing them with a privileged status:

> Since peddling promotes and multiplies the more rapid trade of manufactured products . . . for the benefit of the producers, and also creates the advantage for the greater part of consumers that they may obtain some wares more cheaply than in stores, and given that each individual is free to buy from the peddler or merchant, peddling thus belongs among the useful trades and livelihoods; thus one does not put an end to it because of abuses, which creep into all human interactions, but rather only the abuses are to be dealt with. (Penslar 33)

Those with political power recognized the Jews' crucial place in this system, protecting at least the useful Jews from expulsion and harassment. Not discounting or diminishing the history of expulsions or dismissing the reality that as Jews in deeply religious Christian and Muslim societies they faced a kind of omnipresent danger, in most cases and at most times, Jews did not find themselves cast out and wandering the roads in search of some safe place to live. Trade, whether high end or low end, provided some modicum of security to an otherwise insecure existence (Jersch-Wenzel 95).

Explanations which see trade as liberating for the Jews rather than as the negative result of discrimination have also emphasized the absence of any distrust of business and material acquisition within their religious system. Their holy books which set the terms of Jewish law accepted business dealings as normal but regulated them to soften the worst abuses which could result from individuals pursuing profit. They prayed on their holy days for the blessings not only of health and well-being, but of *parnassah,* literally business.

Jews traded also because they could. Judaism mandated universal male literacy in Hebrew and not coincidentally trade required the ability to read and write, as well as to do sums, keep account books, calculate percentages, even know something about world geography. Throughout the Jewish world, over the course of centuries, young people grew up with trade all around them. They breathed in the idea, almost from the air around them, learning from life itself, that business defined everyday life itself, and since trade depended upon numeracy and literacy, upon linguistic flexibility, young people entered adulthood knowing with a degree of certainty that they would trade. To them, the circumstances of the Jews made business seem just the normal and expected thing to do, whether they entered the field among the lucky few at the higher echelons or the more typical masses who inhabited the lower ones, including the peddlers. The reality that trade demanded literacy and that the Jewish tradition did so also further cemented the bond between trade and Jewish life.

Both their religion and their livelihood pivoted on access to the written word. These two needs for literacy conjoined with each other. Other matters of Jewish life fostered trade, and conversely trade sustained Jewish ties and commitments. Judaism mandated that Jews provide *hachnassat orchim,* hospitality for visitors. It required that they as individuals or through the aegis of their organized communities had to make available places for Jewish wayfarers to lodge, partake of kosher food, and spend Sabbath and holidays. Jewish merchants in pursuit of goods and customers in need of such services found Jewish communities as hospitable waystations on the roads of business.

Trade in fact brought Jews from one region into the homes, synagogues, and communal institutions of others, with the bonds of Jewishness far surpassing the potential suspicion of strangers. Jews in one place, as they hosted Jewish merchants in their time off the road, developed an understanding that Jewishness overshadowed differences in terms of place of origin or dialect. Business essentially forged the Jews' global chain of belonging (Shulvass).

Jewish communities took their shape from trade, in as much as all credit came from within the Jewish world. The well-off gave credit and goods to the poor merchants who in turn extended credit to even smaller operatives, down to the peddlers. The larger Jewish merchants depended upon the more humble ones to sell their goods, and Jewish enclaves functioned as virtual lending institutions, making religious life, collective identity, and business dealings tightly intertwined. When Jews moved either as individuals, families, or as full communities, they turned to the Jews already resident in these places to facilitate their adjustment, to help them settle in, and not coincidentally, to get started in business. In Europe, furthermore, ties of trade, from the top to the bottom, depended on a common language, and from approximately the year 1000, Yiddish in its many variants served as the Jews' *lingua franca*. Hebrew also came to be used by Jews as the language of contracts. Trade, like belief and adherence to the Judaic system, held the Jews together.

While trade united Jews together, it also stimulated intra-Jewish class antagonisms. The concentration of Jews in business, and in particular in a relatively narrow swathe of business, meant that Jews essentially competed with each other. Which peddler had access to the best stash of goods? Which shopkeepers could get their hands on the newest items with which to entice customers? Within families, offspring rivaled each other for an opportunity to get started and make a living in the exact same line of work.

This competition became particularly acute by the latter part of the eighteenth century as the size of the Jewish population skyrocketed, while the first stirrings of industrialization and economic modernization challenged the Jews' long standing economic role. As the poor merchants, whether peddlers or stationery ones, relied upon the same merchants to provide goods and credit and while Jewish law required that they not encroach on each other's livelihood, the fact of being in the same enterprise involved a competitive reality that made for communal tension.

Also, as a few Jews operated businesses which did spectacularly well, and others, in increasing numbers, languished at the bottom, resentment spread from top down and bottom up, challenging Jewish unity. Describing seventeenth century Italy—but it could be applied to other situations—one historian has noted, "two different sorts of Jewry-laws existed, one for the privileged loan bankers and one for the *universita' degli ebre,* a miserable proletariat of peddlers, second-hand dealers, woolcarders and ragpickers" (Wischnitzer xix).

Regardless of the explanation for the Jewish embrace of commerce, it had been a fact of life for them. Certainly some Jews did make a living in crafts and artisans always took their place in Jewish communities. But most of the artisans sold their products directly to the public, erasing the difference between commerce and craft. But even with that, the balance, between trade and craft, favored trade. Within the context of trade, peddling functioned as part of an integrated Jewish economy which descended from wealthy importers and international merchants down multiple steps with the peddlers as merely the bottom of that hierarchy.

JEWS AND THE BUSINESS OF AMERICA

Jews came to America with business opportunities on their mind. It served as the powerful magnet which drew them in and even those who knew that their first American steps would take place as sweat shop operatives and workers in garment factories still came as a result of business. The massive transfer of the Jewish population, mostly from Europe to America came with the dynamic development of the American economy and the mushrooming of business opportunities. In the century from the 1820s to the 1920s one-third of the Jewish population of Europe crossed some national border to find newer and better homes. About 85% of them chose the United States, and also its predecessor colonies, bringing these millions of Jews from places of low productivity and stagnant development to the most dynamic economy in the world.

America from its earliest days until well into the twentieth century experienced a constant and chronic labor shortage, set amidst the vast natural resources waiting to be exploited. This reality undergirded the entire European immigrant flood to America, including that of the Jews. And like all other Europeans Jews left settled places where economic opportunities did not exist for them and opted for America where they did. While the American Jewish communal narrative has emphasized outbreaks of anti-Jewish violence in Europe, the pogroms in particular, as the engines which drove the population transfer, analytically the more mundane story of a group of people, Jews, who sought out places to live better, and ultimately live well, has greater validity. In this draw of America, the world of business loomed large.

The American-Jewish economic fit reflected the long history of Jews and commerce and the long-observed, and often deprecated, American proclivity towards material acquisition. Few foreign commentators on American life failed to notice the desire of its people to acquire and own stuff. Americans, observed from the early nineteenth century onward, seemed to want more and what they wanted had to be bigger and better. No real tradition of asceticism ran through American life, much to the chagrin of a handful of intellectual, ideological, and sometimes religious critiques of American acquisitiveness.

If they wanted more pots and pans, dresses and shoes, table cloths and towels, someone had to provide it. In nearly every period of American Jewish history we can see a confluence between American material needs, or better, wants, and Jewish economic skills, the ability of Jews to sell to Americans the things they wanted.

Let me briefly sketch out three eras in American Jewish history as they reveal this symbiotic relationship. In the earliest decades, in the eighteenth century, the British colonies of North America and the Caribbean existed in large measure to facilitate international trade. Jews, both the Sephardim who actually became the minority by the 1740s, with their roots in the Iberian Peninsula and the Netherlands, and their far flung family members in the "Levant," as well as the larger group of Ashkenazim from Poland who operated at the lower and domestic end of this international commercial network, helped do what the colonial authorities wanted, extract profit. Commerce between the "mother country" and the colonies as well as the importation of slaves from Africa, created a highly lucrative and integrated Atlantic world of trade, designed to benefit Britain. Jews, with their global Jewish trading connections that spanned Europe, the Mediterranean basin, and around the Atlantic, while small in number, helped make possible what we used to call the "triangular trade route." While not alone in fueling the development of the Americas, they used their Jewish contacts to help ensure that goods and capital moved from one point to the next. Jews in the American colonies gained acceptance in the eyes of both colonial officials and the vastly larger non-Jewish population for their contribution to both the Empire's riches and the usefulness which the colonies could show to London-based officials.

From the middle of the nineteenth century into the earliest years of the twentieth as the American white population moved westward to the remote and least settled areas, families and communities of "settlers" articulated a desire for cosmopolitan goods. The westward movement of Americans across the continent made it possible for the commercial interests to gain access to vast stretches of "uninhabited" land which could be farmed, mined, and logged. The nation's penetration of the hinterlands, romantically and jingoistically, described as "manifest destiny," required capital, and it required women and men willing to work the land, fell the forests, dig the mines, lay the railroad tracks, and the like. It also needed intermediaries to bring to these people the kinds of "stuff" that made it bearable for them to live in these undeveloped places.

Some central and east European Jews met America on the shifting peddlers' frontier. Tens of thousands of Jewish men, well-acquainted with itinerant merchandising after centuries of life in Europe, turned their long time economic niche into an American opportunity. The Jewish peddlers, many of whom graduated to becoming the owners of Jewish dry goods stores in the small towns which served the hinterlands, the Jewish retailers in the big cities who outfitted the peddlers, the Jewish owners of scrap and junk yards, and the Jewish tailors who sewed the clothes which then traveled in the peddlers' wagons and ended up on the bodies of rural dwellers, made up a Jewish economy that served the basic needs of the expanding United States. While behind this historic drama lay many complicated economic and political relationships, on the surface what transpired involved a marriage between Americans' desire for consumer goods—buttons, thread, needles, curtains, eye glasses, mirrors, pictures and picture frames, fabric and ready-to-wear clothing—and the willingness of Jews to pick up the familiar peddler's pack and venture out to pretty much anywhere they could find paying customers.

So many of the Jews who began as peddlers graduated to becoming settled merchants who in turn met their non-Jewish neighbors, regardless of race, religion, place or origin, or language, across their store counters, where they made sales, exchanged mundane pleasantries and helped create America's retail life. In white neighborhoods and in African-American ones, Jews sold stuff. In Irish, Polish, and other enclaves peopled by immigrants from central and eastern Europe, stores popped up with Jewish proprietors satisfying the needs of the local residents. Throughout the American South, for example, people referred unselfconsciously to "the Jew store," and if they meant it pejoratively or not, they daily made the connection between Jews and business (Suberman).

By the 1860s yet another match took place between American economic needs and Jewish history, generated by business. The expansion of the garment industry which began with the invention of the sewing machine at nearly the same moment in time as the Civil War, coincided with a series of linked, but independent developments, which transformed not just America but European Jewry. Late nineteenth century urbanization resulted in the movement of hundreds of thousands of young women out of rural areas and off their family farms into the cities. They flooded into industrial and white collar jobs in the years before marriage. This took place simultaneously with the rise of the advertising industry, the emergence of "style" as something within the reach of working class women, new sanitary standards, all of which led to the reality that by the end of the nineteenth century the garment industry took off as one of the most dynamic sectors of the American economy.

Factories, heavily although not exclusively housed in New York, sewed the garments which clothed women and men around America and the world. The ready-to-wear clothing industry spread its dresses and blouses, shirtwaists, hats, and undergarments around the nation and the world fueling American economic development. In this sector Jews as the employers, that is, the business owners, and workers found, and helped create, their special niche. Jews in Europe had long made a living by means of the needle, but in America, they could use that lowly skill to create a vast enterprise which did nothing less than clothe Americans and others, employ in massive numbers successive streams of Jewish immigrants, as well as others, both women and men.

In addition this field with its relatively low need for start-up capital provided to Jews one of the few means by which immigrant industrial laborers could move into the ranks of the employing class. The almost iconic story of the tragic Triangle Shirtwaist Fire of March 25, 1911 stands as a representative moment in the particular history of the garment business as a Jewish enterprise. The two owners of the factory, Max Blanck and Isaac Harris both had immigrated to America from Russian Poland and had begun their American careers, like so many others, as sweatshop laborers. These two managed to scrape together enough money to first open their sweatshop and then move up to owning the largest, most modern factory in the trade, the Triangle Company, housed in the Asch Building. While the details of the fire, the details of the harrowing fate of the victims, the responses of the state of New York, and the powerful words and actions of the union, its women leaders in particular, are enshrined in the annals of American history, the story focuses less on the fact of this as a Jewish business story. Two immigrant Jews went into their peoples' business and by a quite conventional Jewish route made the journey from employee to employer, from laborer to business owner.

These three examples, the many others which cannot be encompassed in either this brief introductory essay or even in the articles which appear in this edited volume, should make it abundantly clear that the business of America involved the Jews as well and the efflorescence of business opportunities exercised a powerful stimulant to the great Jewish migration across the Atlantic. The history of Jewish business in America not only transformed Jewish life but touched the lives of so many Americans.

Let me offer a word of thanks to Professor Steven Ross of the University of Southern California and the Director of the Myron and Marion Casden Institute for the Study of the Role of Jews in American Life for inviting me to conceptualize and edit this volume. Working with him and with Lisa Deborah Ancel and Marilyn Lundberg Melzian, also of USC, who shepherded me and the authors through this process, has been a pleasure. I also want to thank the wonderful group of historians whose works appear here, who agreed to contribute to this volume, which I hope will take a place of pride alongside the other volumes produced by the Casden Institute.

Notes

1. The economic history of the modern Jewish diaspora can be seen in Diner; Teller and Kobrin.
2. Jews clearly functioned as craftsmen as well as traders and a literature exists from the nineteenth century onward trying to prove how artisanship equaled trade as the focus of Jewish economic activity. Most of these craftsmen, however, also sold their goods either directly to the public or, more often, relied on Jewish merchants, including peddlers to get those goods to customers. As such, artisanship did not exist independent of trade.
3. For excerpts from these see Perry and Schweitzer 75–89; see also Mayer.

Works Cited

Arkin, Marcus. *Aspects of Jewish Economic History.* Jewish Publication Society, 1975.

Botticini, Maristella, and Zvi Eckstein. *The Chosen Few: How Education Shaped Jewish History, 70–1492.* Princeton Univ., 2012.

Chazan, Robert. *Reassessing Jewish Life in Medieval Europe.* Cambridge Univ., 2010.

Diner, Hasia R. *Roads Taken: The Great Jewish Migrations to the New World and the Peddlers Who Forged the Way.* Yale Univ., 2016.

Dubnov, Simon. "Voss Felt in Unzer Economisher Geshikhte." *Shriftn far Economic un Statistic,* edited by Jacob Leschinsky, vol. 2, YIV, Economic and Statistical Branch, 1928.

Godley, Andrew. *Jewish Immigrant Entrepreneurship in New York and London, 1880–1914.* Palgrave, 2001.

Israel, Jonathan. *European Jewry in the Age of Mercantilism: 1550–1750.* Clarendon, 1985.

Jersch-Wenzel, Stefi. "Jewish Economic Activity in Early Modern Times." *In and Out of the Ghetto: Jewish-Gentile Relations in Late Medieval and Early Modern Germany,* R. Po-Chia Hsia and Hartmut Lehmann, Cambridge Univ., 1995, pp. 91–101.

Karp, Jonathan. *The Politics of Jewish Commerce: Economic Ideology and Emancipation in Europe, 1638–1848.* Cambridge Univ., 2008.

Kobrin, Rebecca, editor. *Chosen Capital: The Jewish Encounter with American Capitalism.* Rutgers Univ., 2012.

Mayer, Gustav. "German Socialism and Jewish Emancipation." *Jewish Social Studies* vol. 1, no. 4, Oct, 1939, pp. 409–22.

Mendelsohn, Adam. *The Rag Race: How Jews Sewed Their Way to Success in America and the British Empire.* New York Univ., 2014.

Muller, Jerry Z. *Capitalism and the Jews.* Princeton Univ., 2010.

Penslar, Derek. *Shylock's Children: Economics and Jewish Identity in Modern Europe.* Univ. of California, 2001.

Perry, Marvin, and Frederick M. Schweitzer. *Antisemitic Myths: A Historical and Contemporary Anthology.* Indiana Univ., 2008.

Shulvass, Moses. *From East to West: The Westward Migration of Jews from Eastern Europe during the Seventeenth and Eighteenth Centuries.* Wayne State Univ., 1971.

Slezkine, Yuri. *The Jewish Century.* Princeton Univ., 2004.

Suberman, Stella. *The Jew Store.* Algonquin Books at Chapel Hill, 1998.

Teller, Adam, and Rebecca Kobrin, editors. *Purchasing Power: The Economics of Modern Jewish History.* Univ. of Pennsylvania, 2015.

Wischnitzer, Mark. *A History of Jewish Crafts and Guilds.* Jonathan David, 1965.

CHAPTER 1

American Jewish Business:
At the Street Level

by Hasia R. Diner

*T*he history of business as a decisive factor in American Jewish life can be charted as a global matter and as a national one. Jews conducted their businesses from America around the world and across the nation. Business, the buying and selling of goods, the extension of credit and the financing of money-making enterprises grounded Jews in America to constant national and transnational projects, extending over time from the seventeenth century.

But business also took place at the most intimate local level and American Jewish communities, large and small, took their basic shape from business, from commerce and consumption. While Jewish communities served histori-cally as places where Jews worshipped together, provided charity, protected each other, and fulfilled basic religiously-shaped needs including marriage, burial, circumcision, education, and the like, they also derived much from the fact that they existed as places where Jews bought from other Jews and where Jews sold to their co-religionists. These communities functioned as places where Jews extended credit to each other, employed each other, and relied on their co-religionists as customers and purveyors of goods.

Indeed the life of Jewish enclaves hummed around the constant flurry of buying and selling that took place on "the Jewish street" with no clear line sepa-rating the religious, social, and political definitions of "Jewish community" and the flow of goods among Jews. Rather, the commercial transactions, the "buzz" of the Jewish marketplace made the other, presumably loftier functions possible, at the same time that stores and other kinds of commercial places often did double-duty as either formal or informal community centers.

Wherever and whenever Jews coalesced to form communities, they transacted business with each other and made the exchange of goods for money a key element of in-group interaction. What differed from place to place and across time reflected changing Jewish residential patterns, differentials in the size of Jewish communities, technological developments which affected how goods got bought and sold, and the degree to which the state regulated economic activities. But regardless of the historic moment and the geography, commerce and consumption helped make community and provided physical locations for the kinds of interactions among Jews that fostered connectedness, a key element of community.

Buying and selling among and between Jews lay at the heart of Jewish life in as much as Jewish enclaves thrived upon the commercial relationships which brought Jews into constant contact with each other, whereby the marketplace took its basic characteristic from the flow of the Jewish calendar, and according to which Jewish neighborhoods thrummed according to a tempo set by Jewish merchants who provided goods to Jewish customers. They in turn demanded that Jewish entrepreneurs satisfy their yearnings for particular goods, at specified times, and in particular ways. Consumer and entrepreneur depended upon each other, spinning a web of reciprocal relationships which bound them together. While conflict also, and indeed always, characterized intra-Jewish commercial transactions, the degree to which Jews depended upon each other for basic and special goods, invested the entrepreneurial sector with cultural meaning and made it a vehicle for creating and sustaining community.

Whether the commercial transactions functioned smoothly and harmoniously, or conflict arose as the two groups sparred with each other on matters such as cost versus quality, their continuous interactions with each other created a common business zone, forging intimate connections which provided the bedrock of community life. Whole histories of Jewish communities could in fact be told from the vantage point of the mundane reality that wherever Jews lived they sold to and bought from each other, and the shopping street, no less than the synagogue, the study house, the ritual bath, cemetery, or community center, forged the bonds of mutuality.

The sellers and the buyers each played crucial roles in the chain of relationships which made community possible. Those who hoped to make a profit, obviously the merchants, and those who yearned to purchase desired items of the highest quality for the lowest price, the consumers, probably had in mind merely their own instrumental and petty goals when facing each other. Doubtless neither party to the transaction thought "community" when they saw the other across the counters of thousands upon thousands of Jewish-owned shops, nor did they consciously ponder the fact that by purchasing or selling a loaf of bread, a pad of paper, or a pair of socks, that they helped sustain the collective Jewish life and that their behaviors constituted historically significant actions. They probably had no reason to see beyond the shelves and the cash registers in the stores and the larders and cabinets of their homes.

The complicated processes involved in the purveying and purchasing of goods within Jewish communities can and ought to be historicized, divided into categories of analysis, yet always linked to ideas about community. The ordinariness of selling and shopping did not make the matter historically irrelevant. Rather the quotidian commercial concerns of Jewish communities gave them deep social, cultural, and political meanings.[1]

That businesses, large and small, wholesale and retail, served larger communal purposes obviously transcends the history of Jews in America or anywhere. As one historian of shopping as a factor in English social history noted, "Wherever we live, whoever we are, our shopping is very much a reflection of ourselves" (Harrison 5). Most of the literature, however, has tended to emphasize the nature of goods up for sale, patterns of consumption, and changing tastes (see McCracken). Few, either focusing on the United States or elsewhere, and whether historically based or concerned with the contemporary, have twinned the idea of community with that of commerce. Yet shopping streets, wherever and whenever they developed, functioned as common space, places where individuals met, interacted, saw what they shared with each other, and in the process of buying and selling carved out a zone for public life.

Therefore, how and where Jews bought goods, how they used commercial spaces for communal purposes, and what kinds of relationships existed between merchants and customers ought to be part of our scholarly projects. Opening up the category of community to the ubiquitous issue of buying and selling broadens the analytic framework in general and also makes relatively ordinary Jewish people, women as shoppers and sellers, in particular, key players in the creation of community.

Jews did not alone function in communities based on local, everyday business. In the context of American history we have examples from a number of subfields as to the importance of retail space in the forging of community ties. Studies of small town life, both the empirical and the nostalgic, have made much about the country store as a gathering place that bound people together. Lewis Atherton in his 1954 homage to the dying small towns of the midwest, the "middle border," offered an entire chapter to the shopping areas of the towns which served primarily farm families. In particular he pointed to the classic general store, a place where men and women congregated in different areas and where "close to the stove and the conversation" the shopkeeper tallied his ledger and supervised the flow of the shopping. *Main Street on the Middle Border* also made emotionally and historically significant the barbershops, hotels, saloons, and livery stables that lined the village thoroughfares and where men and women met, bought, sold, talked, and made community (44). The Reifel store in Four Corners, Iowa, a town analyzed by historian Carol Coburn, provided the men of this rural, heavily German community with "a gathering place at night . . . where they gathered to exchange the latest news." The store, as analyzed by Coburn, served as the least problematic, and most positive, common denominator for the men who otherwise divided over matters of politics, religious doctrine, and the lure of American culture. Only the store functioned as an uncontested community space (22).

The histories of all minority communities, like the German enclave of Four Corners, could be told from the vantage point of the ethnic marketplace and the multiple functions served by the buying and selling of goods within the community. No immigrant or ethnic community existed without the commercial infrastructure in which group members shopped in stores owned by co-ethnics and in particular imagined those shops to be key places to fulfill group needs. John Bodnar has elevated the ethnic merchants in *The Transplanted* to their rightful place as community leaders, noting in this broad synthetic book, that "In every settlement a group emerged to pursue entrepreneurial ventures which depended upon the support of the immigrant community." He offers then bits and pieces of evidence drawn from numerous histories of various groups which demonstrate how ethnic neighborhood businesses served "neighborhood clienteles," although he does not go much further than that in analyzing the role played by those stores in enabling communities to form (131–38).

The historical scholarship on nearly every ethnic group has been replete with listings and descriptions of food establishments, bookstores, music stores, taverns, and clothing stores which through commerce made it possible to "be" a participant in the ethnic project. The more sophisticated of these studies, like George Sanchez's *Becoming Mexican American* put such ethnic businesses as record shops and clothing stores squarely into the analytic framework, showing how merchants and consumers mediated between "old world" formats and American realities and how the stores functioned as meeting places for Mexicans in Los Angeles, thereby creating sites for the growing community. In Sanchez's Boyle Heights record shops, merchants not only arbitrated between the many musical formats derived from various regions in Mexico and between music defined as Mexican versus American, but the music emanating from the shops drew customers in, put them in conversation with the merchants, with each other, and solidified notions of Mexicanness and community membership. Lizabeth Cohen's *Making of a New Deal* charted the close relationships which existed in Chicago's immigrant neighborhoods between shopkeepers and customers, co-ethnics. The former not only provided needed goods to the latter, but by offering credit to struggling families, the grocers became brokers in the political and economic life of the communities.

Notably, though, few historians, studying any ethnic community in the United States, have done more than mention in passing the vast amount of commerce that linked merchants and customers of the various enclaves. Histories of one group or another contain what might be seen as an obligatory paragraph or two on the range of stores that community members favored and sustained, drawing attention to which goods shoppers preferred. The historians have, by and large, not paused longer to actually study the phenomenon directly, systematically, or thoroughly.

Rather, political scientists and sociologists studying the post-1965 immigration have drawn our attention to the analytic gravitas of entrepreneurship (and consumership) in the construction of ethnic communities. Ivan Light and Edna Bonacich, for example, in their study of Korean *Immigrant Entrepreneurs* in Los Angeles have provided a theoretical model which distinguishes between an entity they called "the ethnic economy" which, unlike the "ethnic *enclave* economy" does not require "locational clustering of ethnic firms, nor does it require that ethnic firms service members of their ethnic group as customers or buy from coethnic suppliers" (xi). Like sociologist Alejandro Portes in his numerous studies of the Cuban enclave economy of Miami, Light and Bonacich, invest significant analytic significance in the social, economic, and political implications of the clustering of Korean-owned businesses located in the heart of Los Angeles' "Korean Town," and the almost inexorable draw of those stores for the residents of the neighborhood.

Historians of ethnic communities in the United States might indeed learn much from the work of the social scientists who focus now on the contemporary processes of immigration and ethnicization. The latter observe these developments as they unfold and see, how crucial a role the ethnic markets play the streets of America's new immigrant neighborhoods.

Enclave commerce ran through American Jewish history and that history points to the intricate links between business and the ways in which American Jews lived in their Jewish communities. Not only did the buying and selling of Jewish "stuff" have long historic roots but those ordinary, constantly repeated commercial acts lay close to the heart of what it meant for American Jews to live in their Jewish communities. American Jews invested meaning in their marketplaces, and defined them as key sites in the construction of both identity and lived life.

In terms of types of Jewish commercial transactions as they lay at the center of the history of Jewish community life a number of categories suggest themselves. First, some of the goods that flowed along the Jewish commercial chain fell clearly in the domain of what has commonly been assumed to be essential to the practice of Judaism. As such the commercial sector never stood apart from the religious. Merchants who sold kosher foods, those who marketed particular delicacies associated with Sabbath and holidays, those who enticed customers with new clothing for festivals, as well as the merchants who displayed new pots and pans, crockery and cutlery in the weeks before Passover provided the material underpinnings that enabled holy time to be marked and lived. Likewise the sellers of books, almanacs, greeting cards, magazines, candles, and various objects which carried religious or ethnic valence, acted through the medium of their commercial transaction as religious functionaries. Their displaying and selling of particular "things" on a weekly or seasonal basis fostered a Jewish tone and helped infuse the streets with a sense of Jewish time.

For those who purchased these goods, their many and repeated acts of shopping and the range of merchants they depended upon to secure these goods, all made possible such sacred acts as marking the Sabbath, making the holiday, and the fulfillment of a continuous set of other religious mandates. Indeed given the degree to which Judaism functioned first and foremost as a home and family based religious system, the masses of Jews depended more upon merchants and their stores in order to perform Jewish rituals than they did upon synagogues and rabbis. As such, not only can the commercial life of the Jewish street not be distinguished from the performance of religious obligations, but rather that life stood at the forefront of getting ready for ritual activities.

The literature as it exists now, despite the fact that few have scholars have devoted much specific attention to the web of relationships which linked

Jewish shops to Jewish community life, already offers many examples of how places of Jewish commerce served simultaneously as places which dispensed Jewish news, fostered Jewish interactions, and the made possible the provision of Jewish services. Ewa Morawska in her study of the small Jewish enclave in Johnstown, Pennsylvania, for example, described how the kosher butcher shop which opened up in 1903 stood next to the railroad station. In her study, that kosher market, "served as a referral service for passengers just off the train. If they were transients, travel assistance was provided by women of the *Hakhnoses Orkhim*, a society constituted to provide aid to wayfarers" (51). The implications of this small detail bear thinking about as we imagine community.

If we understand the making of "community" to be an abstract concept which indicates the process by a set of individuals who consider themselves responsible for others with whom they share some characteristic, transforming them from being merely "a set of individuals" to a collectivity with mutual obligations and expectations, then the butcher shop in Johnstown played a key role for numerous Jews who passed through this western Pennsylvania steel-making and coal mining town. The Jews of Johnstown supported a butcher shop by spending their money there on food which they believed Judaism obliged them to consume and the women of Johnstown banded together to create a formal society that ministered to the needs of Jews in transit from one place to another. Placing the butcher shop near the railroad station may not have been done specifically to fulfill a communal obligation—*hachnassat orchim*—but rather it may have been just good business sense. But its physical location, prominently placed nearby the depot, made possible the intricate fusion of economic, philanthropic, and religious needs, all of which sustained the community of Jews in Johnstown and which by implication made the Jewish community of Johnstown a player in the creation of a larger American Jewish community.

While some kinds of business establishments, like kosher markets, clearly depended upon Judaism and Jewish law, as well as on a network of Jewish religious functionaries, other stores like those that sold household wares, clothing, stationary, and the like also served Jewish functions. Stores that lined the Jewish street did not have to sell specifically Jewish goods to at times play a role in the creation of Jewish community life. Again a small detail in the scholarship winks at us, pointing out that the entrepreneurial sector intersected with the communal, indeed fostered it.

In 1909 a group of Jewish women in Boston's South End, mostly poor mothers, met at Hyman Danzig's Three and Nine Cent Store. No doubt they

exchanged information about a whole range of subjects in this otherwise obscure neighborhood store which served as a convenient gathering place. Among
the issues, they noted among themselves that no medical facility existed in
the neighborhood. They spontaneously formed themselves into a committee
which later that year came up with "a novel fund-raising scheme," construct-
ing and selling "miniature bricks at fifty cents a piece to pay for the building
of an entire hospital. . . . They made the most of nickels, dimes and quarters.
By September, 1911, the little group of women had grown into a fund-raising
society known as the Beth Israel Hospital Association" (Ebert 225). While the
women might have gone about the business of creating a hospital anyway, the
ordinary daily act of gathering at Hyman Danzig's store provided them with a
spring board for community organizing and institution building.

That the women used this commercial space as a social space should
draw the attention of historians. It should highlight to us how community in
the broadest sense of the word depends as much on the street as on the formal
institutions designated as such. This same point has emerged as an analytic
detail in writing about the other end of the century. Historian Gerald Gamm,
in a study subtitled, *Why the Jews Left Boston and the Catholics Stayed*, documented the entrepreneurial Jewish infrastructure of the community that its
merchants and customers abandoned. After ticking off the number of kosher
butcher shops supported by the Jews who shopped along Blue Hill Avenue,
as well as the bakeries, groceries, and fruit markets, Gamm put the G&G delicatessen onto historic center stage, as *the* place which "gave the district its
special character." Quoting from a local newspaper, Gamm offered an insight
into the close connection between the making of Jewish community and the
existence of particular commercial establishments. The article deserves here to
be quoted at some length. Referring to the delicatessens of the neighborhood
the reporter noted:

> Of all the fortresses only one reached the proportion could claim pa-
> latial amenities that testify to high culture, that immense landmark
> which any traveller who has passed down Blue Hill avenue will smile
> in recognition of, the G&G. One the tables of the cafeteria talmudic
> jurisprudence sorted out racing results, politics, the stock market,
> and the student could look up from his "desk" to leer at the young
> girls sipping cream soda under the immense wings of their mothers;
> watch the whole world of Blue Hill avenue revolve through the G&G's
> glass gate.

The dissolution of the Jewish neighborhood of Dorchester, a dense Jewish residential community by all accounts, according to Gamm, can be marked less by the moving of the synagogues than by the final closing of the "glass gate," the end of the food businesses (198–99).

Gamm's reference to this quite mundane eatery did not constitute the first scholarly valorization of it as a dense, powerful, and magnetic Jewish communal institution. Hillel Levine and Lawrence Harmon in their 1992 study of Boston Jewry, aptly entitled *The Death of an American Jewish Community*, also focused on decline, following "the glory years" of Blue Hill Avenue. They placed the delicatessen at the center of the Jewish community's political and social history and went so far as to declare that it "enjoyed the greatest drawing power of any institution in the Jewish community." Politicians, Jewish and non-Jewish eager to win the Jewish vote made an obligatory pilgrimage to the G&G, for example. Indeed, so central a role did it play in bringing Jews together and providing them with a place to be and be with other Jews, that, "if asked to free-associate about Jewish Boston, former residents invariable utter 'the G&G' . . . a place to dine, cut deals, and evaluate prospective sons-in-law." Levine and Harmon asserted, suggestively, that the intellectual and religious leadership of the community expressed disdain, and possibly jealousy, for the G&G and resented the fact that it competed with schools, synagogues, and more refined places of Jewish communal life. The authors asserted that, "those charged with shaping the community," actually "struggled for ways to get people off the Avenue and into the classroom or clubhouse." To no avail, since, at least in the realm of meaning and memory, while many Boston Jews did attend classes as the Hebrew Teacher's College, "few former residents think first of Hebrew College when reminiscing of the old neighborhood." That place of honor belonged to the G&G (13).

While Gamm, and before him Levine and Harmon, identified a few dozen Jewish food establishments alone as key places in the community's self-conception of itself as distinctive and as providing for its own needs, other and larger Jewish enclaves supported even more retail establishments where Jews sold to each other, congregated, and did business in a dense Jewish environment. New York obviously stood in a category by itself, as a mammoth and complicated place for Jewish marketing and Jewish community. An 1899 survey of New York's Eighth Assembly District, which encompassed parts of the immigrant neighborhood, listed no fewer than 631 food establishments that:

catered to the needs of the inhabitants of this area. Most numerous
were the 140 groceries which often sold fruits, vegetables, bread and
rolls, as well as the usual provisions. Second in number were the 131
butcher shops which proclaimed their wares in Hebrew letters. The
other food vendors included 36 bakeries, 9 bread stands, 14 butter and egg stores, 3 cigarette shops, 7 combination two-cent coffee
shops, 10 delicatessens, 9 fish stores, 7 fruit stores, 21 fruit stands,
3 grocery stands, 7 herring stands, 2 meat markets, 16 milk stores,
2 matzo . . . stores, 10 sausage stores, 20 soda water stands, 5 tea
shops . . . 11 vegetable stores, 13 wine shops, 15 grape wine shops,
and 10 confectioners. (Quoted in Rischin 56)

If to every one of these places a steady stream of Jewish women and men
came in and out, stopping to talk to the shopkeeper and to the other customers, exchanging news, finding out about each others' fortunes and misfortunes,
then we can see how the profusion of retail establishments on the Jewish street
created a thick space for making community. The photographic record of that
Eighth Assembly District, that is, the Lower East Side, testified to the intensity
of the street life and the degree which commercial activities drew Jews out of
their apartments and into the public spaces, talking as well as buying, interact-
ing as well as inspecting merchandise, and in the process creating community.

Likewise for decades Jews who had once lived on the Lower East Side
but then moved out to newer areas in the Bronx and Brooklyn, trekked back
to the "old neighborhood" to shop. Memoirs told and retold the details of Jews
from other parts of New York coming to the Lower East Side before Passover to
buy nuts, dried fruit and wine, returning on Sunday mornings for bargains on
clothing as well as for pickles and "appetizing," and finally, in a nearly religious
act tantamount to a pilgrimage, fathers brought their pre-bar mitzvah sons
to the "sacred space" to purchase a *tallith* in anticipation of their thirteenth
birthdays. Each one of these acts of Jewish shopping not only helped make the
Lower East Side the crucible of American Jewish memory culture, but helped
in the process create the key narrative of community in its most authentic form
(Diner, *Lower East Side Memories*).

Jewish commercial life not only sustained ritual practice and provided
the spaces where Jewish socializing and community building activities could
happen, but the ways in which different groups used those places reveal to historians some of the fissures that divided communities. No issue demonstrates
this more sharply than that of gender. That is, Jewish women and Jewish men
had different, albeit linked, histories of commerce and community.

The business sector of the Jewish street, in big cities and in smaller ones, provided a crucial zone for the performance of gender roles, a crucial element in the fabric of community life. For one, street level businesses brought men and women together as both, husbands and wives "manned" the stores, suggesting a host of questions.

To what degree did the small-business sector, the shops along the Jewish main street, employ the labor of all family members versus function as the sole domain of male or female entrepreneurs? What role did married women play in these stores and how did their entrepreneurial activities enhance their authority within the family? How did Jewish women's involvement in these shops and stores limit their options? Here we certainly have a vast range of first-hand accounts which bear witness to the ways in which Jewish women as shopkeepers blurred any kind of line between the public and the private and between the work of business and the business of home.

Countless numbers of Jewish shops doubled as places of residence in as much as families lived above and behind "the store." Mary Antin, for example, offered a description in her lyrical autobiography of how her mother tended the store and "in the intervals of slack trade, she did her cooking. . . . Arlington Street customers were used to waiting while the storekeeper [her mother] salted the soup or rescued a loaf from the oven" (155–56). Hers may be the most famous depiction of a phenomenon which predominated among Jewish entrepreneurial families and existed literally everywhere immigrant Jewish families flocked into self-employment through opening and operating small businesses. To what degree did this pattern affect women differently than men and how did the fusion of family and shop leave its mark on community life?

Small business meant family business. Some women actually operated independent businesses of their own, continuing in America the European tradition of multiple enterprises within a single nuclear family: one belonging to the husband, the other to the wife. However, most Jewish small businesses in America meant husband and wife working together.

While both men and women, recalling memories of the past, may have defined their small business as a place in which women "helped" out in the men's stores,[2] a different kind of pattern emerges in the on-the-ground descriptions of how these stores actually functioned, with Mary Antin's, as an exemplar. Husbands and wives functioned in a symbiotic relationship as they both struggled to make the business a reasonably profitable concern.

Men often decided that they could transition from being someone else's employee to being self-employed precisely when they married.

Entrepreneurship, particularly small scale, street level business, rarely involved single men, and being married meant that they, whether former sweatshop workers, garment factory laborers, or peddlers, now had their life-long partners behind counters and cash registers. The Jewish men who arrived in America and went out on the road to peddle finally married or brought over their wives only when they had the means to open a shop. In numerous cases, the erstwhile peddlers continued, at times, to sell from the road while their wives operated the in-town stores (Diner, *Roads Taken*).

For Jewish women, marriage meant leaving behind the garment factories where they labored as hired hands and becoming "helpers" or better still, un-official co-owners of grocery stores, bakeries, delicatessens, dress shop shops, and dry-goods emporia.

One story, like the hundreds of thousands which left few archived records, involves Harry Cohen who came to Baltimore in 1906 from Chernigov, Russia with his brother. His family had been food purveyors back home, and Cohen hoped to replicate this in America, albeit at a higher level. Realizing this dream, however, had to wait. He first took a job with Schloss Brothers, a garment shop, as a buttonhole maker and presser, living simply and saving his money.

In 1913 he took the first step towards fulfilling his aspirations by marry-ing Sarah Kaplansky, also an immigrant from Russia. He continued working at Schloss Brothers while she took in boarders and laundry, continuing to earn an income after marriage. For six years Sarah and Harry scrimped and saved, and eventually had enough to invest in a business.

By 1919 they had saved enough to buy a building at 1427 East Baltimore Street. Living on the upper floor, they operated a delicatessen on the ground level. Although Sarah continued to take in boarders and do laundry for oth-ers over the course of an unrecorded number of years, she also waited on the customers in the restaurant, prepared kugel, latkes and knishes and baked the challah, while Harry did the work which publicly defined the enterprise as his. He cured and sliced the meat, the "stuff" intrinsically associated with the world of the delicatessen, but she engaged with the customers, presumably using her personal qualities to make them feel welcome and ensure return visits to the business (Kessler 2–7).

Indeed, reminiscence literature is filled with this kind of tale. Sidney Weinberg' *World of Our Mothers*, drawn heavily from oral interviews with Jewish women who had emigrated from eastern Europe to America, resonates with stories about men, women and small businesses. One woman remem-bered wanting to get a job after marriage, but her husband objected. Instead, the two decided to open a small children's clothing store, where they both sewed the clothes and sold to customers. Another of Weinberg's interviewees recalled that her husband "owned" a business selling women's corsets door-to-door in a predominantly Italian neighborhood. Having bought too many of the smaller sizes, which would never do for his potential customers, his wife, "helper" that she was, pointed out to her husband that they could stitch to-gether several of the smaller corsets and not lose too much money on *his* bad investment. Another woman, who assisted her husband in knitting factory, re-lated how "My mind always went a mile a minute and it was necessary because my husband was very conservative and I was the gambler of the family. I ran the factory and my husband was the accountant" (238–39).

One of the interviewees in *The World of Our Mothers* told the following story, demonstrating the shared gender space of the Jewish small business.

> I opened up a hand laundry and I worked like a horse by myself and business was pretty good. And a store opened up around the corner, which was the main street—181st Street—and I took the store and moved in there. And everybody helped. We had an apartment—not far—and my husband was able to go home. He used to get up very early in the morning, open up the store. I went in later and I stayed at night . . . I did all the hard work . . . I worked day in and day out. For eleven years I had the store. (228)

Variations of these themes fill American Jewish oral history and remi-niscence literature. Although these stories have not been systematically studied heretofore, they point to a rich focus for the study of gender. Women and men came together in the realm of small businesses and family stores existed be-cause women and men labored there together. In most cases, at some point or another in the history of these stores, the family lived above or behind the shop, further merging the traditionally male sphere of the market place and the cul-turally sanctioned women's work at home. Their concentration in small neigh-borhood businesses and the subsequent male-female bond defined the world in America for Jewish immigrants very differently than for other ethnic groups.

Business at the heart of Jewish community life in America created a real-ity that the marketplace forced men and women to depend upon each other. However, men and women had different, gendered stakes in their definition of the business, their responsibility in it and its implication for role allocation. By and large, the women's versions emphasize that though husbands considered the business to be theirs by virtue of male norms, as did municipal officials who dispensed the needed licenses, women provided the lion's share of the ideas, serving as the "brains" of the operation. Such rhetoric resonates in women's writings and recollections. Their accuracy matters much less than the reality that business functioned as a space which both women and men occupied and contested.

So too the consumers of the Jewish shopping districts divided and converged along gendered lines, bringing out both Jewish women and men in search of goods. Some sources indicate that they divided their responsibilities as to who bought what. Louis Wirth in the 1927 study, *The Ghetto*, declared that in the Chicago Maxwell Street market, "Thursday is 'chicken day', when Jewish customers lay in their supplies for the Friday evening meal. Most of the purchasing is done by the men, who take a much more active part in the conduct of the household and the kitchen than is the case among non-Jewish immigrant groups. The man sees that the chicken is properly killed for if something should go wrong, he, as the responsible head of the household, would have to bear the sin." Buying the fish, however, he observed, fell more squarely in women's domain on this same Jewish street. As such, Wirth suggested that a gendered shopping world existed and this in turns offers us another way of seeing how the world of consumption in Jewish neighborhoods throbs with analytic possibilities (237).

Statements like these provide tantalizing hints that indicate that gender and gender relations underlie the commercial life of the Jewish street. They lead us to seeing that full-scale histories of Jewish communities as places where Jews bought from and sold to each other have to be refracted through the lens of gender. That Jewish women and men have experienced migration, adaptation, and the process of community building differently, now resides at the center of our historic understanding. That they experienced America as a place of conflict also figures prominently as an accepted element in our understanding of the past (Prell).

The commercial zone can provide yet one other place where this gender struggle played itself out. Paula Hyman has certainly shown this in her classic article on the kosher meat boycotts which raged in New York at the turn of the twentieth century. Those food fights pitted Jewish women, the consumers who considered themselves and their families to be entitled to the right to consume meat at a fair price within their means, against Jewish male merchants, the butchers, who had behind them the communal leadership, the slaughterers and the rabbis. As the women saw it, the merchants, as Jews, had a responsibility to provide kosher meat to them, as custodians of their families;

consumption. They demanded that the business of kosher meat be conducted with their sensibilities and pocketbooks in mind. The women's demands underscored the degree to which marketing and community functioned as fused categories. The drama which got played out in front of the butcher shops, and in the pages of Hyman's article, demonstrate the degree to which commerce, community, gender, and conflict all need to be considered as pivotal forces in Jewish history (Hyman; Frank).[3]

The size of a community as well as the gendered nature of community life reflected itself in the realm of Jewish shopping. From the early twentieth century onward, Jewish visitors who came to New York from the "hinterlands" commented in awe about the great metropolis as a place to buy Jewish goods. The sheer size of New York's Jewish community made possible a diversity of markets whereby Jewish "things" could be consumed. *The Jewish Catalog* (Siegel et al.), perhaps the key text in the Jewish counter-culture spawned in the 1970's, offered its readers explicit advice on how to shop for Jewish goods in New York. The array of items that Jewish merchants in New York could sell to Jewish consumers eager to acquire Jewish "things" demonstrated the city's significance, particularly the Lower East Side. Thus, the *Catalog*, after suggesting, for example, to those eager to buy Jewish books to try book stores in their local communities, directed them to "the Lower East Side . . . a visit to which calls for the time-tested Jewish skills of haggling and striking a bargain with the booksellers" (205–06). For shoppers in search of a ram's horn for Rosh Hashana, it noted, "it helps a lot to be in close proximity to either Jerusalem or (not to mention the two in the same breath) New York. If you are so situated, head for Meah Shearim or its diasporic equivalent, the Lower East Side" (105–06). The ability to buy Jewish goods—books, ritual objects, and pickles—on the Lower East Side added to its sanctity and made it in the process a metaphor for the image of an organic and dense Jewish community.

Likewise, in any number of memoirs or autobiographical fragments American Jews who had grown up and lived outside of New York described, as did art historian Alan Schoener, how a visit to the Lower East Side evoked a sense of Jewish connectedness through what could be bought on its streets. "I found myself," he wrote, "roaming around Delancey Street and Second Avenue, eating food that my mother never cooked" (Introduction). He connected emotionally to a metaphoric sense of Jewish community through those rambles and through those acts of consumption. In order to eat that food, which transported him to a time when the neighborhood had been a dense Jewish enclave, he had to pay money to a merchant, be it the vendor of a cart, the owner of a restaurant, or the proprietor of a store. Schoener, like so many other Jewish voyagers to the old immigrant enclave, reconnected to a mythic community by means of a commercial transaction. (Schoener went on to curate the Jewish Museum's exhibit, "Portal to America," itself a powerful text in the furthering of the idea that the Lower East Side constituted a formative site in the construction of American Jewish communal identity [quoted in Diner, *Lower East Side* 80, 98–99].)

These commercial transactions between Jews, in whichever century they took place, had tremendous impact on the nature of community life and community self-understanding. Although Jews sold to non-Jews historically more often than they sold to other Jews, the close connections which developed between Jewish merchants and local Jewish buying publics helped sustain Jewish space and Jewish community. By patronizing neighborhood merchants and transforming shopping places into community spaces, Jewish consumers in concert with the merchants whom they may at times have conflicted with over quality and price, nevertheless helped make the personal public, and the private communal. Memoirs, autobiographies, as well as a vast number of journalistic sources, described often in exquisite detail the ways in which Jews in cities and towns in many lands and several continents congregated in Jewish stores and shops. Here they mixed together their buying of fish, meat, wine, bread, hats and socks, with the spreading of community news, the selling of notions with debates over notions of community priorities. The stores and shops provided places to gossip, sites for planning public activities, as well as venues for getting the goods defined as both necessary and desirable.[4]

The literature on American Jewish history, despite its relative silence about small neighborhood business as something that mattered, does point to a number of crucial eras. The first era, the one which extended into the early decades of the nineteenth century, relied on the imposition of a pre-modern European Jewish (and also colonial-style) model of high levels of community control in which Jewish merchants who served the Jewish public had to submit to community control.[5] Those goods which Jews saw as crucial to the practice of Judaism, kosher wine, kosher meat and matzah in particular, rather than flowing to customers through independently owned and operated stores which needed to woo the public to come and buy in competition with others selling the same goods, instead, fell into the domain of the congregation—only one per city—which enjoyed a monopoly on the provision of such goods. Those congregations could withhold goods from Jews who deviated from community standards of behavior and enterprising entrepreneurs had no chance of setting up their own businesses. That the goods came from the congregations also made for a kind of subterranean Jewish market. We have no evidence that shops with Hebrew letters, marked with words like "kosher" or "Jewish" graced the streets of early America (Faber 69–70). While the Jewish women and men who inhabited these early communities made a living primarily in commerce, in the selling of various kinds of goods to the general public, Jewish goods came to Jews through the regulated world of the congregations.

Hyman Grinstein in his path breaking history of the Jews of New York, the first of the notable community biographies which dominated the scholarship in the mid-twentieth century, introduced the community-commerce nexus as early as the third page of the book. Grinstein asserted in this introduction that the key moment in the history of the community, a moment which presaged later diversification, seen by some as disunity and the decline of authority, came about in 1812 when a brief, unsuccessful, breakaway from Shearith Israel, the only congregation in the city, went out and hired its own *shohet*. While the "rift was soon healed" and "Shearith Israel continued to supervise the sealing and sale of kosher food," a powerful trajectory had been set on its course. The universal practice that had prevailed in America since the end of the seventeenth century that the one congregation which existed in each city with an organized Jewish presence maintained total control over the selling of kosher food began to unravel.

Instead, under the "broad concept of liberty which existed in America," commercial individualism flourished and competition between congregations and merchants and among those who wanted to be merchants became the norm. The communities unraveled in the face of the "climate of freedom" and a culture of enterprise infused the Jewish commercial world no less than it came to suffuse nearly all aspects of American life (3).

With that unravelling there ensued a long period of time, from the 1820s through possibly the 1960s in which Jewish community life derived much of its impetus and structure from the vibrant and flamboyant tone of the commercial transactions of the Jewish street. In that extended history, in one city after another, Jewish neighborhoods became distinctive in large measure because of what got sold and bought on their streets, and how. Jews went out onto streets in the ordinary course of life, making the purchases of necessities and luxuries in company with other Jews, shopping at stores owned by their co-ethnics. Street, store, and living spaces flowed into one another as being Jewish in large measure meant shopping and consuming Jewish. That marketplace culture flowered in every city where Jews lived and existed in its particular way until

the age of suburbanization, when the rise of the low density, automobile culture, put in place a set of new realities.[6]

In the years that the streets of Jewish neighborhoods functioned as
Jewish marketplaces, merchants had to court the Jewish buying public. The
signs, advertisements, hawking, and pulling-in, all tactics designed to attract
customers, gave the Jewish streets their particular appearance, announcing
to all that these streets constituted Jewish space. Alfred Kazin, describing his
Brownsville of the 1920s, remarked looking backward from the late 1940s, how
the "electric sign . . . lighting up the words Jewish National Delicatessen" made
him and the others who used this Brooklyn street, Pitkin Avenue, as their turf,
feel "as if we had entered into our rightful heritage" (33–34).

The needs of ordinary Jewish women and men to buy particular goods
and the desire of the Jewish shopkeepers, also quite ordinary Jewish women
and men, to win over the consumers meshed. In that meeting place between
Jewish consumers and Jewish entrepreneurs, although conflicts between the
two groups flared with frequency, community flourished.

We can narrate that history of community through commerce from the
narratives of every community which has heretofore been written about. We
can see the communal power of buying and selling Jewish in the primary documents which have survived from each Jewish enclave regardless of geography.
Let me offer a few examples, just to demonstrate the breadth of the material
already available.

Thinking back about all that he had seen in his life, Isaac Mayer Wise
remembered in his 1901 *Reminiscences* the Jewish community that had taken
shape on the east side of Baltimore in the early 1850s, as a place where "there
seemed to be many Jews . . . although everything is very primitive. Women in
the small shops carrying children in their arms, or else knitting busily. Young
men invited passers-by to enter this or that store to buy . . . M'zuzoth, Tzitzith,
Talethim, Kosher cheese and Eretz Yisrael earth were on sale" (quoted in Fein
78). Here in Wise's recollections family life and entrepreneurship, the mixed
male-female presence, community and consumption overlapped in a visible if,
according to him, unappealing way.

In his sociological analysis of Chicago's Jewish community of the late
1920s Louis Wirth may have avoided the word "primitive" and eschewed
the kind of judgmental tone that Wise indulged in, but he offered a similar
kind of observation which put the world of retail squarely into the making
of Jewish community. "The description of the ghetto," opined Wirth, "would
be incomplete without mention of the great number of other characteristic

institutions that give it its own peculiar atmosphere and mark it as a distinct culture area." Here Wirth included, "the Kosher butcher shops, where fresh meats and a variety of sausages are a specialty. . . . the basement fish store to gratify the tastes of the connoisseur with a variety of herrings, pike, and carp, which Jewish housewives purchase on Thursday in order to serve the famous national dish of *gefülte fish* at the sumptuous Friday evening meal . . . Kosher bake-shops with rye bread, poppy-seed bread, and pumpernickel daily. . . . the bathhouse, which contains facilities for Turkish and Russian, plain and fancy, baths . . . basement and second-story bookstores, cafes, and restaurants. . . . the cigar stores, and the curtained gambling houses . . . the offices of the shyster lawyers, the *realestateniks*, and sacramental wine dealers. . . ." Wirth's monograph, published by the University of Chicago Press, came adorned by a series of woodcuts by the artist Todros Geller, identified as "ghetto" types—the "Horseradish grinder" who sat "on the sidewalks in front of butcher shops and fish stores . . . bowed and bearded," sellling to the women and men who walked by, as well as an artistic rendition of the Maxwell Street Market, streaming with people scurrying around buying goods of various kinds (224–28).

That same tone pervaded much of the imaginative literature that grew out of the immigrant communities. Anzia Yezierska's 1923 *Salome of the Tenements* positioned her protagonist Sonya Vrunsky , a fictional stand-in for Rose Pastor Stokes, on New York's Essex Street. Yezierska depicted, with decidedly negative tones, the "jostling throngs, haggling women, peddlers and pushcarts. The smell of fishstalls, of herring stands," all of which gave the neighborhood its distinctive quality. Yezierska peopled her fictional world with Jews who used the streets to provide and consume goods they understood to be crucial to Jewish life. "Holiday hats! Shine yourself out for Passover! Everything marked down cheap!" blared a "puller-in" to Sonya, who, lured by the lights of Fifth Avenue found the life of Essex Street a dismal combination of "the sordidness of haggling and bargaining—all she had ever known till now," with the essence of the immigrant Jewish community (*Red Ribbons* 25–26).

In their history of the Jews of Buffalo, a product of the 1954 Tercentenary commemorations which marked 300 years of Jewish life in North America, Selig Adler and Thomas Connally provided yet another example of how thinking about Jewish community cannot be divorced from considering the role of retail. In charting how "Buffalo's first distinctly Jewish neighborhood" came into being, the two historians noted that, it coincided with the rise of the community's first "shops and business institutions." In particular they noted the centrality of "Rosenblatt's Bakery," where at 268 William Street "Jews met as

they picked bagel, honey-cake and *hallah* out of the bins in the store windows."
The opening up of Rosenblatt's stimulated competition so Joseph Cohen, "went
into the same business." With his purported "secret recipe" brought from
Warsaw, Cohen opened up shop on Strauss Street and "here his son, Albert,
made 'Cohen's rye bread' a household word in Buffalo." The upstate New York
city's Jewish entrepreneurial nerve center extended beyond just bread, and "by
the turn of the century, kosher butcher shops throughout the area had mul-
tiplied rapidly. There were Jewish barber shops in the neighborhood, a bicy-
cle shop operated by Levi Russlander at 136 William Street, and a number of
Jewish shoe repair shops" (186–87).

Studies of individual communities, whether large or small, provide a clear
picture of this Jewish predominance in small business and the intimate link-
ages between it and the patterns of Jewish life. In the small Jewish enclave in
Johnstown, Pennsylvania, nearly all Jews derived an income from their stores.
Their actual purpose in moving to Johnstown, an industrial town in western
Pennsylvania which housed massive steel mills and nearby coal fields, was to
go into business. Shopkeeping brought the Jews to this place (Morawaksa). In
Providence, Rhode Island, a mid-sized city with some industrial options for
Jews, nearly 65% of Russian Jewish men listed themselves as self-employed in
the 1915 state census (Pearlman 43). In New York, approximately 45% of all Jews
earned a living in small businesses of one kind or another in 1909 (Rischin 79).

Throughout this long period of time small business meant family business. Some women actually operated independent businesses of their own,
continuing in America the European tradition of multiple enterprises within a
single nuclear family, with one belonging to the husband, the other to the wife.
However, most Jewish small businesses in America meant husband and wife
working together.

The rabbis, the sociologists, historians, and novelists as well as journal-
ists, reformers, and memoirists have all made a crucial point, each in their separate ways, reflective of the genres in which they worked and the projects they
pursued, that offer scholars of business, community and of American Jewish
history a direction for research. They each saw, like so many other observers,
the profound reality that Jewish communities in the United States functioned
not just as places where Jews prayed, acted politically, and furthered some worthy social goal such as providing for the poor, sustaining education, or supporting Jewish culture. Jewish communities also served as sites for buying and
selling and the entrepreneurial infrastructure of Jewish spaces operated in tan-
dem with the construction of Jewish identity and meaning.

The Jewish streets of Baltimore, Chicago and New York , and all the other places where Jews settled and lived, the commercial hubs of the neighborhoods where Jews planted themselves, provided more than sites for providing ordinary Jews with ordinary necessities. Rather these streets offered Jews informal and organic ways to interact with other Jews. Although the world of Jewish commerce never existed independent of politics and ideology, the reality that some Jews, the shopkeepers among them, needed these stores to make a living, while others, the consumers, needed them to feed, clothe, and supply themselves with a range of goods, made for reciprocity and connectedness, essential elements of the idea of community. The relatively mundane commercial activities, recorded by Wise, Wirth and Yezierska, and the others, the realities they saw of Jews selling and Jews buying, represented a foundational element of life of Jewish communities.

Existing in an intermediate zone between the formal structure of communities—the synagogues, associations, societies with their charters, by-laws, and elections of officers—and the informal, the groups of friends, relatives, neighbors, and even strangers, whose very presence shaped everyday life, stores and shops, the merchants and their customers, made possible Jewish public space.

The business world at the lived level of the street offers a historically rich and analytically complicated vantage point from which to see changing patterns of Jewish community life. While the reality of Jews buying from and selling to each other, both the goods which they believed Judaism demanded of them as well as the ordinary stuff, basic necessities and luxuries, has run continuously through Jewish history, each place and each era reflected differences in context. Those contexts, and in this case the American one, offer historians a new and relatively untapped mine of material from which to imagine community, communities, and their histories. The stories demonstrate the deep bond between the business of Jews and the business of Jewish life.

Notes

Material from this chapter comes from Hasia R. Diner, "Buying and Selling 'Jewish': The Historical Impact of Commerce on Jewish Communal Life," *Imagining the American Jewish Community*, edited by Jack Wertheimer, Brandeis Univ., 2007, pp. 28–46.

1. A quite robust literature on the history of consumption and the significance of shopping has already been developed. A few of the key works of recent years include Benson; Cross; and Cohen.

2. This was the case for Ewa Morawska's interviewees in Johnstown.

3. What is particularly notable in Frank's article is that Jewish women were among the most assertive housewives in New York in demanding that the merchants of their neighborhoods respond to their consumer needs.

4. The one work in American Jewish history which has given the marketplace its due as an analytic construct is Heinze, *Adapting to Abundance*.

5. The scholarship on the pre-modern period in Jewish history has stressed the degree to which business and commerce within the ghetto operated under the control and with the strict regulation by the formally sanctioned community. Rabbis and wealthy elites controlled the commercial sector no less than they controlled the religious sector or the relationship between the community and the larger non-Jewish world. See for example, Katz, *Tradition and Crisis*, where the power of the elite in the economic activities of the community was a major subject of discussion. Katz, for example, noted that the leadership took upon itself the question of "how to regulate competition among Jews," to limit the rights of "strangers," although they were Jews, from settling and doing business in the community (49).

6. A full-scale history of Jewish consumption and Jewish community would have to deal with the late twentieth century and the massive suburbanization of American Jewry as an analytically different era. What impact the low density, automobile-driven nature of suburban life had on Jewish shopping needs to be probed. In essence the realities of suburban design changed the basic nature of "the street" as a place where people walked in and out of stores, congregated on corners, met casually in the mundane course of activities. The development of internet shopping and the privatization of consumption further changed basic patterns and would need to be analyzed in its own terms.

Works Cited

Adler, Selig, and Thomas E. Connolly. *From Ararat to Suburbia: The History of the Jewish Community of Buffalo.* Jewish Publication Society of America, 1960.

Antin, Mary. *The Promised Land.* 1912. Penguin, 1997.

Atherton, Lewis. *Main Street on the Middle Border.* Indiana Univ., 1954.

Benson, Susan Porter. *Counter Cultures: Saleswomen, Managers, and Customers in American Department Stores, 1890–1940.* Univ. of Illinois, 1986.

Bodnar, John. *The Transplanted: A History of Immigrants in Urban America.* Indiana Univ., 1985.

Coburn, Carol. *Life At Four Corners: Religion, Gender, and Education in a German-Lutheran Community, 1868–1945.* Univ. of Kansas, 1992.

Cohen, Lisabeth. *A Consumer's Republic: The Politics of Mass Consumption in Postwar America.* Knopf, 2003.

_____. *Making a New Deal: Industrial Workers in Chicago, 1919–1939.* Cambridge Univ., 1990.

Cross, Gary. *An All-Consuming Century: Why Commercialism Won in Modern America.* Columbia Univ., 2000.

Diner, Hasia R. *Lower East Side Memories: The Jewish Place in America.* Princeton Univ., 2000.

_____. *Roads Taken: The Great Jewish Migration to the New World and the Peddlers Who Led the Way.* Yale Univ., 2016.

Ebert, Susan. "Community and Philanthropy." *The Jews of Boston: Essays on the Occasion of the Centenary (1895–1995) of the Combined Jewish Philanthropies of Greater Boston,* edited by Jonathan Sarna and Ellen Smith, Combined Jewish Philanthropies of Greater Boston, 1995.

Faber, Eli. *A Time for Planting: The First Migration, 1654–1820.* Johns Hopkins Univ., 1992.

Fein, Isaac. *The Making of An American Jewish Community: The History of Baltimore Jewry from 1773 to 1920.* Jewish Publication Society, 1971.

Frank, Dana. "Housewives, Socialists and the Politics of Food: The 1917 New York Cost-of-Living Protests." *Feminist Studies,* vol. 11, no. 2, 1985, pp. 255–85.

Gamm, Gerald. *Urban Exodus: Why the Jews Left Boston and the Catholics Stayed.* Harvard Univ., 1999.

Grinstein, Hyman. *The Rise of the Jewish Community of New York, 1654–1860.* Jewish Publication Society of America, 1947.

Harrison, Molly. *People and Shopping: A Social Background.* Ernest Benn, 1975.

Heinze, Andrew. *Adapting to Abundance: Jewish Immigrants, Mass Consumption, and the Search for American Identity.* Columbia Univ., 1990.

Hyman, Paula. "Immigrant Women and Consumer Protest: The New York City Kosher Meat Boycott of 1902." *American Jewish History,* vol. 70, no. 1, 1980, pp. 91–105.

Katz, Jacob. *Tradition and Crisis: Jewish Society at the End of the Middle Ages.* Syracuse Univ., 2000.

Kazin, Alfred. *A Walker in the City.* Harcourt Brace, 1952.

Kessler, B. "Bedlam with Corned Beef on the Side," *Generations: The Magazine of the Jewish Historical Society of Maryland,* 1993, pp. 2–7.

Levine, Hillel, and Lawrence Harmon. *The Death of an American Jewish Community: A Tragedy of Good Intentions.* Free, 1992.

Light, Ivan, and Edna Bonacich. *Immigrant Entrepreneurs: Koreans in Los Angeles, 1965–1982.* Univ. of California, 1988.

McCracken, Grant, editor. *Culture and Consumption: New Approaches to the Symbolic Character of Consumer Goods and Activities.* Indiana Univ., 1988.

Morawska, Ewa. *Insecure Prosperity: Small Town Jews in Industrial America, 1890–1940.* Princeton Univ., 1996.

Pearlman, J. *Ethnic Differences: Schooling and Social Structure Among the Irish, Italians, Jews and Blacks in an American city 1880–1935.* New York: Cambridge Univ., 1988.

Prell, Riv-Ellen. *Fighting to Become American: Jews, Gender, and the Anxiety of Assimilation.* Beacon, 1999.

Rischin, Moses. *The Promised City: New York Jews, 1870–1914.* Harvard Univ., 1962.

Sanchez, George. *Becoming Mexican American: Ethnicity, Culture and Identity in Chicano Los Angeles, 1900–1945.* Oxford Univ., 1993.

Siegel, Richard et al. *The First Jewish Catalog.* Jewish Publication Society of America, 1973.

Weinberg, S. *The World of Our Mothers: Lives of Jewish Immigrant Women.* Univ. of North Carolina, 1988.

Wirth, Louis. *The Ghetto.* 1928. Transaction, 1998.

Wise, Isaac Mayer. *Reminiscences.* 1901.

Yezierska, Anzia. *Red Ribbons on a White Horse.* Scribner, 1950.

_____. *Salome of the Tenements.* 1923. Univ. of Illinois, 1995.

CHAPTER 2

Common Fortunes: Social and Financial Gains of Jewish and Christian Partnerships in Eighteenth-Century Transatlantic Trade

by Allan M. Amanik

*L*ate in December 1772, George Croghan, notable Ohio Country fur trader and deputy superintendent of Indian affairs, wrote to his partner, David Franks, son of one of early America's most prominent Jewish merchant families to advise on acreage in which they speculated jointly. "As to the contract I made with you and M^r. Plumsted," he added, referencing significant losses that Franks's firm had forgiven after the Seven Year's War, ". . . as I have been so long Indebted to Levey & Franks throu Misfortunes for w^h(ich) I pay No Intrest I wold in frendshipe & gratitude recommend itt to you to hold ye whole y^r Self as by that mains the Sale of those lands will make you an ample mends for my Delay of payment" (Croghan). The goodwill and trust in this exchange stand out, perhaps for just how unremarkable they had become between Christian and Jew. In fact, this was just one in a much larger web of frontier trade and settlement that Franks, Croghan, and their Jewish and Christian partners pursued on the eve of the American Revolution (Stern 25–30; Faber 86). While those ventures played an important part developing regional and imperial markets, of equal significance was the fact that these men's common business interests outweighed ethnic and religious differences that might otherwise have prevented their fruitful and extended collaboration.

Although few early American Jews could boast the wealth or standing of a man like David Franks, in either scale and in scope, they bore many qualities in common. Middling or more accomplished merchants carved out some share of local or transatlantic trade and relied at some point on non-Jewish associates. Even petty Jewish sutlers, at the end of mighty supply chains traversing the Atlantic into colonial frontiers, secured for themselves or benefited along the way from shorter or longer business alliances with Christian counterparts. From the credit they sought or extended, the commercial advice they exchanged, the ships they invested in jointly, or the cargoes they smuggled or sold, early American Jews and their non-Jewish peers looked past religious difference when common commercial ends rendered cooperation advantageous. Those dealings not only contributed to the maturation and ties among colonial and English markets, but the relationships that flowed alongside them laid important foundations for Jews in the colonies.[1] They reinforced commercial rights already won and further propelled North American Jewish standing as it drew wind in its sails from developing English tolerance but deviated in a quicker progression by the decades surrounding independence.

Historians have thoroughly traced the initial connection between early American Jews' perceived economic utility and their ability to settle, trade, and accumulate rights throughout the colonial period. To overlay cross-cultural trade and the calculations that both Jewish and Christian partners made in extended alliances adds a dimension to that story. As most narratives agree, some combination of the pragmatism undergirding colonial commerce, developing Protestant pluralism in England and its holdings, small Jewish numbers in a diverse religious landscape set against stronger anti-Catholic sentiment, and of course the importance of race in doling out rights all factored in to Jewish standing overseas.[2] More recent reflections have also alluded to the power of the market in America "born commercial and capitalist" to level differences for Jews in a field of many newcomers pursuing common profit (Ira Katznelson, "Two Exceptionalisms" 13–14). Others even more specifically consider the increasing sophistication of urban trade in colonial towns and cities and its ability to "erode ethno-cultural demarcation between Jews and non-Jews" (Lederhendler 20).

As much as commerce in the abstract fueled Jewish entry and improving stations overseas, ongoing relationships nurtured between Jewish and Christian partners surely had a hand, too, eroding difference, preempting the repeal of steadily accumulated privileges, or reinforcing rights if challenged. Indeed, even in times of turmoil, historian William Pencak points out, when

early American masses might resent Jewish economic visibility, Christian partners or colonial elites offered ready sources of vocal support to those targeted
Jewish merchants who had cultivated good commercial dealings (Pencak,
"Anti-Semitism" 247). Even soured economic partnerships between Christians
and Jews could bolster Jewish claims as they offered an opportunity for defrauded Jewish businessmen to look to the courts to uphold established rights
or to fortify reputations carefully curated in the court of public opinion.

In that sense these commercial partnerships not only add to historians' recent calls for a deeper understanding of Jewish strategies and engagement with
American capitalism, but also to recent insights into overseas merchants more
generally on the workings of trust and early modern trading networks, within
and across religious communities.[3] To be sure, colonial Jewish merchants commonly sought each other out in trade. They thickened business ties through
marriage matches or apprenticeships, building upon bonds of Jewishness to
deepen commercial networks. At the same time they also branched out and
did not assume Jewishness to be the only or ultimate asset, nor did potential Christian partners shy away from seeking Jewish aid. While studies have
shown that shared family or ethnic networks advanced long-distance trade,
common bonds alone did not automatically foster trust nor mitigate risk. They
also did not deter individuals of one group from looking beyond communal
bonds to partner with members of another. Not exploring trans-group partnerships limited chances for raising capital and accessing markets. Trust or dis-
honesty, though, could never be taken for granted and a host of considerations
shaped business partnerships, beyond intra-group connections. Reputation
and credit-worthiness, social links and wealth which could attract potential
partnerships, and faith in common legal bodies to enforce honest dealings or
punish potential defrauding, mattered too.

To that end, so did wider demographic and legal frameworks governing
English colonial commerce which enabled, and at times encouraged, Jews and
Protestants to form mutually beneficial business partnerships as they weighed
the benefits or costs of joint ventures in regional or transatlantic trade. Despite
early limits of the Navigation Acts which undercut imperial rivals over the
second half of the seventeenth century by obstructing foreign ports and merchants, Jews enjoyed growing access to English colonial markets, particularly by the eighteenth century.[4] Surpassing legal means that Jewish merchants
found to circumvent those acts,[5] the 1740 Naturalization Act gave even foreign-born Jews the right to naturalize in the colonies after seven years' continuous residence and without needing to swear a Christian oath. In British

North America, unlike in England and most other colonies, they no longer faced added tariffs as alien traders. Although Jews born in England and its colonies faced confessional obstacles in office-holding or some other spheres of public life, their ability to trade and transfer assets to heirs did not differ from their Protestant counterparts (Endelman 35–37; Godfrey and Godfrey 34–61; Snyder, "Rules, Rights and Redemption" 154–56). Although Catholic standing would improve over time, Catholics' commercial abilities or path to altered status were far more circumscribed. The Naturalization Act even limited its privileges to Jews, Quakers, and later Moravians to waive the Sacrament and, for those who would take it, it still skewed in the favor of foreign Protestants by requiring it occur "in some Protestant and Reformed Congregation within this Kingdom of *Great Britain*, or within some of the said Colonies of America" (Kettner 74–75).

Common commercial laws intersected with an expectation of legal protections in trade, and this gave Jews in the colonies an added incentive to consider partners beyond religious or communal circles. While policies like the Naturalization Act intended to harness the overseas trade connections of Jewish and foreign Protestant merchants to benefit imperial commerce, they inadvertently provided the basis for Anglicans, Quakers, Episcopalians, Huguenots, and Jews, among others, to forge mutually profitable alliances across boundaries of faith and community.

The present portraits explore the meaning and value that larger- and smaller-scale Jewish and Protestant merchants found in their partnerships in the decades before the Revolution. These merchants diverged in terms of geographic region and commercial scope, in goods exchanged, family stature, place of origin, legal standing as foreign- or native-born, and in some instances failure or success. As with all Jewish overseas traders in England and its American holdings, some stood on the shoulders of towering family names, while others enjoyed far fewer assets when starting out. Despite these differences, Jewish and Protestant associates weighed the costs and benefits of commercial alliances across communal lines and in the context of broader legal and social frameworks of English transatlantic trade making such partnerships both viable and durable. Their decisions and dealings contributed toward markets well beyond them while facilitating new and added commercial opportunities for Jewish and Christian business interests. In the process, those partnerships advanced personal fortunes while adding, incrementally, to larger social, civic, and at times even legal precedents furthering the contours of early American Jewish standing.

INTERETHNIC KINSHIP BONDS AND THE
REPRODUCTION OF STATUS AND WEALTH

The importance of finding and nurturing a partnership across religious borders held for well-off Jewish mercantile families, including those with great resources and prestige. Brothers like David or Moses Franks enjoyed several advantages when they first set out in Pennsylvania and London trade by the middle of the eighteenth century. Indeed each well embodied the ability of wealthy children to build on the financial and social capital of preceding generations to forge independent fortunes. Credit, both financial and reputational, from established relatives fostered their success, but they decided not to limit themselves to connecting only to other Jews (Mathias). Rather, they, and their siblings, sought to forge social bonds with prominent Christian counterparts to enhance business. These ranged from entering into close business partnerships with colonial and English elites to pursuing marital ties with notable Christian families with commercial prowess, as in the case of David and his sister, Phila. In each decision, the Franks children not only accrued social status and wealth, but by deepening personal and commercial bonds to Christian counterparts they extended their resources beyond Jewish circles.

When they had arrived in Philadelphia in 1740 to learn the family trade, Moses and David briefly served their maternal uncles, Nathan and Isaac Levy. Moses soon transferred to London where he grew closer to his father Jacob Franks's family. Through his uncle, Aaron Franks, by then considered the family patriarch and a leading diamond importer, Moses entered the precious gem trade, soon emerging as a largescale exporter of coral (Yogev 152–57). These and other activities gained him access to elite Christian circles that in turn helped him, the family, and their associates win sizeable military contracts during the Seven Years' War (1756–1763). David's share of that larger £750,000 contract provisioning troops flooding the colonies greatly propelled his own commercial ascension in North America. It cemented his standing for at least the next two decades as a preeminent Jewish military supplier while English territorial victories simultaneously opened new ventures for western land speculation and settler supply.

Certainly intra-communal ties at home and abroad counted for much. When Moses departed for London, David stayed behind in Philadelphia and simultaneously, formed the firm Levy & Franks with the boys' uncle Nathan. The firm profited from vending goods on the western frontier and exporting backcountry skins and furs for sale on London and European markets, tying English and colonial merchants and creating, according to historian,

A. T. Volwiler, "a connected chain of credits based in the end upon English capital" (283–84; Byars 10). Jewish merchants like Levy and Franks could not have carried out those activities without the English manufactured goods sold to them on credit by relatives overseas like David's brothers, Moses and Naphtali along with Nathan's brother, Isaac. The privileges conferred them by laws governing colonial commerce ranked equally important. They extended those goods and credit to hinterland agents and traders who bartered for furs or, over time, entrusted them to native nations to promote more successful hunting. As native-born subjects with deep pockets all their own, David and Nathan commanded easy access to vessels that they owned independently or in part with other merchants.[6] They also benefited from well-placed and reliable Jewish contacts in Lancaster who managed their stores and traded on their behalf.[7] Those tangible and intangible assets poised the Levy-Franks men early in their careers to carry out transatlantic voyages in addition to regional trade.

Moses and David's rise in London and North America, respectively, spoke to the importance of these foundations and the Jewish ties surrounding them, but they also reflected the powerful Christian links that these men and their family forged in the colonies and overseas. Those partnerships, in turn, reflect the benefits that Christian counterparts saw in alliances with a Jewish trading house like the Franks. In London Moses had already joined a syndicate of political and banking renown that included Protestant men like James Colebrooke, George Colebrooke, Arnold Nesbitt, Samuel Fudyer, and Adam Drummond. Moses's earlier role in a venture between the Franks and Colebrooke to supply English goods to Jamaica through New York may have facilitated his initial entrée, but the young man's growing London stature only encouraged it.[8] The Franks family's notable wealth of course ranked high, in particular given necessary funds to finance the venture before government reimbursement, but the interethnic supply chains that his background uniquely offered proved perhaps of even greater value. As an American-born son of a well-connected Jewish family which, by his generation, had also begun to marry ever-more prominent Christian counterparts, the specific constellation of Moses Franks' Jewishness actually represented a highly valuable asset.[9]

In the colonies monied men like his father, Jacob Franks, brother David, or brother-in-law, Oliver Delancey, served as important agents in New York, Pennsylvania, and surrounding regions. Likely at Moses's behest, Jacob came to oversee military supply for all of the colonies. The elder Franks had already demonstrated his effectiveness in previous conflicts, provisioning troops in Jamaica during the War of Jenkins' Ear and King George's War (1739–1748).

He also built on existing commercial channels with Jewish agents in Carolina and Georgia to mount a supply chain during Oglethorpe's attacks on Spanish Florida (1740–1743). During the Seven Years' War, Jacob looked closer to home. His son-in-law, Oliver Delancey, worked with his own partner and brother-in-law, John Watts, to supply New York, New Jersey, New England, and Canada. David worked with Philadelphia partners like William Plumsted or his own well-positioned Jewish agents in Lancaster to supply food, arms, finances, and other needs to troops in Pennsylvania, Virginia, and surrounding fronts.

Through each interconnected part the London syndicate reached far across the Atlantic to supply an expanse covering the North American coastal colonies, Canadian provinces, far reaches of the colonial south and west, and troops stationed in strategic islands like Bermuda, the Bahamas, the Lesser Antilles, and Jamaica (Pencak, *Jews and Gentiles* 178; Marcus 2.713). Assessing that network, historian William Pencak observed "the Franks brothers and their connections were effective not because they were richer than Christian merchants and bankers, but because their international network permitted them an especially rapid transfer of funds from one end of Europe to another, and then from Europe to America" (Pencak, *Jews and Gentiles,* 182–83). Far from outpacing Christian peers, these Jewish merchants capitalized on their ability to collaborate alongside them.

The credit and coordination necessary for that kind of agility drew on several factors. The Franks sons' reputations for the competency their father had shown in previous campaigns certainly mattered, but a host of overlapping social ties and transactions proved equally important to draw this cohort together. That Moses and David's sister, Phila Franks, had married Oliver Delancey in 1742 ranked high. The merging of family fortunes clearly promoted close cooperation during the military venture. Jacob even enlisted his son-in-law after the young man's firm, Delancey & Watts, lost its bid for the contract to Moses and his London partners. That Watts and Moses Franks had gone to school together as children and remained close friends clearly also played a hand. Those close social ties proved a shrewd use of resources, particularly given Delancey and Watts' experience in military supply strategies and knowledge of the geography, climate, and infrastructure of the regions at hand. Those combined with similar expertise that the Franks contributed enabling the success of the sizeable and politically important venture (Stern 35–36, 49–50).

David similarly harnessed cross-confessional bonds in family and business for his share of the effort. His own marriage in 1743, for instance, to Anglican Margaret Evans, daughter of Philadelphia's Registrar of Wills, expanded his circle and social standing. Most immediately it fostered his partnership with William Plumsted who assisted in Pennsylvania supply. Plumsted initially replaced Margaret's father, Peter Evans, as registrar general and went on to serve as Philadelphia mayor for three terms over the 1750s. Both also belonged to Philadelphia's Dancing Assembly and Plumsted served as a warden at Christ Church at which David's children had been baptized and where Margaret affiliated.[10] As David's biographer suggests, Plumsted's own social and political advance stemmed in part from his religious fluidity for his conversion from Quakerism to Anglicanism offered "an entrée to all the seats of power" (Stern 46). In this sense, he and David bore something in common, crossing confessional lines in their personal and commercial lives and utilizing that flexibility to accrue material and social capital over time.

While shared bonds of religion and kinship fostered trade and commercial alliances, the Franks brothers successfully harnessed those forces to transcend ethnic and religious lines, as they expanded family ties. They built on close connections amassed in London, New York, or Pennsylvania to Christian elites. They complemented Jewish links with equally important bonds to Anglicans, Episcopalians, Quakers, and even Natives that expanded their commercial reach and furthered their social ascension. The family's wealth, stature, and embeddedness in the Christian world enabled it to overcome any stigma of its Jewishness. Marital and commercial bonds with prominent Christian counterparts expanded the family's resources furthering its trade and elevating its name. Young men like David or Moses Franks might well have been received as partial outsiders, as Jews facing civic limitations in an English or colonial framework that had not yet fully emancipated them and also as American-born merchant princes aspiring to elite English circles. So too among Jews, they might have suffered, a bit, as members of a family tainted by marriages to Christians with offspring being baptized and reared in churches. Yet in fact, those circumstances cast them instead as highly valuable business partners pursued by Jews and Christians alike.

THE LIMITS OF JEWISH NETWORKS

Jews living far south of Pennsylvania, also operated both within Jewish social and commercial worlds, and beyond, crossing over to collaborate with

Christians. One of Savannah, Georgia's earliest Jewish settlers, Abraham Minis built a modest estate and a sound reputation as one of that colony's leading merchants by his death in 1757. While not as successful as the Franks clan, he too saw benefit in intra- and inter-religious business operations and tried both.

Over his years of commercial activity he cultivated good relations with colonial officials and attempted, albeit unsuccessfully, to build extended partnerships with a few Christian merchants. Minis never reached the Franks's heights, but he served as one of their regional agents bolstering a small part of their larger credibility. Whether considering the food for the colony that he received from Jacob Franks or the military provisions that he sent along during Oglethorpe's attacks on the Spanish, Minis occupied a spot in the Franks's expanding Jewish network. He also partnered briefly with one of Franks's nephews until their alliance soured and he aspired to greater independence. In that context, his commercial transactions highlight the benefits as much as the limitations that a Jewish merchant of modest means faced as a small cog in the towering network of a dynasty like the Franks family. So too, his efforts at cross-cultural trade demonstrate the efforts a minor Jewish merchant made to achieve commercial autonomy by looking beyond Jewish circles.

Minis and his wife, Abigail, arrived to Savannah in 1733 from London. They and a handful of others central European Jews arrived there along with a larger party of Sephardic Jews of Spanish-Portuguese descent (Kole 3; Greenberg 552). Despite Minis's intentions to farm, continual flooding of his property dashed those hopes and set him on a path to merchant-shipping. Minis capitalized on the colony's need for basic provisions. By 1736, Thomas Causton, keeper of Savannah's public stores had already written colony trustees of his frustration with "many promises and few performances" of several established merchants from whom he received goods. He also noted the lacking quality of merchandise that did arrive to the colony. "To depend on Carolina at any time is very uncertain," he added, "and the Vessells from New York are generally loaded with Trifling things" (Candler et al. XXI.305).

Minis sought to take advantage of this crisis by tapping into his own New York Jewish supply chain. At Minis's urging, Causton contacted Jacob Franks to arrange the sale of "Two hundred barrils of Beef 50 barrils of Pork and thirty firkins of Butter" (Candler et al. XXI.305). Causton paid Minis in advance and then applied for reimbursement from Savannah's trustees.

Minis gained a reputation for his integrity over the years as well as some local stature for his frequent trade with New York. Fairly soon, however, his dealings with Causton and other local sellers spoiled. By 1738, perhaps in an effort to prevent Minis from cornering the market, Causton and others refused to pay full price for his goods. They even once refused to purchase from him outright. "The Reason given," Minis complained to colonial secretary William Stephens, "was, that they were fully supplied, and wanted no more" despite the fact, he took pains to point out, that they purchased from a non-local seller within a matter of days. Perhaps suspecting his Jewishness as a factor in their motives, Minis stressed his insider status in spite of his treatment to the contrary: "Yet in a few Days after another Sloop came, that was a Stranger, and no Scruple was made of taking all she brought; whilst he who was one of the Town was forced to take all his Cargo into private Stores: From whence he inferred, that a Stranger might expect good Usage, but the same must not be looked for by one of us" (Kole 4; Candler et al. IV.105).

If Jewishness factored in to Causton or others' calculations, it may have drawn less on specific Jewish animus, and more on the commercial benefits that it conveyed through the larger supply chains that Minis uniquely accessed. He remained, after all, the colony's earliest, and perhaps *only*, merchant until at least 1749.[11] He also commanded a valuable monopoly through the stable supply and reliable goods furnished by his northern partner, Jacob Franks. In fact, Causton had just a few years before exhibited enthusiasm regarding Jewish settlement. In 1734 he petitioned Georgia trustees not only to allow freeholders to lease land to Jews with intentions of improving it, but to allow Jewish freeholders to lease their own land to other Jewish newcomers (Pencak, *Jews and Gentiles* 151). When considered collectively, Jews as a group seem to have posed little threat for Causton. One well-connected merchant, however, with the potential to impinge on his trade, led the keeper of public stores and his colleagues to justify their informal boycott.

That Minis shared the episode with Stephens may have reflected his hope of official intervention on his behalf. If nothing else it marked an effort to underscore with local elites the injustice he perceived. So too, as the official record registered his political standing "Mr. Minas, a Jew Free-holder, who had been employing himself in the best Manner," it recognized for posterity, even if no action resulted, the disconnect between his status and his reception by fellow colonists. Nevertheless, Stephens vacillated between his opinion of the Jewish merchant as an individual who "has a fair Character, of being an industrious, honest Man" and a conviction that Causton must have also had good reason for his actions (quoted in Kole 4). If nothing else, the Minis appeal signaled ongoing efforts to ingratiate himself with colonial elites and to build on his credibility over time guarding against comparable social or financial discrimination.

Later in the decade, Minis would respond in a similar manner to another ill-fated partnership with a non-Jewish bookkeeper who arrived to the colony from Jamaica.

When Minis took Samuel Clee into his home and his business in the early 1740s, he had no idea that he would sue the bookkeeper just a few years later for absconding with £400. The move came just after he had dissolved an unfortunate partnership with Coleman Salomons, a nephew of Jacob Franks, whom Minis cast out in 1739 for a "loose Way of Book-Keeping" and suspicions of fraud (Kole 4). Coleman, or Colly as his aunt, Abigaill Franks, often called him in letters to son Naphtali, had already scandalized the family over preceding years. From 1734 to 1738, he rambled from New York to Philadelphia to Europe and back with a brief imprisonment in Pennsylvania (Abigaill Franks, 9 June 1734, 25 Dec. 1734, and 20 Nov. 1738). A partnership with Jacob's nephew initially may have seemed ideal to cement commercial bonds with the American Franks or, better yet, to thicken ties to London's prominent gem-trading Salomons with whom Minis had some association. Colly's irresponsibility, however, brought that pairing to an end highlighting another drawback of allying with looming Jewish dynasties. Minis would profit as one of Franks' regional suppliers during Oglethorpe's attack on Florida, but the Savannah merchant chafed nonetheless under the unanticipated costs of an imbalanced station in larger Jewish networks.[12]

In need of a bookkeeper after his falling out with Salomons, Minis hired Clee to manage his accounts. In a departure from the proximity he had been building with powerful Jewish firms, Minis soon elevated Clee as a full partner. The potential status he might enjoy with a Christian associate may have encouraged the hasty decision, particularly if he suspected local commercial hostility rooted to Jewish ties. Clee's Jamaican connections may have equally enticed Minis as a means to build a presence for himself in West Indian trade. Promise clouded vigilance, however, when the unsuspecting partner entrusted Clee with £400 on a trip to New York to settle debts with the Franks. Rather than resolve those finances Clee fled to Frederica. There, after using Minis's money to purchase and ship a sizeable cargo, he rented a house, establishing himself as a Keeper of Stores (Candler et al. XXV.148). Minis sued Clee unsuccessfully in 1744 and never recouped his losses. Importantly, Jewishness mattered less than a series of technicalities surrounding the summons and other documentation that foiled his first attempt to sue.

Minis took little time to appeal the ruling. As a freeholder and native-born subject who enjoyed a local reputation for honesty, the Jewish merchant likely believed these civic and social qualities would weigh in his favor. Clee evaded final judgement, however, as a two-year delay in the case allowed him to escape once more to Jamaica (Kole 5; Candler et al. XXIV.306–09).

Although Minis lost out financially, the episode highlighted not only his continued faith in colonial institutions, but the favor he thought he had cultivated in officials or the public at large. According to one onlooker, council clerk John Pye, the case did create "much Talk about the Town; and a great part of the Inhabitants inclined to think the Plaintiff hardly dealt with" (Candler et al. XXV.147). Pye also suggested in a letter to colonial trustees that at least two magistrates, Henry Parker and Joseph Watson, had been partial to Minis from the start. "For my own part," he explained, "I am not surprized [sic] at either Mr. Parker or Watsons behaviour, the former having lived on him when in town for many years & is greatly in his debt; and the latter having recd. Great favours of him by the lent of Cash &c. when others refused him" (Candler et al. XXIV.310).

As historians have pointed out in the well-rehearsed context of Dutch New Amsterdam, and perhaps even more frequently a century later, this Savannah court showed no bias against Minis for his Jewishness (Goodfriend 108–10; Snyder, "English Markets" 56–59). Further, rather than pressing for rights through the courts Minis arguably reinforced those he already expected to enjoy. Officials also did not overturn a ruling in his favor because he was a Jew, but rather treated the matter according to legal precedent suitable to a freeholder. Even if only on a small scale, the result and others like it further normalized Jewish status by reinforcing economic and civic parity.

Although larger Jewish networks had afforded Minis an early edge in colonial commerce, he clearly did not intend to rely exclusively on them for support. Rather, in credit, hospitality, and a general effort to establish independent standing as a local man of repute, Minis sought to foster social and commercial alliances with Christian peers. Although his trust may have been misguided in economic partnerships with Causton or Clee, at least in the court of public opinion his financial and friendly investments paid off. So too, the favors he extended to colonial elites also served him well. Although legal technicalities prevented a ruling in his favor, magistrates both accepted his petition to appeal the case and rejected a countersuit that Clee attempted to bring against him.

THE FREEDOM OF LONG-TERM COLLABORATION
AND TRADE ACROSS COMMUNAL LINES

Far more sustained and successful examples of cross-cultural trade played out in Newport, Rhode Island in the business dealings of Aaron Lopez. Continuous cooperation between Lopez and Christian associates played into his outstanding commercial success. After all, after fleeing the Portuguese Inquisition in 1752, Aaron (née Duarte) Lopez arrived to Newport where he began a commercial ascent that eclipsed most of his contemporaries. In just thirty years Lopez controlled a fleet of over twenty ships active in coastal, Caribbean, and transatlantic trade. His business interests spanned the Atlantic in locales like Jamaica, Haiti, Barbados, Dominica, St. Eustatius, Surinam, Honduras, Newfoundland, Quebec, England, Ireland, the Netherlands, Sweden, Spain, Portugal, the Azores and Canaries, and Africa (Chyet 18). Lopez stood out not only for his mighty commercial reach, but also his avid collaboration with Christian partners at nearly all levels.

While not uncommon for Jews to pursue business alliances with non-Jewish agents, captains, or merchants of equal standing, the extent to which Lopez nurtured them over time and, in some instances, preferred them over ready Jewish associates set his dealings apart. They also directly fostered his stunning commercial ascension.

The specialization and expanding roles that Lopez extended to his captains offers one prime example. Valuing loyalty and rewarding proficiency, he elevated several captains over the years into deeply trusted agents or profit-sharing partners. Joseph Reply, for instance, a whaler and shop-keeper in Sag Harbor, Long Island represented one of his earliest partnerships and one of the longest over the course of his career. As of 1755 the two began trading spermaceti for Lopez's budding candle manufacture in exchange for goods sold in Reply's shop. Within a decade collaboration quickly grew. By the late 1760s they engaged in bi-annual joint whaling ventures and Lopez also enlisted Reply to operate the exchanges between Newport, New Bern, and later Edenton, North Carolina (Platt, "Tar, Staves, and New England Rum" 12). They also developed an arrangement for the whaling offseason in which Reply took up residence in North Carolina as Lopez's agent. There, he promoted Lopez's trade and soon played a key role expanding ties to the West Indies. The move came just years after Lopez had abandoned an initial foray into North Carolina trade after realizing that two of his previous captains had defrauded him in small (though no less grating) amounts.[13] Contrary to these earlier deceptions, Reply's skill and proven goodwill outweighed any risk in deepening their alliance. Reply had even previously extended Lopez at least five month's credit on a payment for whale head-matter despite the valuable commodity typically demanding immediate sums in cash. Recognizing the seasonal rhythms of Lopez's trade, Reply correctly understood that longer-term gains in conforming to his partner's timetable outweighed any short term losses (Platt, "Tar, Staves, and New England Rum" 13).

Extended dealings with other captains embodied similar reciprocity. Some became regular specialists, repeatedly overseeing aspects of Lopez's mighty commercial enterprise. When Lopez invested in slaving voyages in the 1760s and 1770s, he increasingly limited his selection of captains to Nathaniel Briggs and William English. The latter had served under Briggs as first mate in the earlier run and clearly impressed Lopez who enlisted him then in his own right the following decade.[14] Similarly, as evading English tariffs on foreign goods took on larger shares of Lopez's business, Nathaniel Hathaway served time and again as the "professional smuggler among the Lopez captains" (Platt, "Tar, Staves, and New England Rum" 9). Finally, when the irresponsibility of Lopez's son-in-law, Abraham Pereira Mendes, threatened to undermine Caribbean commerce in 1769, Lopez replaced the ne'er-do-well relation with Benjamin Wright, a New England captain already in his employ. Wright's savvy made him a natural candidate to become Lopez's new Jamaica agent (Chyet 109–17). Lopez so valued Wright that when the latter threatened to quit during a 1771 disagreement, Lopez abandoned a proposed scheme to retain him in his employ (Platt, "'And Don't Forget the Guinea Voyage'" 610–11). Although typical for captains to serve as agents, the deepening collaboration extended to his pilots spoke to the skills he valued as much as the loyalty and performance he sought to cultivate over time.

Lopez's extended cooperation with Christian merchants reflected similar appreciation, particularly when they shared important commercial knowledge or assisted in navigating English laws governing trade or naturalization, the gateway, at least for a foreigner like himself to greater commercial independence. In 1756, he found an early friend in Boston merchant, Henry Lloyd, who became a close advisor and confidante as much as a partner in business (Marcus 2.629). Early on, Lloyd offered the newcomer key advice in several fields that would become important areas of his trade. When Lopez first ventured into the spermaceti market, Lloyd guided him on best practices to negotiate with Nantucket whalers. Their near monopoly on the raw material not only afforded significant leverage, but the threat that they might circumvent manufacturers and produce candles independently only further tipped the scales in favor of closer collaboration (Chyet 28). As the two regularly traded items like candles, tallow, and head-matter, Lopez's ability to conduct transactions from a place of strength would only benefit Lloyd by extension. That goodwill fed into other partnerships like a scheme to smuggle tea from Holland in which Lloyd offered up invaluable tricks of the trade. These included limiting amounts of illicit goods shipped among legitimate cargo to avoid customs officers' detection, and informing Lopez of increased surveillance of shipping documents to weed out those acquired through forgery or bribery. He also warned Lopez of the presence of spies placed by competing merchants to reveal their illicit trade (Chyet 26–27).

Lloyd may have found Lopez's willingness to smuggle goods a valuable quality to develop in a partner. But smuggling also stemmed from Lopez's foreign standing and his limited ability to trade independently. In light of the Navigation Acts, ships could only trade legally in English ports if owned by British subjects, a status Lopez had to wait for until he met the seven year residency requirement. Even when Lopez did qualify to make his application, an anomalous refusal by the Superior Court to grant him freemanship in 1760 or naturalization in 1762 still posed legal barriers.[15] Then too, Lloyd came to his assistance. Through advice from his brother-in-law, Samuel Fitch, a Boston attorney, Lloyd instructed Lopez on Massachusett's far shorter waiting period, enabling him to naturalize after just three weeks in the nearby port (Pencak 100–03). Out of loyalty as much as much as self-interest, Lloyd again shared valuable knowledge, assisting his partner to navigate local legal structures and, ultimately, to accumulate as many trading powers as possible. Although Lloyd certainly understood the potential gains of helping Lopez in these arenas, the fact that he and other Christian associates did so early in Lopez's career stands out, particularly as they could not know how much financial benefit they would gain from this non-native Jewish refugee. These strong foundational ties that Lopez established with neighboring Christians and those that he nurtured over the course of his career enabled that ascent as much as his ability in the short term to overcome marked limits that his Jewishness or foreign standing would otherwise have posed.

Lopez also benefited from aid he secured from established Jewish merchants, but his growing stature thrived mostly from the non-Jewish networks he developed. He did draw on local Jewish support which included that of his earlier arrived Newport kin, half-brother, Moses Lopez, and his future father-in-law, Jacob Rodriguez Rivera. Both had accrued impressive capital and social standing by the time Aaron joined them. He also benefited from the goodwill of prominent Jewish dynasties elsewhere like the Gomezes, Jacob Franks, or Hayman Levy and Solomon Marache of New York. All extended him much needed credit to begin his activities. Perhaps hoping to win a northern agent, Jacob Franks even hired a clerk to write Lopez in Portuguese and establish a rapport for future dealings (Chyet 24–25, 28).

But as Lopez gained financial independence he increasingly opted to work independently or to seek out Christian partners to fill out his trade. While his initial gravitation to candle manufacture clearly drew on his brother and father-in-law's involvement in that industry after success in the snuff market, Lopez quickly carved out a niche for himself in that endeavor (Snyder, "English Markets" 67). Within a decade among several candle manufacturers who established a collective trust to regulate supply and pricing in the competitive spermaceti market, Lopez signed on as a separate firm from his relations, but he registered as the only Jew without an explicitly stated partner (Chyet 42–51).

As his own standing increased, he also seems to have distanced himself from some of his earlier Jewish creditors. Historian Jacob Rader Marcus suggested that Lopez's inclination to deal with non-Jewish firms in New York like the Crugers or Ludlows may have served as strategy to detach himself from earlier dependence on Jewish correspondents in that city. So too, his notable decision to "bypass the American-born Frankses to deal almost exclusively with Gentiles" in London or his preference for Christian agents in locales like Amsterdam with plentiful Jewish suppliers may have further sought to edge out Jewish competitors (Marcus 2.585–86).

Even some of Lopez's most audacious schemes late in his career drew wind in their sails from the multilayered support he had developed over the years with an array of Christian partners. A massive 1775 whaling expedition to the Falkland Islands seemed to Lopez a viable enterprise despite the £40,000 necessary to finance the run. This said nothing of the political nerve it required to partner with men like Francis Rotch, of Boston Tea Party infamy, or the delicate balance he had to recognize among larger colonial powers amid pre-Revolutionary tensions. His long dealings with the Rotches since at least 1760 clearly contributed to the bold undertaking. From early exchanges of coffee, chocolate, molasses, and rum on his account for significant amounts of whale matter, their collaboration had evolved by the 1770s to encompass a fleet of fifteen whaling vessels (Marcus 2.259; Chyet 28, 142–53). In an equally notable initiative in 1772, he attempted to build on years smuggling Madeira wine into Rhode Island by folding regular voyages to Lisbon into expanding coastal and West Indian trade. Enlisting trusted captains like Nathanial Hathaway and Joseph Reply may have softened the speculative nature of the enterprise's trial voyage. Whether Lopez anticipated the vessel's seizure, though, he probably factored in his close relations with colonial officials like customs collector, Charles Dudley, or former chief justice and governor, Samuel Ward as protection against losses too severe. As most studies of the episode excitedly point out, Ward even jovially returned a barrel of wine that had washed up on his property after crewmembers cast it overboard to minimize detection upon the ship's capture. Little wonder that friend and famed minister, Ezra Stiles, noted in his diary, "The vessel and wines will be condemned—but it is said they will be set up at a trifle and Lopez will bid them off at far less than duties; so that he shall make his voyage good. Favor and partiality!" (quoted in Chyet 126). Whether captains, fellow investors, or fellow colonial elites, the longstanding relationships that Lopez fostered and sustained with Christian associates over the years served as the backbone for his commercial empire as much as his commercial aspirations.

Merchant-shippers like David or Moses Franks, Abraham Minis, or Aaron Lopez focused on divergent markets, varied in their respective capacities, and drew on very different resources whether trading networks, social stature, or personal wealth. Nonetheless, precisely because these figures cut across region, trade, places of origin, and socio-economic or political standing they represent a wide spectrum of early American Jewish merchants whose careers demonstrated the limits and opportunities of regional or transatlantic trade. Despite their differences in situation and outcome, though, all looked to Christian partners as a strategy to advance their profits and all did so early on in their careers.

Their different starting points inflected those alliances with very different tenors. So too, that dynamic shaped the benefits or calculations that their Christian partners weighed when deciding to engage with Jewish associates. Albeit near-economic equals, they still occupied social and civic marginality that cannot go ignored. Sustained and profitable cooperation or recourse to legal protections that mattered more than their Jewish identity played some part in their demarginalization, for Christians in their immediate circles and toward a longer and larger popular perception.

Indeed, these men's respective careers show, too, that Jewishness did not register as a liability whether it intersected with wealth or lack of obvious status. Rather, at least for this array of early American Christian and Jewish entrepreneurs, and likely many others in need of extended study, interethnic partnerships in trade and religious non-uniformity proved something of an asset, promoting wealth and standing among those who already possessed it and presenting a path for Jews who sought alternatives to established Jewish networks. At the same time, it afforded an entry point to Christian merchants seeking to tap into Jewish supply chains or ever-valuable credit flows that enabled them to function. It allowed economic adventurers to pool their funds and resources in pursuit of greater profits. Although forces well beyond Jewish and Protestant business alliances clearly underwrote the maturation of English transatlantic commerce over and a related phenomenon of Jews' steady accrual of social and civic rights within that bigger world the course of the eighteenth century, the ability of individuals to forge alternative business paths registered too in each expanding realm. Alongside improved information flows, more sophisticated systems of credit, and the military or geographic consolidation that all developed English markets overseas, the legal and social contours enabling extended trade beyond communal or religious lines added to that mix. To that end, so too did individual Jewish and Christian profit-seekers who tested the limits of that system and, by making the most of it, reinforced it and furthered it along. They did so in their local business dealings, but also on a global scale.

Notes

1. On the role of Jewish merchants developing distribution and consumer networks linking colonial markets to one another and English goods see Snyder, "English Markets."

2. Just some recent overviews that consolidate these themes include Katznelson, "Between Separation and Disappearance"; Diner 18–26; Jaher; Sorkin 178–87; Lederhendler 1–25.

3. On Jews and American capitalism see Kobrin. On trading networks just a few recent examples include Hancock; Trivellato; Aslanian; Trivellato, Halevi, and Antunes; and Bregoli.

4. The first act in 1651, for instance, prohibited goods not shipped directly through England or English provinces in order to undercut Amsterdam as a competing center of trade. Subsequent acts of the 1660s closed off colonial commerce to foreign-born merchants so that only recognized subjects could profit from English holdings (Godfrey and Godfrey 50–51).

5. Although barred as alien merchants from colonial trade, Jews could initially pursue the letters of endenization that the Crown granted fairly liberally. Non-naturalized foreign traders received an in-between status as denizens that compensated Jews for the need to swear an Anglican oath for full naturalization offering a gateway, despite foreign tariffs, to colonial exchange (Godfrey and Godfrey 50–51).

6. In 1745 they co-owned the *Sea Flower* with ships named for David's sisters, *Richa* (1746) and *Phila* (1750), also registered to Levy and Franks. Their ship, *Myrtilla*, regularly sailed twice a year for London, importing and exporting manufactured goods for colonial commodities (Wolf and Whiteman 27).

7. For a thorough reconstruction of those Jewish ties see Pitock, "'Separated from us as far as West is from East.'"

8. In 1740 Moses assisted Jacob in trading English goods received from Naphtali in London for building materials and other supplies that they sent on to Jamaica via John Colebrooke, the London firm's representative (Marcus 2.713–16).

9. Marcus even goes so far to suggest that Franks' limited civic standing as a Jew shielded him from political infighting and allowed him to remain one of the few steady members of the syndicate over the course of the war (2.713–16; Pencak, *Jews and Gentiles* 182–83).

10. Perhaps as a function of his recognition and ties to well-connected men like Plumsted, by 1757 Franks had also joined the prestigious Library company of Philadelphia and within five years won coveted membership to the select Mount Regal Fishing Company (Stern 46; Pencak, *Jews and Gentiles* 181; Wolf and Whiteman 33).

11. Minis imported and traded for at least a decade before the 1749 establishment of Harris & Habersham, long considered Georgia's first merchants. See "The Minis Family" 48.

12. Minis transferred supplies from New York between Savannah and the British base at Frederica. Rounding out those efforts, Samuel Levy and Colly's brother, Moses Salomons supplied military goods in Charleston that they received from New York (Marcus 2.713).

13. In 1762 Lopez had given up the trade after realizing that captains either underreported sales or charged his account for duties that never actually paid (Platt, "Tar, Staves, and New England Rum" 6).

14. Between 1764 and 1769, Nathaniel Briggs captained three of six initial slave voyages that Lopez financed among Africa and the Caribbean. When Lopez reentered the trade between 1770 and 1775, Briggs captained or consigned four out of seven voyages with William English overseeing the rest (Platt, "'And Don't Forget the Guinea Voyage'").

15. Pencak reasons that fears of Lopez or fellow Jewish applicant, Isaac Elizer association with an elite mercantile political faction and thereby swinging closely contested colonial elections may have fueled the refusal (100–03).

Works Cited

Aslanian, Sebouh. *From the Indian Ocean to the Mediterranean: The Global Trade Networks of Armenian Merchants from New Julfa.* Univ. of California, 2011.

Byars, William Vincent. *B. and M. Gratz: Merchants in Philadelphia 1754–1798; Papers of Interest to Their Posterity and the Posterity of Their Associates.* Hugh Stephens, 1916.

Bregoli, Francesca. "'Your Father's Interests': The Business of Kinship in a Trans-Mediterranean Jewish Family, 1776–1790." *The Jewish Quarterly Review* vol. 108, no. 2, 2018, pp. 194–224.

Candler, Allen D., Kenneth Coleman, and Milton Ready, editors. *The Colonial Records of the State of Georgia,* vol. XXI. Franklin Printing, 1904–.

Chyet, Stanley F. *Lopez of Newport: Colonial American Merchant Prince.* Wayne State Univ., 1970.

Croghan, George. Letter to David Franks. 27 Dec. 1772. Franks Family Papers, P-142, Box 1, Folder 10. American Jewish Historical Society, New York, NY, and Boston, MA.

Diner, Hasia R. *The Jews of the United States, 1654–2000.* Univ. of California, 2004.

Endelman, Todd M. *The Jews of Britain, 1656 to 2000.* Univ. of California, 2002.

Faber, Eli. *A Time For Planting: The First Migration, 1654–1820.* Johns Hopkins Univ., 1992.

Franks, Abigaill. Letter to Naphtali Franks. 7 Oct. 1733, in *The Letters of Abigaill Levy Franks, 1733–1748,* edited by Edith B. Gelles, Yale Univ., 2004, p. 11.

————. Letter to Naphtali Franks. 9 June 1734, in *The Letters of Abigaill Levy Franks, 1733–1748,* edited by Edith B. Gelles, Yale Univ., 2004, pp. 19–21.

————. Letter to Naphtali Franks. 25 Dec. 1734, in *The Letters of Abigaill Levy Franks, 1733–1748,* edited by Edith B. Gelles, Yale Univ., 2004, p. 34.

————. Letter to Naphtali Franks. 20 Nov. 1738, in *The Letters of Abigaill Levy Franks, 1733–1748,* edited by Edith B. Gelles, Yale Univ., 2004, p. 64.

Gelles, Edith B. *The Letters of Abigaill Levy Franks, 1733–1748.* Yale Univ., 2004.

Godfrey, Sheldon J., and Judith C. Godfrey. *Search Out the Land: The Jews and the Growth of Equality in British Colonial America, 1740–1867.* McGill-Queen's Univ., 1995.

Goodfriend, Joyce D. "Practicing Toleration in Dutch New Netherland." *The First Prejudice: Religious Tolerance and Intolerance in Early America,* edited by Chris Beneke and Christopher S. Grenda, Univ. of Pennsylvania, 2011, pp. 98–122.

Greenberg, Mark I. "A 'Haven of Benignity': Conflict and Cooperation Between Eighteenth-Century Savannah Jews." *The Georgia Historical Quarterly,* vol. 86, no. 4, 2002, pp. 544–68.

Hancock, David. "The Trouble with Networks: Managing the Scots' Early-Modern Madeira Trade." *The Business History Review,* vol. 79, no. 3, 2006, pp. 467–91.

Jaher, Frederic Cople. "American Exceptionalism: The Case of the Jews, 1750–1850." *Why is America Different: American Jewry on Its 350th Anniversary*, edited by Steven T. Katz, Univ. Press of America, 2010, pp. 28–53.

Katznelson, Ira. "Between Separation and Disappearance: Jews on the Margins of American Liberalism." *Paths of Emancipation: Jews, States, and Citizenship*, edited by Pierre Birnbaum and Ira Katznelson, Princeton Univ, 1995, pp. 157–205.

———. "Two Exceptionalisms: Points of Departure for Studies of Capitalism and Jews in the United States." *Chosen Capital: The Jewish Encounter with American Capitalism*, edited by Rebecca Kobrin, Univ. of Rutgers, 2012, pp. 12–32.

Kettner, James H. *The Development of American Citizenship, 1608–1870*. Univ. of North Carolina, 1978.

Kobrin, Rebecca. "The Chosen People in the Chosen Land: The Jewish Encounter with American Capitalism." *Chosen Capital: The Jewish Encounter with American Capitalism*, edited by Rebecca Kobrin, Univ. of Rutgers, 2012, pp. 1–11.

Kole, Kaye. *The Minis Family of Georgia 1733–1992*. Georgia Historical Society, 1992.

Lederhendler, Eli. *American Jewry: A New History*. Cambridge Univ., 2017.

Marcus, Jacob Rader. *The Colonial American Jew, 1492–1776*, vol 2. Wayne State Univ., 1970.

Mathias, Peter. "Risk, Credit and Kinship in Early Modern Enterprise." *The Early Modern Atlantic Economy*, edited by John J. McCusker and Kenneth Morgan, Cambridge Univ., 2000, pp. 15–35.

"The Minis Family." *The Georgia Historical Quarterly*, vol. 1, no. 1, 1917, pp. 45–49.

Pencak, William. "Anti-Semitism, Toleration, and Appreciation: The Changing Relations of Jews and Gentiles in Early America." *The First Prejudice: Religious Tolerance and Intolerance in Early America*, edited by Chris Beneke and Christopher S. Grenda, Univ. of Pennsylvania, 2011, pp. 241–62.

———. *Jews and Gentiles in Early America, 1654–1800*. Univ. of Michigan, 2005.

Pitock, Toni. "'Separated from Us As Far As West Is from East': Eighteenth-Century Ashkenazi Immigrants in the Atlantic World." *American Jewish History* vol. 102, no. 2, April 2018, pp. 173–93.

Platt, Virginia Bever. "'And Don't Forget the Guinea Voyage': The Slave Trade of Aaron Lopez of Newport." *The William and Mary Quarterly*, vol. 32, no. 4, 1975, pp. 601–18.

———. "Tar, Staves, and New England Rum: The Trade of Aaron Lopez of Newport, Rhode Island, with Colonial North Carolina." *The North Carolina Historical Review*, vol. 48, no. 1, 1971, pp. 1–22.

Snyder, Holly. "English Markets, Jewish Merchants, and Atlantic Endeavors: Jews and the Making of British Transatlantic Commercial Culture, 1650–1800." *Atlantic Diasporas: Jews, Conversos, and Crypto-Jews in the Age of Mercantilism*, edited by Richard L. Kagan and Philip D. Morgan, Johns Hopkins Univ., 2009, pp. 50–74.

———. "Rules, Rights and Redemption: The Negotiation of Jewish Status in British Atlantic Port Towns, 1740–1831." *Jewish History*, vol. 20, no. 2, 2006, pp. 147–70.

Sorkin, David. "Is American Jewry Exceptional? Comparing Jewish Emancipation in America." *American Jewish History* vol. 96, no. 3, 2010, pp. 175–200.

Stern, Mark Abbot. *David Franks: Colonial Merchant.* Pennsylvania State Univ., 2010.

Trivellato, Francesca. *The Familiarity of Strangers: The Sephardic Diaspora, Livorno, and Cross-Cultural Trade in the Early Modern Period.* Yale Univ., 2009.

Trivellato, Francesca, Leor Halevi, and Cátia Antunes, editors. *Religion and Trade: Cross-Cultural Exchanges in World History, 1000–1900.* New York: Oxford Univ., 2014.

Volwiler, A. T. "George Croghan and the Westward Movement." *The Pennsylvania Magazine of History and Biography,* vol. 46, no. 4, 1922, pp. 273–311.

Wolf, Edwin, and Maxwell Whiteman. *The History of the Jews of Philadelphia from Colonial Times to the Age of Jackson.* Jewish Publication Society of America, 1957.

Yogev, Gedalia. *Diamonds and Coral: Anglo-Dutch Jews and Eighteenth-Century Trade.* New York: Leicester Univ., 1978.

CHAPTER 3

Jewish Immigrant Bankers, New York Real Estate, and American Finance, 1870–1914

by Rebecca Kobrin

What an extraordinary episode in the economic progress of man that age was which came to an end in August 1914!

—*John Maynard Keynes[1]*

The summer of 1914 is most often remembered for the eruption of the war that transformed Europe; fewer recall how during the same summer a crisis of confidence unfolded on American shores that led to the end of the era of immigrant banking. The private unincorporated businesses that were known in America as "immigrant banks" may have faded into history, but the debates they launched over immigration, access to credit and banking reform have reverberations until today. The crisis was set in motion by thousands of East European immigrant Jews in New York City who ran to withdraw their savings from their "banks," a network of unregulated immigrant businesses that sold ship tickets, kept deposits, granted small loans and processed currency exchanges for overseas transfer—to transmit back to Europe. Overwhelmed by the sea of depositors rushing in, several immigrant banks closed their doors ("Depozitors un der bankn kampf" 1). As a result, Eugene Lamb, New York State's Banking superintendent, decided to intervene, taking over the books of the banks of A. Grochowski, the Deutsch

Brothers, Adolf Mandel, M & L Jarmulowksy, and Max Kobre because they did not have enough funds in reserve to return their depositors' assets. The Jarmulowsky bank alone had 15,000 depositors with over $1,667,000 in deposits in the bank. But that paled in comparison to the banks of Max Kobre, who had branches on the Lower East Side and in Brooklyn that claimed over 23,000 depositors who had entrusted $3,700,000 to him ("Information RE: Private Bankers").

Figure 1: Depositors protest outside a failed bank, July 24, 1914. Lot 7178, Library of Congress Prints and Photograph Division.

Riots soon broke out as many immigrant banks could not distribute their funds to their depositors who feared the worst and wanted to send funds back to Europe (fig. 1). These riots concerned New York City's officials as it raised questions about the stability of banking institutions in New York City, the financial capital of the United States. Since 1863, New York had served as the backbone of the United States' expanding banking system (Sylla).[2] Many believed in 1914, that New York's banks would remain unscathed by the rumblings in Europe (Ahamed 29–32). But New York's immigrant Jews, whose extended families still lived in Europe, did not see the war as some distant menace.[3] Uncovering the fact that much of these institutions' missing assets were tied up in real estate investments that could not be quickly liquidated, the

New York State Banking Superintendent, Eugene Lamb would set in motion legislative and judicial efforts that would forever doom the world of immigrant banking. These new laws fundamentally altered the practice of "private banking" in New York City, a city that functioned as America's financial capital, Jewish immigrant capital and the pre-paid ship-ticket sales capital of the world. Within a few years, hundreds of other small immigrant businesses that similarly made a profit from selling ship tickets and investing in real estate were forced to shut down. But such drastic measures were deemed necessary by New York State banking authorities who believed such regulation would protect New York State from the world of immigrant banking that was threatening to not only economic life in New York but in America itself (Hochfelder 340; Lears).

This chapter aims to raise questions about the place of Jewish immigrant banking in early-twentieth century New York, highlighting the historic interplay between banking regulation, New York real estate development and immigration history. Through its close analysis of the world of Jewish immigrant bankers by means of a focus on the business of Max Kobre, I seek to reinsert East European Jewish immigrant entrepreneurs into the narrative of American economic history. To be sure, the influence of Jews on banking in the United States is far from unchartered territory (Birmingham; Carosso; Supple; N. Cohen; Pak). But when asked how immigrant Jews and their business practices shaped twentieth-century American banking, most scholars would rattle off the names of famed Jewish investment bankers such as Jacob Schiff, Paul Warburg, and Henry Lehman, whose successes shaped the sector of investment banking (Chernow; N. Cohen; Pak). However, that isolating of a few prominent exemplars of Jewish economic achievement obscures the formative roles played by unregulated East European Jewish-run immigrant banks at the turn of the twentieth century. Part of a broader trend in banking catering to "unbanked" immigrant masses, entrepreneurial Jewish immigrants deployed innovative credit mechanisms and speculative investment strategies that shaped not only American commercial banking but also urban development in cities such as New York. The credit that these institutions offered to immigrants directly contributed to their ability to come to America and to their economic practices once they arrived. While some of these experiments succeeded and others failed, they all deserve attention because, as American historian David Hollinger points out, the lack of a straightforward historical and social-scientific study into what enabled East European immigrant Jews to succeed economically in the United States has perpetuated a mystification of Jewish history (Hollinger 596). In short, this chapter seeks to highlight the ways in which East European Jewish immigrant bankers who have been placed in the dustbin of history actually transformed not only the Jewish immigrant world, but commercial banking and its regulation in the United States as America's system of banking regulation took shape in direct response to risks taken by these unregulated financial institutions and their failures.

THE PROBLEM OF THE IMMIGRANT "BANKER" IN THE UNITED STATES

In 1907 the US Congress created a commission to investigate what many Americans saw as a national crisis: the unprecedented number of immigrants flowing into the United States. Led by Senator William Dillingham, this commission made observations and recommendations that became codified into law concerning such varied issues as instituting a literacy test, a quota system based on national origin, continuing Asian exclusion, and granting greater federal oversight of immigration policy (Benton-Cohen). Among the many problems this commission identified was the pressing issue of "Immigrant Banks." As the commission noted in 1910:

> Numerous instances are at hand where strangers have gone into communities and established themselves as steamship agents and foreign-exchange dealers. Their only qualification was that they were Italians among Italians, or Magyars among Magyars. Even a former evil reputation does not seem to injure their ability to attract patronage. In the course of the investigation, knowledge was gained of two fugitive swindlers, two clerks discharged for dishonesty, several laborers dismissed for dishonesty . . . who have established themselves successfully as bankers. (United States, Congress, Senate, The Immigration Commission, 24 Feb. 2010, 22)

Max Kobre, who arrived in the United States in 1891, became one of the most prominent immigrant bankers through his sale of ship tickets from his "banks" on the Lower East Side and in Brooklyn (fig. 2). Kobre also became infamous among representatives of the British and Dutch shipping lines for his practice of selling tickets on installments—offering credit—through these agents. Kobre introduced new selling methods, such as cheaper cash-orders, enabling him to further pierce the divided ethnic markets common in the sale of ship tickets. In fact, Kobre sold so many tickets that the Holland

American line secretly sent an agent to investigate his business practices in 1894. As Van den Toorn, the representative of the Holland-American Line in New York, reported, Kobre exemplified the corrupt business practices of East European Jewish agents who sold on installments through peddlers. Agents of the Continental Lines posing as migrants caught Kobre underselling their established rates. While fined for his practices, Kobre was up and running again in less than a week: he sold too many tickets on installment to be put out of business.

Figure 2: Max Kobre. Image courtesy of Shaw Kobre.

Indeed, it was Kobre's expansive offering of credit through the sale of tickets on installment that raised the ire of shipping companies in 1895 as they tried to seize control of the increasingly competitive New York pre-paid ticket market. Other groups also used peddlers to sell tickets, but the shipping lines targeted Max Kobre's "Banking, Passage and Exchange office," seeing it as an exemplar of the problem (Feys ch. 3).

In short, many officials throughout the country were concerned with the growing ranks of unqualified immigrant "bankers who sold ship tickets and in contrast to traditional bankers did all their business in a foreign language and operated out of other commercial enterprises, such as saloons, grocery stores, bakeries, or boarding houses (Day; Jenks and Lauck xv, 96). In New York City, the nation's financial capital, banking authorities were concerned about these so-called banks as they knew that aside from selling ship tickets, they also offered loans. Yet they were not chartered or regulated by any governmental authority. Thus, they did not hold funds in reserve as state-chartered banks were expected to do. As the Senate Commission on Immigration bemoaned, this lack of regulation enabled these enterprises to use the deposits left with them for a myriad of speculative investments, such as stocks or real estate.

> As regards the tendency among immigrant bankers to invest funds entrusted to them in real estate and stocks, it is only necessary to state here that many of these bankers who receive deposits are property holders to an extent not warranted by the legitimate profits they would derive from their steamship, foreign exchange or other business. It was found that real estate, first and second mortgages and speculative securities were favored forms of investment. Deposits have undoubtedly been the greatest resource these bankers have in making such investments. (United States, Congress, Senate, Reports of the Immigration Commission, 2011, 244)

Immigrant bankers' involvement in urban real estate development can be clearly seen through the world of Jewish immigrant banking in the years leading up to 1914. East European Jewish immigrant businesses' credit-accessing strategies transformed the ever-expanding world of New York real estate. Starting at the end of the nineteenth century, real estate emerged as the ideal industry for ambitious immigrants who lacked capital and were willing to take risks. Scholars have long pondered Jewish immigrants' embrace of real estate investment that took place in numerous cities throughout the world at the end of the nineteenth century.[4] The Jewish world that saw real estate as a commodity in New York demonstrates what Sara Stein has observed in another commodity market, namely, the ways in which "ethnicity [acts] as a powerful force in the shaping of commodity networks and, conversely, [how] particular commercial networks . . . impact on the identity formation of their participants" (Stein 777). Unlike other commodities in which Jews were overly represented during this period, real estate did not present its investor with an easily portable asset (Stein; Oltuski; Vanden Daelen). Rather, it did present great profits to those willing to take large risks. Jews appreciation of real estate as a commodity, according to some scholars, was directly linked to their pre-migration experiences in which they "never developed an attitude of reverence and permanence toward land." As historian Edward Shapiro sums up, they appreciated "what was important were land values, not the land itself " (121).

The ways in which immigrant bankers became involved in real estate is illustrated through the numerous banks of Max Kobre with branches in Brooklyn and the Lower East side (fig. 3). His most lucrative branch was in Brownville, Brooklyn, a center for East European Jewish immigrant settlement at the turn of the twentieth century. Brownsville, as Alter Landsman recalled, possessed one of the most dynamic real estate markets in New York City before 1914:

> Real estate values jumped. Hundreds of buildings were erected to provide housing for newcomers. Between 1907 and 1909, the entire section of west Rockaway was cluttered up with diggers and excavators. Whole streets were cut through and piled with building material and sewer pipes. In 1909, Dr. Coyne, president of the Brownsville Tax Payers Association, stated that lots originally costing $50 or more had been sold within the previous two years at an average price of $3000. (83)

Figure 3: Advertisement for Max Kobre's Bank, Yidishe tageblat *January 2, 1912.*

From Kobre's 1914 Bankruptcy trial, one can clearly see how he tapped into this exploding real estate market. In addition to running a bank that made small profits off of placing deposits on which he offered 3% interest into chartered

banks in Brooklyn that offered 6% interest, Kobre also established two companies in which he served as secretary and Moses Ginsburg served as the treasurer.
As his bookkeeper, Elias Frankle testified, "The Saratoga Improvement Company
and the Canal Realty Company were both real estate arms of Kobre's business.
Kobre still made some profit from steamship tickets sold through the "foreign
department," in Manhattan but his real estate investments drove his profits starting in 1910 ("In the Matter of Max Kobre and Moses Ginsburg" 15).

In many ways, one can say Kobre actually provided the Jewish immigrant
community with a service, since most aspiring real estate investors had no collateral and needed several thousand dollars, and at times, over ten thousand
dollars (Kobre v. Kramer Mortgage Company, 1914). To be sure, there were
other credit accessing institutions—such as the Hebrew Free Loan Society or
Jewish hometown associations [landsmanshaftn]—but these institutions rarely
offered loans over $500 (Tenenbaum 6). As scholar Shelly Tenenbaum high-
lights, the business model for these credit-accessing organizations was that
they raised capital from supporters contributions. In New York City, wealthy
German Jews now and then loaned small amounts under $300 to approved
borrowers without interest. Kobre, on the other hand, loaned out thousands to
individuals lacking collateral as he trusted them.

Jews were far from the only immigrant group to invest in real estate. Such
behavior was common, as the Senate Immigration Commission noted: "there
is a great tendency about immigrant bankers to invest funds entrusted to them
in real estate and stocks . . . Speculation in real estate is not infrequent" (United
States, Congress, Senate, Reports of the Immigration Commission, 2011, 244).
Though not the only ones to engage in this venture, Jewish immigrant bankers
became particularly heavily involved in real estate at the turn of the century.
As the main institution granting loans to ambitious immigrants, immigrant
banks became central to New York City real estate development, a fact many
contemporary observers noted (Wheatley 324–27; also see Shachter 10). As
Richard Wheatley claimed in his 1892 survey of the "Jews in New York," Jews
not only owned close to $200,000,000 in real estate but their constant trade of
real estate holdings was responsible for more "than five-eights" of all real estate
deals in New York City (325).

Where Jews may have differed from other immigrant groups lay in their
lack of sentimentality and forward-looking attitude: when other groups began
moving into specific neighborhoods, Jews moved elsewhere and developed new
communities by buying up lots, erecting cheap buildings and renting them out
quickly to prospective residents. Rather than just being involved in Manhattan,

Jewish immigrant real estate entrepreneurs relished investing in developing the outer boroughs of New York City. As George Cohen noted in 1904,

> Whole stretches of hitherto uninhabited territory, like the Bronx, Borough Park and Bensonhurst in New York City, Douglas Park section in Chicago and similar sections in the other cities have been converted into veritable cities, where block after block of fine suburban residences house the Jewish population. Land values within ten years have risen to an extent undreamed of. Barren and deserted spots have been turned into fine residential sections with all the latest advantages of a modern community. The tenement sections into which they migrated several decades earlier have been to a certain extent rebuilt; numbers of old private houses and slum dwellings have been converted into up-to-date double decker apartments.
>
> [In New York City] These Jewish operators do not confine themselves to the East side, but extend their activities to all parts of the Greater City and its environs. There is more than an accidental connection between the tremendous rise of real estate values in New York City since the [18]90's and the expansion of the Jewish community in the metropolis. In critical times, however, more than one fortune went with greater rapidity than it came. Nevertheless, as a result of the unparalleled expansion, a large number of erstwhile Jewish pushcart peddlers and shopkeepers marched triumphantly through the portals of homes in New York's most exclusive residential section. (127–28)

Jewish immigrant bankers of all groups relied on their ethnic networks to build the types of dwellings that would entice other immigrants to move (Gabaccia).[5] But the system that built up the tenements and new neighborhoods was heavily dependent on credit access and risk. A 1903 report by an investigator for the New York State Tenement House Commission, Elgin Gould, explains the vital centrality of credit and risk for New York City real estate development:

> The work is done as cheaply as possible [on borrowed funds]. Every penny saved means so much more profit to the building as he is not a holder for investment but builds to sell as soon as the building is completed or even before completion, should he be fortunate enough. Such a tenement built on an inside lot, would cost at the present time from $16,000 to $19,000. The cost of the lot varies, let us say, from $15,000 to $18,000. The total investment would therefore amount to about $34,000. Rentals are fixed so that if the building keeps full and all rents are collected, from 12 to 12.5 percent gross would be received. (358)

Playing a disproportionate role as a result of their credit accessing strategies, immigrant Jews became a central force in the expansion of new areas of
New York City (Gabaccia). So many Jewish immigrants tried their luck in New
York City's real estate market that Abraham Cahan, editor of the *Jewish Daily
Forward*, the most popular Yiddish daily newspaper, would coin the Yiddish
term "realestatenik" (combining the words real estate and *alrightnik* [nouveau
riche]) in reference to the growing ranks of speculators in the Jewish immigrant world. As Cahan evocatively depicted in his classic tale of Jewish immigrant life, *The Rise of David Levinsky*, "huge fortunes seemed to be growing like
mushrooms all over New York . . . I saw men who three years ago had not been
worth a cent and who were now buying and selling blocks of property" (480).
The "intoxicating" real estate "boom," Cahan explained, attracted all "the small
tradesmen of the slums" to "invest their savings in houses in lots" (464). These
"realestateniks" would gather in Harlem on the corner of Fifth Avenue and
116th Street, where their "gesticulating, jabbering, [and] whispering," made
them resemble "the crowd of curb-brokers on Broad Street" (486). But the
commodity they were trading was not stocks but building lots.

Beyond Abraham Cahan, there was a general sense in New York City
that tenement construction was a particularly Jewish economic niche. As
George Cohen stated:

> The purchase of real estate and building of new homes has become a
> Jewish business in New York . . . A perusal of the real estate columns
> of the daily newspapers bring out the fact that the overwhelming ma-
> jority of buyers of real estate are German and Russian Jews. The vast
> heterogeneous population of New York City are sheltered in Jewish
> houses. The Real Estate Record and Guide might be mistaken for a
> Jewish directory of the city. (128)

Max Kobre with the help of Moses Ginsburg became one of the most
successful "realestateniks" around in Brooklyn. The lawsuits following the
banks closures revealed the extent of their holdings throughout Brownsville.
But their lofty ambitions were thwarted by events that transpired in Europe. As
thousands of Jewish immigrant depositors ran into Max Kobre's three banks to
withdraw their funds to send back to Europe, Max Kobre's real estate investments caused the bank to have insufficient funds in reserves.

THE JEWISH COMMUNAL RESPONSE TO THE
JEWISH IMMIGRANT BANK CLOSURES

Jewish communal leaders realized that they had to respond immediately to the growing ranks of Jewish immigrant depositors who could not access their money after news of war in Europe. As a group, most Jewish immigrant depositors often teetered on the brink of destitution. Living in the densely packed Lower East side and in Brownsville, in tenements which one contemporary observer called "great prison-like structures," the neighborhood, as scholar Gerard Wolfe points out, "soon became synonymous with [immigrant Jews'] grinding poverty and squalid existence."[6] The sixty thousand depositors who could not access their funds immediately became impoverished, underscoring that America at the turn of the twentieth century was no promised land for immigrants. As essayist S. L. Blumenson recalled several decades later: "the same poverty that existed among the denizens of the Judengassen [Vienna's Jewish district] was duplicated on the [Lower] East Side" (65).

The frightened and infuriated depositors realized that despite all their hard work and frugal saving, they were no longer just struggling immigrants. With their savings eviscerated, they fell into the growing ranks of the "Jewish poor" or "near poor," as one social service provider termed their situation, akin to what they had sought to escape in Tsarist Russia.[7] Immediately, Jewish social workers realized that the reverberations of the banks' failures would be felt by many far beyond the depositors themselves. Indeed, Kehillah worker Dr. Paul Abelson stressed the growing ranks "in very great financial straits" whom he encountered daily who found themselves dependent on soup kitchens for their daily sustenance. On the heavily populated streets of the Lower East Side, as economist and statistician Isaac Rubinow commented in 1905, "almost every newly arrived Russian-Jewish laborer comes into contact with a Russian-Jewish employer; almost every Russian-Jewish tenement dweller must pay his exorbitant rent to a Russian-Jewish landlord" (Rubinow 104). Indeed, without Jewish communal action, the whole economy of the Lower East Side could collapse.

But the bank closures took place in late July and early August, when most of the New York Jewish banking elites had decamped to the Adirondacks for the summer. Perhaps unaware of the unfolding crisis, they offered no immediate response to their co-religionists growing need. After the riot at City Hall, Judah Magnes sent a panicked telegram to Louis Marshall, who tersely responded, "I am on vacation until September 1, at which point I will address this issue" (Magnes, Internal correspondence). With no other Jewish private banker stepping up to bail out these failed East European Jewish immigrant bankers, Felix Adler, Mortimer Schiff, Cyrus Sulzberger, Bernard Semel, and Julius Goldman, the leading figures of the New York Kehillah, penned the following letter to their friends and fellow Jewish leaders:

> The failure of the banks on the East Side which tied up the savings of sixty thousand depositors to the amount of more than ten million dollars ($10,000,000), coming in combination with existing conditions of unemployment, has produced a state of affairs which has not heretofore been paralleled in our community. Thousands of thrifty and self-supporting persons have been reduced to the verge of penury. These are people who have never been recipients of charity and do not now wish charitable gifts to meet their requirements.[8]

As these leaders noted, the angry, rioting depositors were not criminals. They painted them instead as models of self-reliance who needed help in a desperate time. Forming the New York City East Side Emergency Loan Fund, Adler, Schiff, Sulzberger, Semel, and Goldman asked anyone who could afford it to make a donation of $5 that "a generous donor" would match so that a new "popular loan fund" could be established "to deal with making loans to persons not willing to apply to charitable institutions" (Files of the New York City East Side Emergency Loan Fund). Appreciating the general uncertainty and financial strain of the time, they emphasized that the "amount they requested from each individual is so small that we felt we may indulge the hope that we shall receive a favorable response for every person to whom this letter is addressed." But these pleas for help fell on deaf ears, and the depositors remained penniless.

Indeed, the first effort to address the Jewish immigrant banking crisis came from a most unlikely corner of the world: Russia. Realizing the centrality of the remittances sent by Jewish immigrant banks for the relief of Russian Jewry, a group of noted Jewish bankers and public men in St. Petersburg penned a "Memorandum on a Proposed Jewish Immigrant Bank," in which they decried, "the recent failure of many private banks. . . . causing misery and hardship to hundreds of thousands of our poor people, the losses in the transmission of monies abroad (estimated by the Russian minister of Finance in 1910 at 26% of the twenty million sent to Russia annually)."[9] They went on to deplore "the swindlers" and argued for "the necessity for a responsible and unselfish agency to care for this very real need of the immigrant."

They concluded their memorandum with the following offer:

With these considerations in mind, a group of noted Jewish bankers and public men of St. Petersburg organized before the war a society whose avowed purpose was to establish a bank in St. Petersburg to take care of the financial operations of Jewish emigrants. It was to have a capitalizaion of five million rubles and branch offices in Vienna, London, New York, and wherever else needed. The officers of this society are B. Mandel (lawyer Supreme Court of Petrograd), President; Dr. Bomash (Member of Duma), 2nd vice president; J. Pumpionsky (Director of AsoffDonBank) Tresurer; A Soloweitchik, (Director of Asiatic Bank) Hon Secretary.

Despite the good intentions expressed, however, because of the worsening of the war and conflict in Tsarist Russia, their offer could not be fulfilled. So instead of looking overseas, Jewish immigrants began bringing their financial grievances to the courts. The two cases with the most appearances in front of a Bankruptcy court judge between 1914 and 1916 were the bankruptcies of Max Kobre's bank and M & L Jarmulowksy bank. The depositors hired lawyers to represent them, who did not shy away from taking up the court's time: lawyers visited the court over 382 times to discuss the closing of Max Kobre's bank and 371 times in relation to the Jarmulowsky closure (Bankruptcy docket Vol. 42). Max Kobre and Meyer Jarmulowsky joined forces and sued Eugene Lamb for closing their banks, since they argued, their private banks were not under his regulatory jurisdiction and he had no right to place them in bankruptcy (Max Kobre & M & L Jarmulowsky v. Eugene Richards Lamb, 1914). Trying to avoid court and reopen his business as soon as possible, Meyer Jarmulowsky agreed to make a payment of 15% on each dollar, followed by an annual payment of 10% for the next six years. This did not satisfy the depositors who convened a meeting between themselves, their lawyer, William Sulzer, and Meyer Jarmulowsky ("Tush!" 6). One depositor at the meeting "with fury blazing from his eyes," as the *New York Tribune* reported, "made a prodigious leap, snatched a weapon from his pocket. Before the startled banker could raise an arm to guard his life a keen blade was at his throat . . . if not for Sulzer's quick hands, in another instant Jarmulowsky's life's blood would have spotted the carpet" ("Tush!" 6).

Seeing the violent rage of the depositors, Judah Magnes, head of the Kehillah, realized that immediate action was necessary. The Kehillah could not wait until the New York Emergency Loan fund tried again to raise sufficient sums to repay each insolvent depositor. Thus, Magnes decided to pursue legal action, as well, forming the Depositors' Protective Committee to shield those who had fallen into penury. Appreciating immigrants' desire for legal and governmental action, Magnes had the committee authorized by the State Banking Department to act in the interests of depositors of the private immigrant banks of the East side. In a promotional leaflet, Magnes claimed the "committee agrees to represent, without charge," but he warned his prospective clients:

> CAUTION!!!
> Engage no lawyers.
> Under no circumstances give up your pass book.
> Have patience and confidence in the Banking Department of the
> State of New York.[10]

But far from reassuring the depositors that there was no need for lawyers, Magnes and his Depositors' Protective Committee appears to have not discouraged disgruntled depositors from turning to the courts to help them with their claims. Jewish immigrant depositors' search for remuneration led them to the bankruptcy courts in Brooklyn and New York, and formatively changed these courts and their vision of immigrant banking.

JEWISH IMMIGRANT BANK DEPOSITORS AND
THE NEW YORK BANKRUPTCY COURTS

Three days after Eugene Lamb closed Max Kobre's bank Bessie Weinstein, represented by Morrison and Schiff, lodged the following petition in Brooklyn's United States District Bankruptcy court for the Southern District of New York. Claiming she was owed $1,500, Bessie Weinstein, who was joined in her claim by Hyman Zukerman and Phillip Stillerman, sought not just a full repayment but to make sure that all fraudulent bankers were put out of business. Claiming that Max Kobre was a co-partner with a man named Moses Ginsberg, she wanted to make sure that both paid for all the funds lost. As the petition claimed, both were full partners in the "private banking business and steamship agent and as agent for transmission of moneys under the name and style of Max Kobre's Bank with offices at 1783 Pitkin Aveune and 81 Grand Street in Brooklyn and 41 Canal Street in the Borough of Manhattan" ("In the Matter of Max Kobre and Moses Ginsberg" Case #5295).

The central questions of this petition and the numerous cases that would occupy the bankruptcy court for the next two years concerned the business

practices of Jewish immigrant bankers. Weinstein and her lawyers would con-
tinually argue over how these banks were run and how they invested their assets. One case would involve whether Kobre ran his business as a partnership
with Ginsberg or as a partnership with his wife. Could Ginsberg, who was central to the establishment on 1783 Pitkin, be held responsible or did he just work
for Kobre who really owned the bank? Creditors wanted all help finding those
who could repay them. Other cases revolved around the legal issue of consolidation, as Jewish immigrant bankers often had several branches scattered
throughout New York City in immigrant enclaves in Manhattan and Brooklyn.
Many in Brooklyn feared that only depositors in Manhattan would be repaid,
as that was where the riots took place and as Kobre transferred funds between
his banks. As Weinstein's lawyers' petition argued,

> Your petitioners are informed and believe that said alleged bank-
> rupts with intent to hinder, delay and defraud their creditors, and
> with intent and for the purpose of giving preference contrary to the
> provisions of the Bankruptcy Law. . . . [as they] transferred and set
> over unto said diverse persons, firms and corporations large valuable
> property consisting of merchandise, accounts and dues receivable of
> the value of $10,000 applicable to the payment of debts of the alleged
> bankrupts.
>   Your petitioners are informed and believe that said alleged bank-
> rupts conveyed, transferred concealed or removed or permitted to be
> concealed or removed, a large part of their property of considerable
> value not exempt from levy and sale under execution. . . . the alleged
> bankrupts have their domicile and residence at the time of the filing
> of this petition. ("In the Matter of Max Kobre and Moses Ginsberg,"
> Case #5263, 30–31)

In short, the lawyers for Weinstein argued that depositors should not
only be able to make claims on Kobre's real estate holdings, including his private home in Manhattan, but that Kobre had to consolidate all the banks' assets
from his bank businesses at 41 Canal Street, 1783 Pitkin Ave in Brownville and
81 Grand Street, Williamsburg Brooklyn ("In the Matter of Max and Sarah
Kobre" 8; "In the Matter of Max Kobre and Moses Ginsberg" Case #6101).
Residents of Manhattan should not be given preference, according to Section
24B of the Bankruptcy Act, the petition argued—all of Max Kobre's assets
had to be consolidated so that he could pay off debts in his Pitkin Ave bank
branch in Brooklyn with funds from his Lower East side establishments ("In
the Matter of Max and Sarah Kobre").

To be sure, the cases involving the closed Jewish immigrant banks of 1914 may have not set legal precedent but they did occupy much of the courts' time. The history and evolution of bankruptcy legislation and code is one of the least-often studied areas of American legal history.[11] The evolution of the bankruptcy code from the mid-1800s to 1914 can be viewed from a larger point of view as the story of American legislators coming to terms with America as it was. By 1914, it can be seen as New York State judges trying to shape America as an emerging world power populated by immigrant risk-takers and speculators, not just idyllic agrarians. To be sure, the story of bankruptcy legislation in the United States is also a distinctly American and political one. As exemplified by the reaction to the failed Jewish immigrant banks of 1914, code was slow to change as a result of conflicts between state and federal rights, as well as the system of checks and balances.

By looking at specifically how New York's bankruptcy courts dealt with the onslaught of cases resulting from the 1914 Jewish immigrant bank closures, one is constantly reminded that the roots of the bankruptcy code, as John Witt points out, lay in ideas of religious moralism. When bankruptcy laws did not keep debtors in line, prominent preachers in the nineteenth century turned to religious rhetoric to shame debtors into good behavior. As Witt notes, moral and religious language was used to supplement the legal action. But in 1914, New York State bankruptcy judges quickly realized that religious language would not curb the behavior of these non-Protestant immigrant bankers. Thus, the court exhibited a more stringent approach to Jewish immigrant bankers. While the US Bankruptcy Code may have been the most liberal debtor relief bankruptcy system to come into existence since the Jubilee Year of the Old Testament, as late-nineteenth century US bankruptcy law enabled the debt-strapped corporation to set its debts to one side, and continue in business, rather than shutting down, Jewish immigrant bankers were not given the same leeway, depriving the economy as a whole of its products and (what should be) its contribution to the common good.[12]

On November 13, 1914, all filed into the courtroom of Thomas I. Chatfield. Representing the people, Jeremiah Mahoney would spend the next five days making sure "the truth [is] brought out" concerning whether Moses Ginsberg was "a partner in the entire Max Kobre Bank" or just a partner in his Brownsville branch ("In the Matter of Max Kobre and Moses Ginsberg" Case File 5263). As the bankruptcy court hearing suggests, "The Brownsville Branch may have been far more profitable than the New York business" (4). The profits were derived from the fact that the bank also ran the Saratoga Improvement

Company as well as the Collective Holding Company, two corporate entities that invested in real estate in Brooklyn led by Moses Ginsberg, Louis Weinstein and Elias Frankle. Frankle had worked at Kobre's original bank at 40 Canal Street since 1908. But he moved to the Brownville bank in 1913, which employed around fifteen people, because of the numerous real estate deals being conducted there with bank assets.

In the end, Kobre did not have his full day in court. On June 5, 1916, the *New York Times* attracted readers with the headline: "Max Kobre Dead on Eve of Trial." All were intrigued about the details of his death, since he had once threatened suicide during his two-year indictment for the failure of his private banks on the Lower East Side and Brownsville during one of the many heated exchanges he had with assistant district attorney, Leslie Tompkins. In one particularly charged encounter, Kobre railed that he would rather commit suicide than see his family lose their Harlem home at 115 West 122nd Street. So when Kobre was found on his kitchen floor, "lying under an open jet of a gas stove," just hours before his trial was to start, many became suspicious. One police officer declared it suicide, only to be corrected shortly thereafter by the city coroner: Max Kobre died of heart disease, falling to the ground from a massive heart attack while heating himself some milk so that he could fall asleep. As the coroner summed up: "a man does not commit suicide standing up . . . [the abrasions] found on Kobre's body indicated that the banker had falled [sic] to the floor near the gas stove."

The controversy that surrounded Max Kobre in his death mirrored the conflicting attention his bank's failures received in its demise after 1914. Did Kobre deserve jail time? Or was he just an overextended immigrant entrepreneur who was caught in a precarious position by the unexpected events of the summer of 1914 as a result of his real estate investments and offers of credit to those willing to invest in developing new areas of New York City?

IMMIGRANT BANK CLOSURES AND THE EXPANSION OF NEW YORK STATE BANKING LAW

The new banking laws passed in the years immediately following the closures of the Jewish immigrant bank failure marked a watershed moment in the history of commercial banking in New York City. While historian Jared Day argues that the era of immigrant banking came to an end during the early 1920s after "Americanized" immigrants began their own attack against immigrant banks, the aftermath of the closing of the Jewish immigrants banks suggests that it was increased state regulation that ultimately led to the strangulation of the immigrant banking system. As Day notes, "the numerous immigrant bank failures of 1907," prodded "the New York state legislature to pass what came to be known as the "Wells Law." This law provided that all private bankers who accepted money for the sale of steamship tickets or for transmission abroad had to file a $15,000 bond to assure that the transactions were faithfully executed (Day 75–76; W. and M. Hamm). While the Wells Law addressed issues of corruption in the world of immigrant banking, Max Kobre had not actually done anything corrupt or illegal; rather he had invested heavily in real estate that he could not liquidate quickly. In response, banking and legal authorities crafted the Banking Law NY §156, that gave "persons making deposits for safekeeping or transmittal preferred claims against certain funds upon a private banker's insolvency," and to recover any "money which he can trace and identify."[13] The law would enable depositors to make claims against the Kobre's massive real estate holdings. Banking Law NY §156 would go on to define banking insolvency law until 1930.

But the most revolutionary change set in motion by the immigrant bank closures of 1914 concerned the world of private banking, of which immigrant banks and bankers constituted a large segment. While several court cases in the years leading up to 1914 had "recognized" the definition of a private banker as "a person or a firm engaged in the banking business without authority from the banking department and not subject to the banking law or the supervision of the superintendent of banks" (5–6). But as the *New York Times* reported, just months before the war broke out, the Senate Banking Committee held a hearing and decided that immigrant bankers must be supervised and regularly checked to avoid failure.

Thus, New York State revised its banking laws in 1914, declaring in chapter 369 of section 2 of the Consolidated Banking Laws of New York that anyone who wanted to call himself a "private banker," or who "makes use of any office sign bearing thereon the word 'bank' in his business must be regularly supervised by the New York State's Banking Superintendent." Moreover, the new Banking Superintendent in 1921, George McLaughlin, pushed the New York State Senate and the governor to pass a new bill to further amend the 1914 state banking law. As he explained to Governor Franklin Delano Roosevelt, "The purpose of the new proposed bill is to broaden the powers of savings banks so that they may make foreign transmissions through banks or trust companies that incorporate under the laws of the State of New York. They do expect . . . they will attract the foreign born into their institution . . . [and will] educate them [from the problems with their immigrants banks] (George McLaughlin to Hon. C. Tracy Stagg, Counsel to the Governor, 1921). This note pushed Governor Roosevelt to support the amendment proposed by State Senator Cotillo and approve it on April 9, 1921. McLaughlin lauds this endorsement, claiming it would represent "a step in the right direction" in his effort to erase the need for the services provided by immigrant banks.

Beginning in 1921, the Banking Department's regulatory push led at least thirty-six private banks to incorporate as state banks or become a part of other financial institutions (Table 1). Meanwhile, from 1914 to 1932, the Department liquidated approximately 101 private banks. While it is undocumented as to why these banks were liquidated and whether it was voluntary, it is clear that the Banking Department utilized its authority to close immigrant banks more than other institutions run by private bankers as it waged a war against institutions catering to the foreign-born that they believed were financially unsound.

The Banking Department's efforts to liquidate immigrant banks and pressure them to become incorporated transformed the strategies used by those remaining Jewish immigrant bankers to earn money. The percentage of real estate and mortgages of total assets these banks held dropped significantly. In 1915, real estate and mortgages comprised 36% of the total assets of these banks, and this figure dropped to as low as 7% in 1923 and 1926.

In the decades after the 1914 Jewish immigrant bank failures, banking regulators became convinced that the informal financial institutions used by immigrants were suspect and fraudulent. They mobilized public pressure and lobbied for new banking laws to suppress immigrant banks' capacities. As the New York State Superintendent of Banks Joseph Broderick declared in support of amendments to New York State banking laws in 1930, "The amendment will not only act as a deterrent to the formation of new bootleg banking concerns, but will serve either to drive those in existence under the supervision of the Banking Department or out of business."[14] Drawing on prohibition era discourse, Broderick made clear that unregulated immigrant bankers were akin to renegade bootleggers.

By 1930, Broderick had made credit access for immigrants as difficult to find as an alcoholic drink. He made it illegal for private banks holding deposits under $500 to accept any sums, thereby preventing those surviving immigrant banks from providing the basic service it clients needed (Van Horn 116). With private banks' capacities significantly stricken by the efforts of the Banking

Department, by 1932, only seventeen private immigrant bankers remained under the Superintendent of Banks' supervision while in 1909 the Dillingham commission had found over one thousand operating in New York City alone (*Annual Report of the Superintendent of Banks, 1932*).

Table 1: *Number of Private Banks Authorized, Liquidated and Incorporated as State Banks, 1915–1932 (Annual Reports of the Superintendent of Banks, 1914–1932).*[15]

Year	Number of Private Banks	Number of New Private Banks Authorized	Number of Private Banks liquidated	Number of Private Banks that became incorporated banks or were absorbed by incorporated institutions
1915	75	29	3	1
1916	76	11	5	1
1917	80	9	4	1
1918	84			
1919	91	10		2
1920	101	10		
1921	98	3	4	
1922	95	3	5	
1923	90	0	6	
1924	82	1	5	
1925	74	0	0	4
1926	68	0	4	8
1927	59	0	7	2
1928	50	0	6	
1929	44	0	7	17
1930	33	0	18	
1931	20	0	21	
1932	17	0	6	
Total			101	36

CONCLUSION

In the decades following 1914, the world of immigrant banking would virtually disappear from the streets of New York City. As the banking capital of the nation, its legislations and actions served as a model for other states to address the problem of "immigrant banking." As ships used were seized to transport troops, the business of mass migration came to a halt. The world of open borders irrevocably gave way to regulations and border control that ended an era of global free movement of people, capital, and credit (McKeown 156). So what is the historical significance of the lost world of Jewish immigrant banking and immigrant banking writ large? First and foremost, Jewish immigrant bankers were far from exceptional: dozens of other immigrants inserted themselves in the American economy through conducting businesses that depended on connections on both sides of the Atlantic. The virtual erasure of these businesses from the annals of history because of the business' ultimate collapse has obscured the transnational ties shaping early-twentieth century American business. The narrative of East European Jewish migration has been shrouded for far too long by American nationalist mythology and Emma Lazarus's powerful imagery. But East European Jewish migration was embedded in a larger system of distribution in which a migrant served as a lucrative commodity. This commodity was expertly speculated on by Jewish immigrant bankers like Max Kobre. Once the regulation of ship ticket prices made the sale of ship tickets no longer profitable, men like Max Kobre turned their attention to real estate speculation as well. By offering credit to prospective migrants and other business practices, East European Jewish bankers both fueled and shaped this mass population shift. Once their immigrant clientele arrived in America, the continued access to credit offered by men like Kobre transformed not only immigrant economic adaptation to America but also the physical landscape of New York City.

Notes

1. John Maynard Keynes, "The Economic Consequences of the Peace," 6.
2. Under the national banking system, national banks outside of New York were required to maintain 15% of their reserves, of which three-fifths, or 9%, would be held as deposits in New York. If a bank was seen as failing in New York City, it could create a panic throughout the country.
3. The editorial pages of the Yiddish press capture the terror that seized the Jewish immigrant community upon seeing the events of July 1914 unfold. See *Forverts*, 31 July 1914, p. 4; *Forverts*, 14 Aug. 1914, p. 5; *Varheyt*, 1 Aug. 1914. For a discussion of the larger reaction to the outbreak of war in the Yiddish press see Rappaport.
4. For a discussion of Jews in New York real estate see Schepper 24; Freed 719; Hirsch 183; Morris 187; also see editorial "New York Structural Progress and the Jew" 181; Dolkart. For a discussion of Chicago, see Satter.
5. Indeed, scholarship on Jew's role in New York real estate development has focused mostly on the interwar years when the outer boroughs became speckled with small apartment buildings erected by Jewish entrepreneurs in the Bronx along the Grand Concourse or in Brooklyn, along Eastern Parkway. These Jewish builders, as Deborah Dash Moore points out, relied on their ethnic networks to build the types of dwellings that would entice middle class Jews. See Moore, *At Home in America* 19–59.
6. The Lower East Side housing stock was described in Century Magazine, Nov. 1888, quoted in Rischin 93; Wolfe 27.
7. The Metropolitan Council on Jewish Poverty (51) discusses the dire predicament of the "near poor" who barely manage to "make ends meet" with their paychecks and can easily join the ranks of the destitute.
8. Magnes Archives, File P3/1803. Also see Files of the New York City East Side Emergency Loan Fund.
9. This memorandum is undated but probably was penned in August 1914 as it is reprinted in the *American Hebrew*, Sept. 1914.
10. "Depositors' Protective Committee." I would to thank Arthur Goren for giving me this document.
11. Several noteworthy works on the history of Bankruptcy law include Skeel; Witt, and Warren, a 1935 history written from the study of Congressional debates; and Bays, written as part of an informative American Commercial Law Series in 1920.
12. Under the traditional Anglo-American "rule of law"—modeled on Roman law—contracts are considered sacrosanct, and debts must be repaid at all costs, in former times often at the cost of the life or liberty of the debtor. Thus, to be bankrupt was considered a crime to be punished.
13. This law can be accessed and read in full through Westlaw, Document 14_39_33_4300.

14. I would like to thank Shira Poliak for sharing her Barnard thesis with me. See Shira Poliak, "Protecting and Assimilating Foreigners: Immigrant Banks and New York State Banking Regulation, 1907 to 1932."

15. A "0" indicates that the Report specified that no new private bank was authorized or liquidated. A space indicates that the Annual Report did not specify if new banks were created, liquidated or became incorporated banks in the given year.

Works Cited

Abelson, Paul. Letter to Cyrus Sulzberger. 16 Mar. 1915. Magnes Archives, File P3/1803, Central Archives for the History of the Jewish People.

Ahamed, Liaguat. *Lords of Finance: The Bankers Who Broke the World.* Penguin, 2009.

Annual Report of the Superintendent of Banks. New York State, 1922.

Annual Report of the Superintendent of Banks. New York State, 1924.

Annual Report of the Superintendent of Banks. New York State, 1927.

Annual Report of the Superintendent of Banks. New York State, 1932.

Bankruptcy docket Vol. 42: RG 021. 6 Aug. 1914—8 Dec. 1918. National Archives. Bays, Alfred W. "The History and Purposes of Bankruptcy Legislation."

American Commercial Law Series. 1920. Part 1, chestofbooks.com/business/law/ American-Commercial-Law-Series/Bankruptcy-Chapter-1-The-History-And-Purposes-Of-Bankruptc.html. Accessed 19 Aug. 2018.

American Commercial Law Series. 1920. Part 2, chestofbooks.com/business/law/ American-Commercial-Law-Series/The-History-And-Purposes-Of-Bankruptcy-Legislation-Part-2.html. Accessed 19 Aug. 2018.

American Commercial Law Series. 1920. Part 3, chestofbooks.com/business/law/ American-Commercial-Law-Series/The-History-And-Purposes-Of-Bankruptcy-Legislation-Part-3.html. Accessed 19 Aug. 2018.

Benton-Cohen, Katie. *Inventing the Immigration Problem: The Dillingham Commission and Its Legacy.* Harvard Univ., 2018.

Birmingham, Stephen. *Our Crowd: The Great Jewish Families of New York.* Syracuse Univ., 1996.

Blumenson, S. L. "Culture on Rutgers Square." *Commentary*, vol. 10, 1950, 65–74.

Broderick, Joseph. Memorandum to Mr. Samuel Rosenman, Counsel to the Governor, n.d. Legislative Bill Jacket 1930, ch. 678, Reel #5, New York Public Library—Science, Industry and Business Library, New York, NY.

Cahan, Abraham. *The Rise of David Levinsky.* 1917. Penguin Classics, 1969.

Carosso, Vincent P. "A Financial Elite: New York's German-Jewish Investment Bankers." *American Jewish Historical Quarterly (1961–1978)*, vol. 66, nos. 1–4, 1976–1977, pp. 67–88.

Chernow, Ron. *The Warburgs: The Twentieth-Century Odyssey of a Remarkable Jewish Family.* 1993. Vintage, 2016.

Cohen, George. *The Jews and the Making of America.* Stratford, 1924.

Cohen, Naomi. *Jacob H. Schiff: A Study in American Jewish Leadership.* Univ. Press of New England, 1999.

Day, Jared N. "Credit, Capital and Community: Informal Banking in Immigrant Communities in the United States, 1880–1924." *Financial History Review*, vol. 9, no. 1, 2002, pp. 65–78, doi.org/10.1017/S0968565002000045.

"Depositors' Protective Committee." Papers of Judah Magnes. "Depozitors un der bankn kampf." *Forverts*, 1 Aug. 1914, p. 1.

Dolkart, Andrew. "From Rag Trade to Riches: Abraham E. Lefcourt Builds the Garment District." *At Home in America*, edited by Deborah Dash Moore, Columbia Univ., 1981, pp. 19–60.

Feys, Torsten. "A Business Approach to Trans-Atlantic Shipping: The Introduction of Steam-Shipping and Its Impact on the European Exodus, 1840–1914." Dissertation, University of Ghent, 2008.

Files of the New York City East Side Emergency Loan Fund, 25 Mar. 1915, American Jewish Historical Society, Center for Jewish History.

Forverts, 31 July 1914, p. 4.

Forverts, 14 Aug. 1914, p. 5.

Freed, Clarence I. "The Romance of Realty: Men Who Became Makers of the Metropolis Through Real Estate Enterprise." *American Hebrew*, vol. 120, 1927, p. 742.

Gabaccia, Donna. "Little Italy's Decline: Immigrant Renters and Investors in a Changing City." *The Landscape of Modernity: Essays on New York City, 1900–1940*, edited by D. Ward and O. Zunz, Russell Sage Foundation, 1992, pp. 235–51.

Gould, Elgin. "Financial Aspects of Recent Tenement House Operations in New York." *The Tenement House Problem*, vol. 1, edited by Robert DeFrost and Lawrence Veiller, Macmillan, 1903, pp. 355–66.

Hirsch, Helen. "Jewish Pioneers in the Construction of NYC." *Jewish Forum*, vol. 31, 1948, 183–84.

Hochfelder, Daniel. "Where the Common People Could Speculate": The Ticker, Bucket Shops, and the Origins of Popular Participation in Financial Markets, 1880–1920." *Journal of American History*, vol. 93, no. 2, 2006, 335–58.

Hollinger, David. "Rich, Powerful, and Smart: Jewish Overrepresentation Should Be Explained Rather Than Mystified or Avoided." *Jewish Quarterly Review*, vol. 94, no. 4, 2004, pp. 592–602.

"In the Matter of Max Kobre and Moses Ginsberg, co-partners doing business as Max Kobre's Bank at 1783 Pitkin Ave, Brooklyn, NY." United States Bankruptcy Court Case no. 6101, p. 8. Folder 5271, National Archives and Records Administration, New York, NY.

"In the Matter of Max Kobre and Moses Ginsberg, copartners doing business under the name and style of Max Kobre's Bank." United States Court of Appeals for the Second Circuit Case File 5263, p. 2. RG 276 Box 2038, National Archives and Records Administration Folder. New York, NY.

"In the Matter of Max Kobre and Moses Ginsberg individually and a co-partners doing business as Max Kobre's Bank, Jan. 13, 1915." United States Court of Appeals for the Second Circuit Case #5295. National Archives and Records Administration Folder. New York, NY.

"In the Matter of Max and Sarah Kobre doing business as Max Kobe's Bank." United

States Bankruptcy Court Case no. 6101, p. 8. Folder 5271, National Archives and Records Administration Folder. New York, NY.

"Information RE: Private Bankers." Judah Leib Magnes Papers, P3/1542, Central Archives for the History of the Jewish People, Jerusalem.

Jenks, Jeremiah W., and W. Jett Lauck. *The Immigration Problem: A Study of American Immigration Conditions and Needs*. Funk and Wagnalls, 1911.

Keynes, John Maynard. "The Economic Consequences of the Peace." *Collected Writings: The Economic Consequences of Peace*, vol. 11, by John Maynard Keynes, Macmillian, 1971.

Landesman, Alter. *Brownsville: The Birth, Development and Passing of a Jewish Community in New York*. Bloch Publishing, 1969

Lears, Jackson. *Something for Nothing: Luck in America*. Penguin, 2003.

Magnes, Judah. Internal correspondence with Louis Marshall. File P3/1543, Central Archives for the History of the Jewish People.

Magnes Archives, File P3/1803, Central Archives for the History of the Jewish People.

"Max Kobre Dead on Eve of Trial: Under Indictment Two Years after His Three Private Banks Had Closed; Had Hinted at Suicide." *New York Times*, 5 June 1916.

McKeown, Adam. *Melancholy Order*. Columbia Univ., 2008.

McLaughlin, George. Letter to C. Tracy Stagg, Counsel to the Governor Franklin Roosevelt, 31 March 1921. Legislative Bill Jacket 1921, Chapter 679, New York Public Library— Science, Industry and Business Library.

"Memorandum of Proposed Jewish Immigrant Bank." C. Aug. 1914. Magnes Archives, Folder P3/1544, Central Archives for the History of the Jewish People. Reprinted in *American Hebrew*, Sept. 1914.

Metropolitan Council. *Report on Jewish Poverty*. Jan. 2004.

Moore, Deborah Dash. *At Home in America*. Columbia Univ., 1981.

Morris, Jack. "Twentieth Century Achievements in New York Real Estate and Construction." *Jewish Forum*, vol. 31, 1948, pp. 187.

"New York Structural Progress and the Jew." *Jewish Forum*, vol. 31, 1948, p. 181.

Oltuski, Alicia. *Precious Objects: A Story of Diamonds, Family, and a Way of Life*. Scribner, 2011.

Pak, Susie. *Gentlemen Bankers: The World of J. P. Morgan*. Harvard Univ., 2013.

Poliak, Shira. "Protecting and Assimilating Foreigners: Immigrant Banks and New York State Banking Regulation, 1907 to 1932." Senior Thesis, Barnard College, 2013.

Rappaport, Joseph. "The American Yiddish Press and the European Conflict in 1914." *Jewish Social Studies*, vol. 19, nos. 3–4, 1957, pp. 113–28.

Rischin, Moses. *The Promised City: New York Jews, 1870–1914*. Harvard Univ., 1962.

Rubinow, Isaac. "Economic and Industrial Condition: New York." *The Russian Jew in the United States*, edited by Charles S. Bernheimer, Philadelphia, 1905, pp. 102–21.

Satter, Beryl. *Family Properties: Race, Real Estate and the Exploitation of Black Urban America*. Metropolitan, 2009.

Schepper, Abraham. "Jews as Builders in New York." *American Hebrew*, 4 July 1913, p. 24.

Shachter, Abraham. "Jews As the Builders of New York." *American Hebrew*, 4 July 1912, p. 10.

Shapiro, Edward. *A Time for Healing: American Jewry Since 1945*. John Hopkins Univ., 1992.

Skeel, David. *Debt's Dominion*. Princeton Univ., 2001.

Stein, Sarah A. *Plumes: Ostrich Feathers, Jews, and a Lost World of Global Commerce.* Yale Univ., 2008.

Supple, Barry E. "A Business Elite: German-Jewish Financiers in Nineteenth-Century New York." *Business History Review*, vol. 31, 1957, pp. 143–78.

Sylla, Richard. "Federal Policy, Banking Market Structure, and Capital Mobilization in the United States, 1863–1913." *The Journal of Economic History*, vol. 29, no. 4, 1969, pp. 657–86.

Tenenbaum, Shelly. *A Credit to Their Community: Jewish Loan Societies in America* (Wayne State Univ., 1993).

"'Tush!' Says Sulzer Foiling Assassin." *New York Tribune*, 3 April 1915, p. 6.

United States, Congress, Senate, The Immigration Commission. Immigrant Banks, presented by Mr. Dillingham, 24 Feb., 1910. 61st Congress, 2nd Session. Serial Set Vol. No. 5662, Session Vol. No. 63.

United States, Congress, Senate, Reports of the Immigration Commission: Immigrant Banks. 61st Congress, 3rd Session. Vol. 37, Senate Doc. 753. Washington, DC., 1911. Reprint, 1970.

Van Horn, Patrick. "The Small Private Banker in New York and Regulatory Change, 1893–1933." *Essays in Economic & Business History*, vol. 28, 2010, pp. 107–21.

Vanden Daelen, Veerle. "Negotiating the Return of the Diamond Sector and Its Jews: The Belgian Government During the Second World War and in the Immediate Postwar Period." *Holocaust Studies*, vol. 18, 2012, 231–60.

Varheyt, 1 Aug. 1914.

Warfield, David, and Margherita Hamm. *Ghetto Silhouettes*. Trieste, 2017. Warren, Charles. *Bankruptcy in United States History*. Beard, 2000.

Westlaw, Document 14_39_33_4300. *Thomas Reuters Westlaw*, legal.thomsonreuters.com/en/products/westlaw.

Wheatley, Richard. "The Jews in New York." *The Century Magazine*, vol. 43, 1892, pp. 323–42.

Witt, John. "Narrating Bankruptcy/Narrating Risk." *Northwestern University Law Review*, vol. 98, 2003, pp. 303–33.

Wolfe, Gerard. *The Synagogues of New York's Lower East Side*. New York Univ., 1978.

CHAPTER 4

Far Away Moses & Company: An Ottoman Jewish Business between Istanbul and the United States

by Julia Phillips Cohen

*I*n the fall of 1867, a small photograph inscribed with the words "Guide at Constantinople—Far away Moses" (fig. 1) made its way across the Atlantic in the baggage of Colonel William R. Denny of Winchester, Virginia. Likely the source of inspiration for an illustration Mark Twain later included in his account of his journey with Denny through Europe and the Middle East, it is now filed away in Twain's archive.[1] However ephemeral, this material exchange across continents provides a unique window into nineteenth-century Americans' experiences of the "Orient" and the self-exoticizing performances of the Ottomans they met. The man pictured here, known by the name Far Away Moses, was among the most successful guides of the late Ottoman era (see Wayne; Çelik 18; Kirshenblatt-Gimblett, *Destination Culture* 103, 105; Kirshenblatt-Gimblett, "A Place in the World" 71–72; and Nance, *Arabian Nights* 41–42, 143). Understanding his role in shaping both American perceptions of the East and Ottoman commercial endeavors highlights Ottoman Jews' participation in the business of orientalism as well as empire.

Far Away Moses's career was made possible by a changing landscape of travel, tourism, and mass consumption. Once steam and rail travel made global tours increasingly accessible, growing numbers of European and American travelers began to appear in Ottoman lands. In cities across the empire,

Figure 1: Photographic calling card of Far Away Moses, bearing the words "Guide at Constantinople." (Courtesy of the Mark Twain Project, The Bancroft Library, University of California, Berkeley.)

people seized the new opportunities this development brought with it (Nance, "A Facilitated Access Model"). Some served as guides and dragomans for the many foreign visitors who sought to tour the Ottoman "East." Others peddled oriental wares to tourists desirous of items they associated with times and places far removed from their own. By the second half of the nineteenth century, the global market for oriental carpets and other Eastern items was booming, as middle-class individuals across Europe and the United States introduced oriental-style smoking parlors and cozy corners into their domestic interiors (Quataert, *Ottoman Manufacturing* 141–42; Spooner; Hoganson, "Cosmopolitan Domesticity"; Hoganson, *Consumers' Imperium*). Ottoman vendors responded accordingly, attempting to further cultivate their clients' tastes for the stuff and styles of their empire. Turkish tobacco, foodstuffs, metal lamps, tables of inlaid wood, swords, Islamic manuscripts, Qur'an stands, carpets, and tapestries lined their shops in Istanbul's bazaar. Their entrances as well as the merchants within welcomed passersby in an increasingly dizzying array of languages.

Although Armenian, Greek Orthodox, Muslim, Jewish, and other Ottomans all participated in this trade across the empire and beyond, our limited understanding of their commercial, social, and political networks has continued to obscure the lives and careers of these Ottoman traders. Indeed, though both the labor and art histories of the Ottoman carpet, tile, tobacco, and other Islamic art industries are well documented, the merchants who trafficked in these items have attracted scant attention.[2]

Thanks in part to American travelers such as Mark Twain, it is possible to tell the story of one of the nineteenth century's best-known marketers of the Orient to the United States and of the company that used his name. Although he left no papers of his own, Far Away Moses—and, later, the company that grew up around him—produced an array of travel writings, photographs, print illustrations, newspaper articles, advertisements, commercial displays, souvenirs, letters, and government and business contracts in English, French, German, Hungarian, Ladino, and Ottoman and modern Turkish. Recovering this archive requires reconstructing not only Far Away Moses's career but also the process by which different individuals appropriated his persona as icon and trademark, both in the United States and back in the Ottoman Empire. In the Ottoman context, the Jewish and Muslim merchants who established a company bearing his name eventually found that this act of appropriation enabled their firm's transformation into a global enterprise with ties to the Ottoman state and a broad international clientele. Aided by new technologies, including the steamship, telegraph, and new and ever-cheaper forms of mass media, the members of this company, along with their associates, left an indelible impact on global styles as well as Westerners' ideas about the Ottoman Empire.

One of the aims of this essay is to suggest that this process was reciprocal—that the various members of the firm not only left an imprint on different global markets but that these markets also left an imprint on them. This approach falls into a rarely trodden territory between fields. While economic histories have illuminated much about merchants' networks and the cultural practices that sustained their bonds of trust, the ways that practices of self-fashioning have intersected with the politics of the marketplace seldom figure in such studies.[3] Although an extensive literature details the transformative effect of consumption on the modern consumer, meanwhile, far less attention has been paid to how both the experience and the demands of the marketplace might be transformative for the seller.[4] Finally, though the growing number of studies on Jewish economic niches have exposed the extent to which the trade in particular products—rags, liquor, ostrich feathers, Hollywood films, modernist art—became associated with Jews, we know little about cases in which Jewish traders' public personas were so thoroughly associated with their product.[5] Yet, this article argues, the success of Ottoman Jewish oriental-goods merchants hinged equally on the alliances they forged and the expertise they accrued, on the one hand, and their ability to sell both themselves and their wares as "authentically" Eastern, Ottoman, and Jewish, on the other. This process not only shaped the way these individuals marketed their merchandise, it also had repercussions in realms both personal and political.

THE MAKING OF FAR AWAY MOSES

Around the year 1860, a self-styled "oriental" Jew who went by the name Far Away Moses began to earn the attention of foreign audiences as he offered tours of Ottoman Istanbul to American and European travelers. Far Away Moses was catapulted from obscurity into the international arena by a series of serendipitous encounters and by his skill in selling himself as he presented and sold the Orient to inquisitive tourists. He quickly became a celebrity on both sides of the Atlantic, inspiring myriad illustrations and colorful travel writings, in addition to a company that would soon bear his name. For all that was subsequently written about his life and work, however, many of the most basic details remain a mystery.[6] The playful moniker he used with his clients enveloped his public persona so completely that it is difficult to find mention of any other name for the man. He appears to us simply as Far Away Moses, Ottoman Jewish dragoman, guide, and "dealer in rugs, embroidery, and all kinds of Oriental goods" (Stoddard 280).

Far Away Moses began his career as a dragoman, or translator, and local guide for Western tourists to the Ottoman capital. He was said to have known many languages but apparently knew English particularly well (Stoddard 280; "Far-Away-Moses: Jew"; "The Troubles of 'Far-Away Moses'"; Willard 194; Thacher; "Finishing the Fair"). In 1863, a British doctor who traveled to the empire described Far Away Moses as a well-known part of the Istanbul landscape and the best dragoman the "City of the Sultan" had to offer (Radcliffe 721). Just five years later, an American chronicler claimed that "[n]ext to the Sultan, and possibly his grand vizier, the most noted person in the capital of the Mohammedan world is Far-away Moses." Thus it was that this man, "by profession a dragoman, by residence a Byzantine, by race and religion a Jew," gained a reputation so extensive throughout the Levant that it was as notable, "though in a different channel," as that of the Ottoman military general Omar Pasha or the Algerian war hero 'Abd al-Qadir, the same author claimed (Swift 424). The comparison was not an obvious one, since by all accounts Far Away Moses was neither a political figure nor a communal leader.

Yet his fame continued to grow.[7] Londoner John Murray's handbook for travelers to the Ottoman capital recommended Far Away Moses as "an intelligent and honest dragoman" who could "be heard of at the Liverpool Steam-packet Office" in the Perşembe Bazaar of the Galata district of Istanbul—a rare compliment from a guidebook culture that often denigrated dragomans as either untrustworthy or unnecessary for those tourists looking to strike out on their own (Murray, *Handbook* 1871, 18). British and American travel writers soon began to mention their encounters with the man and to praise his honesty, reliability, and intelligence, no doubt in large part because they had learned of his various good attributes from Murray's guidebook.[8] To many, hiring Far Away Moses as a guide became a requisite part of the tour of the city, no less important an experience than visiting the Hagia Sophia or the Topkapı Palace of Old Istanbul.

Tourists did not simply seek Far Away Moses's services because they found him reliable, however. His image as an Eastern Jew particularly appealed to his largely Protestant Anglophone clientele, many of whom regarded him not merely as an exotic oriental but also as a biblical figure worthy of their admiration.[9] One English author who published a travelogue describing his time in Istanbul in 1877 made the religious dimension to his choice explicit, writing, "If the traveller is wise, he will immediately show a proper respect for his Old Testament by selecting Far Away Moses."[10]

The Ottoman Jewish tour guide and dragoman played the ancient Hebrew type well. By the 1860s he was no longer a young man. His "flowing beard" was "thickly streaked with gray," according to an American journalist who added that the Ottoman Jewish cicerone had the "saddest of eyes," having "often looked upon the weary side of life" (Leech 60). His outfit also struck his foreign clients as appropriately exotic and antiquated. With his turban, baggy pants, waist sash, and short loose vest—a traditional mode of men's dress that the introduction of the Ottoman uniform of frock coat and fez in 1829 had rendered "unmodern"—Far Away Moses took on the aura of a different era (Quataert, "Clothing Laws").

The *carte de visite*, or photographic calling card, he had made by 1867 suggests that Far Away Moses was aware that his success hinged on creating a

memorable image of himself. Doing so involved playing on an evolving stereo-
type of the Ottoman Jew. An 1863 photograph of a group of Jewish men who
posed in the studio of the imperial photographers Abdullah Frères shows them
dressed in outfits similar to—though more ragged than—the one Far Away
Moses would wear in his *carte de visite* just a few years later (fig. 2). It was no co-
incidence that the "Jewish types" depicted in the photograph were portrayed in
rags: Jews had a reputation for being among the poorest groups in the Ottoman

*Figure 2: "Jewish Types" from Istanbul. Photograph of Abdullah Frères. Pierre de Gigord Collection of
Photographs, Getty Research Institute, Los Angeles (96.R.14; A37.F30).*

capital.[11] Many European and American travelers would have been familiar with
such stereotypes. Some may have even seen this particular photograph, as various English-language guidebooks recommended the Abdullah Frères studio to
their readers, suggesting that a photograph produced by the Ottoman studio
was "one of the most valuable curiosities" that tourists could take home from
Istanbul.[12] Far Away Moses thus embodied and performed for tourists the role
of the generic Ottoman Jew whom they had come to expect.[13] Rendered among
the sundry objects that he helped them acquire, he too became a curiosity.

It did not take long for others to begin to propagate their own images of
Far Away Moses. When in 1869 the private secretary of a US admiral published

his account of their squadron's goodwill tour of Europe and the Middle East, he included an illustration of the Ottoman Jewish dragoman made by the well-known American caricaturist Thomas Nast (fig. 3). Nast's drawing offers a mirror image of the photograph that originally appeared on the Ottoman Jewish guide's *carte de visite*, suggesting that the American author who contracted his services was among those who had received a personal copy of Far Away

CONSTANTINOPLE. 373

through those wonderful passages or corridors, making a rapid survey of the valuable merchandise from all parts of the Oriental world, and purchasing little articles as souvenirs, to be presented to absent friends in token of remembrance. These bazaars are peculiarly an Eastern institution, and afford much pleasure. Each trade has its distinct quarter, and the dealers, sharper and more cunning than

the shrewdest Vermonter that ever whittled a clock, expose their goods to great advantage, and invariably demand for them four times the sum they hope to obtain from a chance purchaser. Conscience is an attribute of nature to them unknown, and their sphere of happiness

Figure 3: Thomas Nast's rendering of Far Away Moses based on his photographic calling card, James Eglinton Montgomery, Our Admiral's Flag Abroad: The Cruise of Admiral D. G. Farragut, Commanding the European Squadron in 1867–68, in the Flag-ship Franklin (G. P. Putnam & Son, 1869), p. 373.

Moses's photographic calling card.[14] Although he remained faithful to the photograph in his depiction of the Ottoman Jewish guide, Nast took liberties elsewhere, adding to the originally empty background the silhouette of a mosque flanked by two minarets. Standing in the foreground of a scene now set in the "Land of the Sultans," Far Away Moses became at once more exotic and less (exclusively) Jewish.[15] In Nast's rendering he was no longer simply a wise old Hebrew but also an Eastern subject from a Muslim country. The insertion of Islamic architecture added a new dimension of oriental allure to the relatively unadorned image that Far Away Moses had circulated of himself.[16]

More fortuitous still than his portrayal by the famous American caricaturist was Far Away Moses's inclusion in a second book published that same year.[17] This was Mark Twain's *The Innocents Abroad, or the New Pilgrim's Progress*, an account of the American author's travels to Europe and the Levant in 1867. There, at the start of chapter 35, appeared a description and engraving of Far Away Moses, who had served as Twain's guide and translator in Istanbul

Figure 4: Far Away Moses as portrayed in Mark Twain, The Innocents Abroad, or the New Pilgrim's Progress *(Hartford, 1869).*

882   OUR KIND RECEPTION IN RUSSIA.

was a sufficient *visé* for our passports. The moment the anchor was down, the Governor of the town immediately dispatched an officer on board to inquire if he could be of any assistance to us, and to invite us to make ourselves at home in Sebastopol! If you know Russia, you know that this was a wild stretch of hospitality. They are usually so suspicious of strangers that they worry them excessively with the delays and aggravations incident to a complicated passport system. Had we come from any other country we could not have had permission to enter Sebastopol and leave again under three days—but as it was, we were at liberty to go and come when and where we pleased. Every body in Constantinople warned us to be very careful about our passports, see that they were strictly *en regle,* and never to mislay them for a moment: and they told us of numerous instances of Englishmen and others who were delayed days, weeks, and even months, in Sebastopol, on account of trifling informalities in their passports, and for which they were not to blame. I had lost my passport, and was traveling under my room-mate's, who stayed behind in Constantinople to await our return. To read the description of him in that passport and then look at me, any man could see that I was no more like him than I am like Hercules. So I went into the harbor of Sebastopol with fear and trembling—full of a vague, horrible apprehension that I was going to be found out and hanged. But all that time my true passport

FAR-AWAY MOSES.

(381–82) (fig. 4). With 69,500 copies sold in its first year, *Innocents Abroad* was an immediate success ("Europe and the Holy Land"). It did not take Far Away Moses long to realize the opportunities that this development afforded him. Almost immediately after it appeared, he began to take regular trips to the American consulate in Istanbul in order to borrow the book and "read the chapter about himself" to English and American tourists (Twain, Letter to Bliss). He also requested a copy of the chapter (and, later, the book) through the offices of the consul, so as to be able to use it as an advertisement (Letter to Cox).[18] Mark Twain obliged his old guide, as an 1870 note to his publisher makes clear (Letter to Bliss).

Far Away Moses had a habit of adapting his persona to the travel literature that described him.[19] According to an American customer he met during the 1860s, he began to use his famous alias only after a guidebook had given him that title (Leech 61). Now he again fashioned his image accordingly. The "baggy trowsers," "silken jacket," "voluminous waist-sash," and "fiery fez" Twain had described became Far Away Moses's signature style, one from which he would deviate only slightly over the years when posing for photographs (Twain, *Innocents Abroad* 381; "Troubles of 'Far-Away Moses'" 8; Smith). His outfit—unremarkable from the perspective of mid-nineteenth-century Ottoman dress—now became the costume he wore in order to play himself.

He also appears to have compiled his own personal dossier of the various endorsements he received from satisfied customers over the years. This included not only a copy of chapter 35 of *Innocents Abroad* (or, at times, the entire book) but also a letter of recommendation from an American general whom he had toured around Istanbul in the late 1860s as well as various other testimonials (Swift 431–32; "Far-Away Moses: The Girls Visit an Eastern Bazar"; "Faraway Moses, Mark Twain's Famous Guide"). By the 1870s, Far Away Moses also updated the inscription on his business card to include the page number (382) on which his image appeared in Twain's famous travelogue (Morris 649; Audenreid).

The more attention he received, the more mysterious Far Away Moses became. Stories about how he earned his famous nickname began to multiply: certain authors suggested that the British Bradshaw's travel guides had given him his title (Leech 61). Others ventured that it was an edition of Murray's handbook that had chosen the name for the Ottoman Jewish dragoman.[20] Still others attributed the name to Mark Twain, writing that the American author had devised the nickname as Far Away Moses toured him around Istanbul in 1867 (Adler, Letter to Sulzberger Adler, 24 Dec. 1890; Bancroft 5.854; Donlon). In one American author's rendition,

> The humorist and the guide strolled along together, the former being so intensely interested in what he saw that he often stood stock still in the road to admire the strange architecture of the houses and shops. But Moses kept plodding away, with the result that when the humorist resumed his tramp the Turk was so far ahead of him that it was with difficulty that he was called back. So often did Twain find himself alone in his tramps through the crooked streets of Constantinople that he facetiously dubbed his guide and chaperone "Far Away." ("Finishing the Fair")

There was only one problem with each of these explanations: no one appears to have been reading the literature they cited. Had they done so they might have seen that Bradshaw's guide was among the rare sources *not* to call Far Away Moses by his famous sobriquet or that Murray's guide to Constantinople recommended the Ottoman Jewish dragoman in a matter-of-fact manner, without giving any indication of having invented his nickname ("Guide and Interpreter" 638; Murray, *Handbook*, 1871, 18). Finally, Twain's chapter in *Innocents Abroad* makes quite clear that Far Away Moses already had his name when the two met. "Ignoring the fanciful name he takes such pride in," Twain wrote, "we called him Ferguson, just as we had done with all other guides," so as to avoid having to pronounce "their dreadful foreign names" (*Innocents Abroad*, 381).[21] Although the precise role Far Away Moses played in the proliferation of these various origin stories about his unusual nickname is unclear, he seems to have actively cultivated the sense of mystery that continued to grow up around him.

Another uncertainty that soon presented itself to travelers was the question of whether they had met the "real" Far Away Moses. So great was the Ottoman Jewish guide's fame that various individuals across the Ottoman capital reportedly presented themselves to tourists as the man or, when that proved impossible, as his relation. Travelers began to write of spending their days in Istanbul trying to evade "the Moses family," which increased "by continued accessions" and formed "a sort of procession" that followed them wherever they went (Swift 428). In some cases a group could spend many days in the company of a guide they believed to be Far Away Moses before realizing they had been deceived. One author described his experience, suggesting that about the fourth day he and his travel companions were in Istanbul "the proof came in so strong against" their guide "that he confessed himself not the genuine, but the brother of the original." As the same author explained, "Far-away-Moses had ceased to be Far-away-Moses" (Swift 431).

Others claimed to see through such schemes from the start. A young woman who went shopping for oriental curiosities in a market in Nice, France, reported an encounter with a man bearing a letter of recommendation from the "American minister at Constantinople" certifying the "remarkable integrity of 'Far-away Moses.'" "Then you are 'Far-away Moses'?" she asked him before receiving the cryptic reply, "Yes, and my big brother at Constantinople" ("Far-Away Moses: The Girls Visit an Eastern Bazar" 329). The American journalist and travel writer Thomas W. Knox mocked the claims of various characters to

on hand to accommodate you. But if you have not met the original you are introduced to some English-speaking Turk, Jew, or Christian who affectionately inquires after Mark Twain and hopes he is well and happy.

I think about seven dozen "brothers of Far-Away Moses" were pointed out to me, and they resembled him, each other, and

themselves, about as much as a cup of coffee resembles a row of mixed drinks in an American bar room. Moses admits that like the friend of Toodles "he had a brother" but he denies fraternal relations with all the "brothers" that hang about the bazaars and hotels.

Moses narrates an experience of his mercantile life such as we sometimes hear of in America. He shipped a lot of goods to Vienna at the time of the Exposition, and on these goods he figured a handsome profit on his mental slate. They were

SOME OF THE BROTHERS OF FAR-AWAY MOSES.

sent by steamer to Trieste, and thence by rail to Vienna. On arrival the boxes were found to contain old iron, straw, and pieces of wood, and Moses was in great grief, for the original lot had cost him about six hundred pounds sterling.

He tried to recover, but the two companies—steamboat and railway—played " Spenlow and Jorkins" on him most admirably. Each said that the robbery must have occurred while the boxes were in charge of the other concern, and after much trouble Moses received nothing by way of indemnity. Neither company would pay a centime until the locality of the robbery had been proved, and as this could not be shown, there was no payment. And to add to the loss he could not even recover the freight charges, which he had paid in full before removing the boxes from the railway station and discovering his loss.

Figure 5: Far Away Moses's many brothers, Thomas Wallace Knox, Backsheesh! Or Life and Adventures in the Orient (Hartford, 1875), p. 178.

be Far Away Moses, suggesting that his "seven dozen 'brothers' . . . resembled him, each other, and themselves, about as much as a cup of coffee resembles a row of mixed drinks" (178). To illustrate his point, Knox included a caricature of "some of the brothers of Far-Away Moses" in the travelogue he published of his journey east (fig. 5). An American man named Lee Meriwether, who authored a low-budget travel guide of Europe, wrote that by the time he left Istanbul he had met so many claimants to the position of Far Away Moses that he "began to think the woods full of them" (188).[22] "That the guides think the mere name Far-away-Moses a passport to your good graces is a great compliment to Mark Twain," Meriwhether concluded (188–89). The "real" Far Away Moses no doubt agreed. His "mere name" opened many doors for him and—it would seem—for many of his "brothers" as well.

FAR AWAY MOSES & COMPANY

Still others discovered they could use Far Away Moses's name as a trademark. When in 1868 a Jewish merchant named Elia Souhami partnered with the Muslim merchant Sadullah Bey to form a company specializing in oriental items in Istanbul, they drew Far Away Moses into their business, using his fame to build their reputation.[23] Thus was Far Away Moses & Company formed. Soon enough, the famed guide graduated from his first career. Trading places with the tourists he had so often greeted at Istanbul's docks, Far Away Moses embarked for the United States, where he helped establish various branches of the new business he represented ("Troubles of 'Far-Away Moses'" 8). Among these were a headquarters at New York's Union Square and shops in the Palmer House Building of Chicago, beneath the Grand Union Hotel in Saratoga, and on Chestnut Street in Philadelphia ("Far-Away Moses—He's Back in Turkey"; *Memorial of John Eliot Bowen* 89; Hutton 101; Putnam; Adler, Letter to Sarah Sulzburger Adler, 26 Dec. 1890). He also displayed the firm's merchandise at different world's fairs during this period, crossing the Atlantic to attend the 1873 International Exhibition in Vienna before traveling stateside again to sell the company's wares at the 1876 Centennial Exposition in Philadelphia (Knox 178; Putnam; "America's Trade in Oriental Rugs").

When he finally returned to the Ottoman capital at the close of the de-cade, the company continued selling its carpets to American clients through auctions and through a Muslim representative named Hasan Bey ("Rugs at

Figure 6: Far Away Moses as he appeared in Innocents Abroad, in an advertisement in the Chicago Daily Tribune, 14 Dec. 1888.

Auction"; "Far Away Moses—Grand Collection"; "Far Away Moses"). In advertisements for one such auction from the late 1880s, an etching of Far Away Moses taken directly from the one featured in *Innocents Abroad* graces the page, although now with a smoking pipe placed in his hands, presumably to give the image an extra exotic flare (fig. 6). Evidently the former dragoman no longer needed to appear in person to sell his sundry items: instead, the logo of the mysterious and quirky Eastern figure that one of Twain's illustrators had limned two decades earlier did his work for him. Far Away Moses's newly gained popularity had rendered him iconic.

Yet Far Away Moses's iconic status meant that those who sought to malign the Middle Eastern merchants in their midst found in him an easy target. Among the first to make this clear was an American woman who penned an 1879 editorial in the *New York Times* entitled "The Age of Bric-a-Brac."

Bemoaning the "Japanese fever" then sweeping the United States as well as the profusion of "cabinet-maker's rubbish" and "Oriental pots and pans from the bazaars of Faraway Moses and his tribe," the author not only dismissed all of the "Eastern" merchants who sold items she considered worthless but also suggested that all such merchants were essentially indistinguishable from one another. Writing just a few years later, another American traveler lamented that before going abroad her knowledge of "Turks had previously been limited to the Far-away-Moses sort, who come to America as missionaries to convert us to a correct taste in carpets" (Pitman 190). For this author as well, there was reason not to allow "the Far-away-Moses sort" to serve as the de facto ambassadors of the Orient in the West, nor to dictate so fully Americans' views of the East. Despite their dismissive tone, both editorials signaled the extent to which Far Away Moses's name had become synonymous with the trade in "Eastern" goods for American consumers in the late nineteenth century.

Others were vexed by Far Away Moses and his "tribe" because of the direct competition they represented. Among such individuals was the American department-store mogul John Wanamaker. Anxious to undermine his Middle Eastern competitors, Wanamaker launched an advertising campaign during the early 1890s that drew on Far Away Moses's fame and quoted from Mark Twain's description of his one-time guide.[24] Seeking to discredit the Ottoman carpet and curiosities dealer whose name they used to capture readers' attention, Wanamaker's ads suggested that there was no longer any reason to buy oriental objects from orientals since their goods could now be had cheaper, and with greater transparency, at his store ("Wanamaker's," *Philadelphia Times,* 17 Sept. 1891). Dismissing the whole "Far-away-Moses business," one such ad suggested that the "solemn merchandise and the serious manner" with which they approached their work hardly made the "Turk or Arab a model of honest trading."[25] Another ventured that although the "humbug of Far-away Moses" had often been exposed, "[d]evious and crafty Armenian ways" were taking over the oriental embroidery and rug business in the United States ("Wanamaker's," *Philadelphia Times,* 6 Apr. 1892). Although these ads referred to all sorts of "Easterners"—including Turks, Arabs, and Armenians—as wily and unreliable, Far Away Moses stood in for them all.

Wanamaker may also have had more personal reasons for his campaign against the former Ottoman Jewish dragoman and guide. It was in 1876, during the very period in which Wanamaker opened the first department store in Philadelphia, that Far Away Moses brought his company's merchandise to the Centennial Exposition in that city and, soon after, helped establish a branch of the Istanbul-based firm not far from Wanamaker's new department store. Given their shared involvement with the 1876 exposition and the close proximity of their stores, it is likely that Wanamaker and Far Away Moses knew each other.[26] In the years that followed, the two men and their businesses also competed for customers in advertisements placed side by side in the same newspapers (see, e.g., "No Laggards Here" and "Far Away Moses"). For all his criticism of the "Far Away Moses business," Wanamaker clearly felt threatened by the Ottoman Jewish man and those he represented—both the partners of his company and, more broadly, the growing numbers of Middle Easterners who had by this time arrived in the United States to sell their oriental wares.[27]

As Far Away Moses's name and image became commonplace—if contested—among consumers and vendors of oriental goods in the US, back in Istanbul the company that had formed with his name now adopted the less whimsical title Elia Souhami Sadullah & Company, after its two partners Perhaps Souhami and Sadullah believed that the din of voices that had come to question the reliability of Far Away Moses, his "brothers," and his wares were drowning out those who spoke and wrote admiringly of him, harming the firm's business prospects in the process. Perhaps they believed that their company had finally come into its own and no longer needed the gimmick of the quirky Eastern Jewish figure who had once appeared on their ads.[28] Whatever the reasons, the company's new title had the effect of normalizing the firm and de-exoticizing its image. Rather than building its reputation purely on the fame of the elusive literary figure of Far Away Moses, the company now became a company like so many others, bearing the name of its founders. Its choice to switch from an English-language title to one with names that were more recognizably Ottoman also signaled the firm's growing interest in appealing to local audiences.

Yet, despite the change in name, the company's approach to advertising changed little. Just as the items Far Away Moses had shipped to America in the 1870s and 1880s had included "antique carpets," "embroideries, silk draperies, Persian-Moorish lanterns," and "oriental bric-a-brac," advertisements for the rebranded Elia Souhami Sadullah & Company published in the French, English, and Ladino presses of the empire touted its extensive selection of oriental antiques, embroideries, platters, carpets "large and small," and "oriental ornaments and curiosities" from regions as diverse as Central Asia (Dagestan), Persia, and Western Anatolia (Izmir, Kula, and Gördes) ("Grand choix varié de tapis orientaux"; "Large and Choice Selection"; "Sadula i Robert Levi"). The geographical diversity featured in Elia Souhami Sadullah & Company's advertisements or in Far Away Moses's all-encompassing—if somewhat perplexing—

"Persian-Moorish lanterns" illustrated the great assortment of goods that the company offered from across the Islamic world.

As it announced its eclectic offerings of antiques, embroideries, and carpets from diverse corners of the Islamic Orient, the firm responded to a Western demand for various oriental items displayed and consumed side by side. Equally telling was its use of expressions like "oriental bric-a-brac" and "oriental ornaments and curiosities," demonstrating the extent to which the company's representatives had adopted an outsider's view of the items they procured and produced. There was a long history to such language, of course. Although elites had been engaged in the collection, display, and sale of natural and manmade "curiosities" in Europe for hundreds of years, by the nineteenth century the process had been democratized, allowing members of the global middle class access to the curious and exotic—or at least to things fashioned in this style (Pomian; Greenblatt; Hooper-Greenhill; Daston and Park; Impey and MacGregor; Mauriès; MacGregor; Bleichmar and Mancall; Davenne; Molineux 90–93).

It was during this period that the market for all that was curious caught on in the Ottoman Empire as well. Commercial directories published in Istanbul throughout the late nineteenth and early twentieth centuries listed "Oriental Curiosities" as a regular rubric for advertisers.[29] In this sense, Elia Souhami Sadullah & Company promoted its merchandise using the extant professional vocabularies of the day. Yet as the century came to a close, the firm's interest in providing Westerners with oriental curiosities as well as the self-exoticizing performances of its most famous representative began to compete with new pressures to present the company as one that promoted the goods—and thus also the economic interests—of the Ottoman state.

THE STUFF OF EMPIRE IN AN AGE OF NATIONS

The final decade of the nineteenth century witnessed a significant shift in Elia Souhami Sadullah & Company's public profile. The firm grew substantially, adding branches in Paris, London, Cairo, and Izmir, drawing nearly six hundred weavers and embroiderers into its employ and expanding its warehouse in Istanbul to seven large adjacent shops of three stories.[30] Different commentators proposed that this new layout made the store unique and quite possibly the largest in the entire vicinity of Istanbul's Grand Bazaar (*Cook's Continental*

Time Tables 202; Jacob 58; Willard 194). Others suggested that the company had become the "most important," the "most progressive," and the "most popular" firm dealing in Eastern antiquities in all of Istanbul ("M. Elia Souhami"; Adler, *I Have Considered the Days* 86; Jacob 58). By the 1890s, the firm also boasted that it was the only establishment of its kind in Istanbul to use fixed prices at a time when this trend was catching on in stores across the United States and Europe (Coufopoulos 6; Leach 123). A new emphasis on the shop's style similarly reflected a broader turn toward harnessing the "marketing power of interior design," much as managers of department stores and other commercial venues across the globe had begun to do during the same period (Roxburgh; Rappaport; Miller; Whitaker).[31]

The company's promotional literature now drew attention to the style of its shop's interiors for the first time. The firm's 1892 advertisement in *Cook's Continental Time Tables and Tourists' Hand Book* described Elia Souhami Sadullah & Company not only as "the largest House in Turkey in Oriental Articles," boasting "all sorts of rugs and carpets, silken sashes, dresses and curtains in all hues and colours," but—crucially—also one whose shop was "decorated and adorned in Turkish style" (*Cook's Continental Time Tables* 202). The new 1893 edition of Murray's *Handbook for Travellers in Constantinople* employed similar language. In the guidebook's "Bazar" section, readers could now find an endorsement suggesting that the best firm "in the Stambul Bazar" was "Sadoullah & Co., 'Faraway Moses', whose shop is decorated in Turkish style, and . . . [whose] carpets . . . are made for them in Smyrna and the interior" (156).[32] In a late nineteenth-century photograph that captures a section of this shop's inner courtyard, one glimpses low tables of inlaid wood, carpets, tapestries, portieres, metal lamps, and other decorative items hanging from walls, spread across the floor, and draped from a passageway leading to a second story. In the company's own version of a cozy corner, two men smoke a nargileh. The man seated in the right back corner is a now-gray Far Away Moses (fig. 7) (Beaugé et al. 70.).[33] The identification of the store's style as "Turkish" also reflected a meaningful transformation in the firm's approach to self-promotion. Whereas in the previous decade the company's advertisements had highlighted the great variety of oriental objects in its warehouses, references to the diverse origins of its goods increasingly gave way to a new advertising strategy. Wares from Ottoman locales—including Smyrna, in western Anatolia, and the Anatolian "interior"—remained in descriptions of the company's stock while mention of the Dagestani, Persian, and "Moorish" items it had once advertised fell away.

Figure 7: Interior of the shop of Elia Souhami Sadullah & Co., Istanbul. Pierre de Gigord Collection of Photographs, Getty Research Institute, Los Angeles (96.R.14; A12.F44).

Elia Souhami Sadullah & Company's new marketing techniques were the product of the Ottomanization of the firm's image, which occurred serendipitously during the 1890s. During the preceding decade—since Far Away Moses had left American shores to return to the Ottoman capital—the business had grown primarily by selling its wares to individual European and American tourists in that city and to private buyers in the United States and England, although representatives of the firm also showed up at world's fairs in London in 1884 and Antwerp in 1885, earning two gold medals, a bronze medal, and an honorable mention for their displays (*Exposition universelle d'Anvers* 88; Corneli and Mussely 331; Meriwether 189; Carathéodory Effendi). By the late 1880s the friendship that Sadullah Bey, Elia Souhami, and a new junior partner named Robert Levy developed with Oscar Straus, the US envoy extraordinary and minister plenipotentiary to the Ottoman Empire from 1887 to 1889, helped the firm secure the position of purveyors of oriental rugs to R. H. Macy & Company, which was run by Straus's brothers Isidor and Nathan (Straus, Letters to Isidor Straus, 21 Mar. 1889; 28 Mar. 1889; 11 Apr. 1889; [?] May1889; and 28 May 1889). Soon after Straus's tenure as minister ended, the young American Jewish scholar Cyrus Adler, then an assistant professor at the Johns Hopkins University, appeared in Istanbul as a special commissioner in charge of arranging various Middle Eastern exhibits for the upcoming Columbian Exposition in Chicago.[34] While in the Ottoman capital, he made the acquaintance of the firm's members and spent long hours with Robert Levy, whom Straus had personally recommended he meet.[35] In a letter he sent home from Istanbul, Adler remarked that he was impressed by these men and also by their shop in the bazaar, which he described as the "handsomest" he had seen. Noting that he considered Levy "hospitable by nature," Adler wrote that he also had reason to believe that Levy was interested in working with him in order "to do a big thing at Chicago—get a monopoly for the Constantinople exhibit." Levy was not disappointed (Adler, Letter to Sarah Sulzberger Adler, 24 Dec. 1890). With Adler's support, his company won the bid to run the Ottoman exhibit at the upcoming Chicago World's Fair.

The firm's partners were now tasked with representing their government on an international stage by creating a space that could be judged to be authentically Ottoman, or "Turkish," as Americans and Europeans were more inclined to call it ("La Ekspozision de Shikago"; "L'Exposition de Chicago"). The contract, prepared by the Ottoman Ministry of Trade and Public Works, specified that Elia Souhami Sadullah & Company would model the empire's government building at the fair after the Sultanahmet fountain that stood at the entrance to the Topkapı Palace in the imperial capital. It also sanctioned the construction of a mosque, a bazaar, a theater, and a replica of the Egyptian obelisk at Istanbul's Sultanahmet Square. Proper Islamic etiquette was to be observed at all times and visitors allowed into the mosque only at the discretion of the directors. The carryings-on in the theater, too, were to be regulated: nothing that would cause harm to the reputation either of Muslim women or of the empire as a whole was to be permitted. Not surprising in this context, the contract made clear that—under Elia Souhami Sadullah & Company's stewardship—only Ottoman goods were to be sold (Ottoman Ministry of Trade).[36]

In a matter of months, the company became the custodian of Ottoman prestige and products abroad. To be sure, Elia Souhami, Sadullah Bey, and Robert Levy's enterprise in Chicago remained a private one.[37] Yet once preparations for the exhibit were set into motion, the distinctions between the imperial government's official and unofficial representatives were often blurred. In preparation for the fair, Robert Levy accompanied the Ottoman commissioner İbrahim Hakkı Bey to the imperial Hereke carpet factory in order to select the choicest examples of rugs produced at the government-run factory for shipment to Chicago (Yıldız Perakende). Ottoman entrepreneurs interested in displaying their merchandise as part of the empire's exhibit were also instructed to make their arrangements directly with representatives of Elia Souhami Sadullah & Company in Istanbul ("La Ekspozision de Shikago" 2). Later, after they had arrived in Chicago, İbrahim Hakkı Bey charged both Levy and his assistant commissioner to act on his behalf when he was obliged to return to the empire for a time ("Calls from Foreign Representatives"). Whether for this reason or simply as a result of their unfamiliarity with his position as a private contractor for the Ottoman government, local press reporters in Chicago referred to Levy with titles like "Effendi Levy, the Imperial Commissioner to the World's Fair" ("Never Ending Stream of People") and "the Sultan's representative" ("Orient at the Fair"). The author of one such report fashioned Levy into the "Turkish Commissioner to the World's Fair," suggesting not only that the carpet merchant of Istanbul was a governmental representative but also that he might be considered Turkish ("Rare Turkish Embroideries").[38]

Levy actively cultivated this image of himself. Like Far Away Moses, he donned elaborate "oriental" outfits for cameras and crowds in Chicago and beyond. Yet in other respects he departed from his older colleague in his choice of attire. Unlike Far Away Moses, who was rarely caught in anything other than the robe, waist sash, and turban that had become a hallmark of his style, Levy playfully switched between an array of outfits on a regular basis, dressing variously as an Aegean Zeybek warrior, an Islamic legal scholar, and a modern Ottoman decked in frock coat and fez or a tailored suit with no hat.[39] Whereas Far Away Moses had continued to publicly embody one Ottoman type—that of the Ottoman Jew—over many decades, Levy chose instead to appear as various Ottoman types, including those associated with Ottomans of other religions. A photograph from this period of Levy together with four other employees of his firm (including Far Away Moses, who appears to his left) shows him in the embroidered vest, tapered billowing trousers, and curved *yatağan* sword associated with West Anatolian Zeybek irregulars (fig. 8). The nargilehs, inlaid wood tables, and clothing in the photo were, no doubt, among the items available for sale in Elia Souhami Sadullah & Company's shops. In such cases, the different personas that Levy and other employees of the company adopted were directly shaped by the products they sold.

Levy's ambiguous status in Chicago also inspired American entrepreneurs, who used his likeness to advertise their products. His self-exoticizing displays convinced various American observers that he could be considered a captivating oriental, a "true Turk," and even—it would seem—a Muslim.

Figure 8: Robert Levy (center) "with his personnel." Prétextat Lecomte, Les Arts et métiers de la Turquie et de l'Orient (Paris: Société d'Éditions Scientifiques, 1902), p. 317.

An 1893 advertisement for Kirk's American Family Soap gave this impression when it featured the "Noble Robert Levy" leading members of a local branch of Shriners in prayer as part of the dedication of the Ottoman mosque, which his company had helped build and oversee on Chicago's Midway Plaisance.[40] By presenting Levy kneeling and with hands upturned in the position of Muslim prayer, with a caption suggesting that the dedication ceremony had united "Christian and Mohammedan" alike, the advertisement left open the question of his religious affiliation, using mystery, and the exotic scene, to sell its soap (fig. 9) ("Kirk's American Family Soap").

Meanwhile, the now-aging Far Away Moses, who had also shown up at the Turkish Village in Chicago, similarly confused Americans' categories. To some he appeared as a clearly Jewish type, whereas others simply identified him as an oriental. Although his self-presentation changed little over the years, different observers projected onto Far Away Moses a variety of identities. At times, he seemed to encapsulate the Orient of *One Thousand and One Nights*, appearing to one American observer to be an "Eastern magician."[41] At other times he became a "remarkable Israelite," unmistakable as a "Hebrew," or even a Shylock (Cox, *The Isles of the Princes* 8; "Far-Away Moses: The Girls Visit

Noble Robert Levy—Concessioner of the Sultan of Turkey—is assisted by Medina Temple, A. A. O. N. M. S., in dedicating the Turkish Mosque at the World's Fair.

Brothers all, Christian and Mahommedan, united in nothing more strongly than their belief in the superiority of

Kirk's American Family Soap

—America's Favorite Laundry Soap—Pure—Lasting—Full Weight—Washes the most delicate and precious lace without injury, washes the heaviest woolens and clothes thoroughly.

Kirk's Dusky Diamond Tar Soap—used by laborers because of its cleansing and healing qualities.

Figure 9: Using "Noble Robert Levy" to sell Kirk's American Family Soap, Chicago Daily Tribune, 29 Apr. 1893.

an Eastern Bazar"; Knox 177; Smith). Despite these authors' reassurances and the clue offered by his unforgettable sobriquet, other observers appear to have taken Far Away Moses for a Muslim.[42] As for his nationality or place of origin, commentators labeled him as Turkish, Egyptian, Persian, Algerian, and Syrian in turn, suggesting that the exchangeability of the various objects he sold under the larger rubric of "oriental" had come to apply to him as well.[43]

However they characterized him, different observers continued to portray Far Away Moses as emblematic. Perhaps not by chance, an illustration printed in a pictorial record of the fair depicted a "Turk in Costume" dressed in a nearly identical fashion to Far Away Moses's now-famous outfit. Like the older Far Away Moses present at the fair, the illustrated figure sported a white beard, baggy pants, waist sash, and turban (fig. 10) (Bancroft 5.854.).[44] Far Away Moses also appears to have been the model for the "Semite" head that Otis T. Mason, an ethnographer at the National Museum in Washington, DC (today's Smithsonian), selected as one the keystones of the Library of Congress's Thomas Jefferson Building, alongside the various other ethnic types that adorn its façade (Wayne 18). Far Away Moses thus came to embody various categories—whether Turkish, oriental, Muslim, Semite, Jew, or some combination thereof.

ı in this half rood of canvas; for
e impression be conveyed; is the
of
ıs
st
re
n-
e,
ɔn
ɔe
ts
o-
at
re
ɔn

ːd
ıe
al
ıe
ʿe

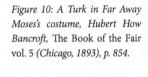

Figure 10: A Turk in Far Away Moses's costume, Hubert How Bancroft, The Book of the Fair *vol. 5 (Chicago, 1893), p. 854.*

A TURK IN COSTUME

n as he sought refuge in the sea.
ɔf canvas, whereon is depicted "the

Yet the Ottoman Jewish guide-cum-enterprising merchant seems to have been less preoccupied with these numerous rubrics than with preserving the image Mark Twain had bestowed upon him. As one chronicler of the fair put it, he was so "very proud . . . of his distinction" that "if questioned as to his identity," he would reply: "If you do not believe that I am he, look on page 382 of the book" (Pierce 363). A visitor to his shop similarly mentioned that while her group rested "from the fatigue of looking over the large stock" he had displayed before them, Far Away Moses produced a copy of Mark Twain's book, where his picture could be found. "This was conspicuously marked," she explained, and "it was evident that he wished our memory freshened by what the author had said of him" (Barber 127).

Far Away Moses took an active role in refreshing people's memories of him. He regularly inquired after Mark Twain and asked his American interlocutors to send his personal greetings to the famous author (Wadsworth; Cox, *Orient Sunbeams* 164). Upon realizing that the young man named Theodore Roosevelt whom he had spirited through the Ottoman capital many decades earlier had now become president of the United States, he quickly penned a letter to the American head of state.[45] The autographed correspondence that he received in response now joined Twain's book, his letters of endorsement, and various other publications featuring his likeness, all of which Far Away Moses reportedly kept with him in order to display them to his customers ("Faraway Moses, Mark Twain's Famous Guide"). Some of these items even made their way onto the walls of his store: one American commentator who undertook a trip of "nearly 20,000 miles" across Africa, Asia, and Europe, wrote home to Troy, New York, in 1894 to report that while "in Constantinople one day in the bazaar of 'Faraway Moses,'" the Ottoman Jewish carpet merchant had "proudly exhibited on the wall a framed copy of the *Troy Times*," which had given an account of him and featured his picture ("Personal"). The texts and images that others had produced to describe Far Away Moses to foreign audiences thus became part of his performative repertoire, which he used to promote both his business and himself.[46]

In the hands of the firm's new partner Levy, however, the self-exoticizing self-promotion of the company's early days came to overlap with a new impulse toward state promotion. In contrast to his older business associate, Levy made clear the links he drew between his engagement with things oriental and his broader allegiance to his empire—a position that coincided with growing pressures to create a unified and loyal Ottoman citizenry back in the empire.[47] It was in this context that—almost immediately after arriving in Chicago—

Levy made a great show of his patriotism to the local press. In an article describing a gathering of fair organizers at the Palmer House Hotel in downtown Chicago—the very same building in which Far Away Moses had established a branch of his business two decades earlier—a journalist for the *Chicago Daily Tribune* introduced Levy as an "enthusiastic Turk" who was "thoroughly patriotic" and who declared that he "would lose his last drop of blood . . . in defense of his country" ("Turkey Holds the Key"). While on the fairgrounds he gave public speeches in Turkish and orchestrated an Ottoman Day celebration replete with Ottoman flags, food, and patriotic speeches ("Faithful Subjects"). He also promised that the stuff of his empire on display there would help promote the Ottomans' place in the world ("El Sabah"; *Picturesque Chicago* 15).

Levy's performances of his political attachment to his empire were not the only signs of growing imperial identification among Elia Souhami Sadullah & Company's representatives. Well after the fair had ended, the company—now renamed Sadullah, Levy, and Madame Souhami following Elia Souhami's death—continued to announce itself as the Ottoman concessioner of the Chicago exhibition, as it did in an advertisement the company placed in Demetrius Coufopoulos' *Guide to Constantinople*, published in 1895 in London. Although this advertisement employed the familiar language of the oriental (suggesting that the company was the "only reliable dealer of Oriental goods"), it also boasted the specifically Ottoman focus the company had developed in recent years, touting both the company's production of "Turkish Carpets and Embroidery" and its collection "of Turkish Antiquities, Carpets, Old Arms, Embroidery, Porcelain, and Silver Ware," which it claimed was the largest such collection in the world (6). Even after it added "Eastern" wares from non-Ottoman locales (such as Dagestani and Persian carpets) back into its advertised repertoire, the company announced its new identification with the empire in other ways, as in 1895 when it placed an Ottoman flag on its advertisement in an Istanbul businesses directory and on a new version of its business letterhead (fig. 11) (Cervati 1179; for the letterhead, see Receipts from Sadullah, Levy and Vve Souhami).

Figure 11: Sadullah, Levy & Vve. Souhami advertisement in Cervati 1179. Collection of the Greek Patriarchate of Istanbul, courtesy of SALT Research Center.

CONCLUSION

Although the memory of both have been all but erased, Far Away Moses and the company whose name he inspired were wildly successful in their day, capturing the attention of influential American authors, illustrators, entrepreneurs, collectors, and politicians (including Mark Twain, Thomas Nast, John Wanamaker, George Vanderbilt, and Theodore Roosevelt) and working with interests as varied as R. H. Macy & Company, the Smithsonian and Victoria and Albert Museums, and the Ottoman government.[48] Their multistory production site, warehouse, and shop in Istanbul competed in both its stocks and its approach to interior design with many of the large department stores of the day, while the firm's claim to be the "only reliable dealer" in oriental goods and its adoption of the fixed-price system similarly echoed the language and policies of its contemporary competitors in the retail trade (Coufopoulos 6). Even those who dismissed Far Away Moses and his imitators as swindlers and vendors of inferior goods testified to the extent of his influence. Indeed, by the late nineteenth century his had become a household name associated, across the United States, with oriental carpets and decorative items—to the point that it came to stand in for Middle Easterners of various backgrounds who had come to the country as vendors of Eastern wares.

Dealing in the global oriental-goods trade was in turn transformative for the company's members: the various markets in which they operated inspired them to continuously reinvent both their products and themselves. Allowing life to imitate art, Far Away Moses regularly made reference to himself as Far Away Moses the literary—and illustrated—figure, both replicating and embellishing a version of himself that others had imagined, carrying around the pages and engravings that described him, and keeping newspaper articles about himself framed on the walls of his shop in Istanbul. Whatever his "real" name may have been, the stage name others had bequeathed to him enveloped his public persona almost completely.[49]

With time, Elia Souhami Sadullah & Company also altered its image according to the evolving demands of various imperial markets—not just American and European but also Ottoman—changing its name and increasingly emphasizing the Turkishness of the company, its interior design style, and its wares. Meanwhile, Robert Levy's image as Ottoman patriot coincided with his increasing involvement with Ottoman goods. Although this was apparent by the time he showed up with the official concession to represent his state in Chicago in the early 1890s, it had begun before: as early as 1886, a group of Ottoman merchants who displayed their merchandise at the Ottoman exhibit at the Exposition Universelle in Antwerp wrote their government on Levy's behalf, suggesting that the state honor him for his activities promoting the business of their empire at the fair (Carathéodory Effendi). Even as the different members of the firm adapted and readapted their personas and marketing strategies, however, their ability to sell both their goods and themselves as "authentic" orientals remained crucial to their success over the course of many decades.

This imperative—to be "oriental" and, later, Ottoman, in order to propel their business—meant that their Jewishness at times went unremarked. Yet, although their American and European interlocutors often treated the Jewish members of the company first and foremost as "orientals," there is no indication that they ever attempted to hide the fact that they were Jewish. Of course, there were those who identified both Far Away Moses and Robert Levy primarily, or even exclusively, as Easterners or "Turks," as well as those who mistakenly took them for Muslims or conflated them with Armenians, for that matter; but their misidentification by others need not be read as straightforward acts of intentional passing. Back home in their own communities, and among fellow Ottomans, their Jewishness would have been an uncontested fact of life. It was thus inscrutable only to outsiders, and even then only partially.

In this context the firm's members did not need to hide or even down-play their Jewishness in order to develop their oriental and Ottoman perso-nas. Even as they sought to present themselves and their wares as genuinely "Eastern," the company's Jewish members actively cultivated both their Jewish ties and personas. There was good reason for this. Although their Jewishness gave pause to certain observers, it often proved an asset.[50] Far Away Moses ap-pealed to Anglo-American audiences in large part because they perceived him as an enigmatic and quirky biblical type. The "East" he represented was at once (or, sometimes, in turns) Jewish and Islamic. Elia Souhami and Robert Levy not only befriended but also found willing business partners and customers in their American coreligionists Cyrus Adler and Oscar Straus, both of whom they hosted in their homes, synagogues, and Jewish communal balls.[51] It was Levy's connections with Straus that allowed his company to become the pur-veyor of Turkish carpets to R. H. Macy & Company; his acquaintance with Adler—made on Straus's recommendation—helped secure his firm the con-cession to represent the Ottoman Empire at the Chicago World's Fair. It is thus that, in an ironic twist of history, the company's American and Jewish ties helped it become more "Eastern" and more Ottoman.

Just as selling oriental items had once fostered the oriental persona of Far Away Moses—who became an oriental who sold "orientals" (a contemporary term for oriental carpets), a curiosity who sold curiosities, and a man many considered as ornamental as the items he helped his customers acquire—the experience of favoring Ottoman goods allowed mercantile and state-building projects to overlap, turning the likes of Robert Levy, and all members of Elia Sadullah Souhami & Company for that matter, into Ottomans. They became, in a sense, what they sold.

But that is not all. The material exchanges that engendered this pro-cess shaped not only the public and political personas of different members of the firm but also spheres more intimate. The oriental goods in which they traded figured among their most prized possessions, which they displayed in their own homes and passed down to members of their families over many generations (Rosenspitz 613–14; Adler, Letter to Sarah Sulzberger Adler, 26 Dec. 1890; Bishop, 23 Feb. 2013, 5 June 2014, and 24 Oct. 2014; Valensi, 25 Feb. 2013, and 20 Mar. 2014). Contacts with the individuals who helped them launch their careers also appear to have had a meaningful impact on their personal lives. Far Away Moses reportedly named his son Marco in honor of Mark Twain, whom he claimed as a friend as well as a patron ("Faraway Moses, Mark Twain's Famous Guide"). Robert Levy followed suit by naming his son

Oscar Straus Levy, after Oscar Straus, the American envoy to the Ottoman Empire with whom he sustained a friendship over many decades (Adler, *I Have Considered the Days* 89; "Se. Izidor Straus" 3). This last relationship engendered new material exchanges in turn. Among the cherished items Robert Levy boasted in his home were the cup and saucer his son Oscar Straus Levy had received from his namesake.[52] Nearly half a century after William R. Denny transported Far Away Moses's photographic calling card on a ship across the Atlantic, these items had made the reverse journey, leaving a tangible trace of the personal connections forged in the midst of business transactions. Robert Levy, who had dedicated his life to selling carpets, objets d'art, and souvenirs to tourists, now had a souvenir of his own.

Notes

I am indebted to Aviva Ben-Ur, Paris Papamichos Chronakis, Jonathan Karp, Niki Lefebvre, Lisa Leff, Noam Maggor, Catherine Molineux, Katherine D. Moran, Devin E. Naar, Sarah Abrevaya Stein, Ruth Toulson, and Edward Wright-Rios for their incisive feedback on different versions of this article. The article was originally published as "The East As a Career: Far Away Moses & Company in the Marketplace of Empires," *Jewish Social Studies: History, Culture, Society*, vol. 21, no. 2, Winter 2016. pp. 35–77.

1.   For the image in his travelogue, see Twain, *The Innocents Abroad* 382.
2.   The story of the participation of Armenians in the oriental carpet trade in the United States is perhaps the best known: see "America's Trade in Oriental Rugs"; Mirak; and Jenkins-Madina. Although various works record the participation of Ottoman Jews in the global oriental-goods trade, we still know relatively little about such individuals' lives and business practices. For Ottoman Jews and their descendants in Turkish tobacco and oriental-carpet work in Europe, see Guttstadt 111–12, 118, 123, 127–29. For Ottoman Jews and oriental products in the United States, see Angel 143–44; Papo 21, 29–30, 277; Bali; Ben-Ur 23, 29, 49, 131, 287; and Cohen, *Becoming Ottomans* 135–37. For the Istanbul Jewish firm that eventually employed Far Away Moses, see Grossman and Ahlborn 44, 52, 128; Bali 61; Cohen, *Becoming Ottomans* 62–73; and Cohen, "Oriental by Design."
3.   Recent studies on the role that trust played in commercial transactions include Trivellato; and Aslanian.
4.   Exceptions include recent works in modern Jewish history such as Stein, *Plumes*, and Karp, "Blacks, Jews," which argue that Jews' involvement in different economic arenas affected people's perceptions of them as more or less white, respectively. See also Chiswick, and Shandler, for how the experience of the marketplace shapes Jewish practice and piety. For some of the recent work on consumption in modern Jewish history, see Heinze; Joselit; Auslander, "'Jewish Taste'?"; Auslander, "The Boundaries of Jewishness"; and the various essays in Reuveni and Roemer.
5.   For a fascinating example of the intersection of persona and product in modern Jewish history, see Shandler. On rags, see, among others, Mendelsohn, and Diner. On alcohol, see M. Davis, and Dynner. On feathers, see Stein, *Plumes*. Among the many studies, too numerous to recount here, that treat the association of Jews and Hollywood and modernist art, see Gabler, and Bilski. Other recent work detailing Jewish participation in different economic niches includes Lerner, and various essays in Kobrin. For new scholarship on Jews and modern economies more broadly, see Penslar; Godley; Schroeter; Slezkine; Teller; Chiswick, Lecker, and Kahana; Karp, *The Politics of Jewish Commerce*; Lederhendler; Muller; Reuveni and Wobick-Segev 1–20; Chiswick; Kobrin; and Kobrin and Teller.
6.   As of yet, I have been unable to ascertain either his birth or death date. His precise relationship (both commercial and personal) to the other members of the firm he

eventually joined similarly remains uncertain, although most sources indicate that he was an employee rather than a partner.

7. According to different authors, word of the Ottoman Jewish guide spread across the Middle East, from Cairo to Damascus and Beirut to Izmir. Swift 425; Glazebrook 85; Stevens 205.

8. Various travel writers of the period, including Mark Twain, explicitly referenced what guidebooks said about the places they visited. One author playfully made light of this, writing in his preface: "Mistakes of fact, when they occur, are not my own, but must be laid at the door of John Murray, Esq., of London," Swift 6. For writers who praised Far Away Moses's trustworthiness and knowledge, see, for example, Montgomery 372; Murray, *Handbook*, 1871, 18; Leech 61; Swift 425; Buckham 1.381; Stoddard 280; and Jacob 58.

9. A number of the American and British travel writers who described Far Away Moses made explicit their identification as Christians. Some were missionaries. Others visited missionary and Bible societies or portrayed their journeys as pilgrimages to the holy sites of the Holy Land and Near East. See, for example, Montgomery, and Buckham; Noble; and Morris 2.657. For the American and British interest in exploring the lands of the Bible during this period, see J. Davis; Obenzinger; Long; Bar-Yosef; Wharton; and Rogers.

10. Baker 8. Other references to Far Away Moses as a patriarchal figure include "Race Types at the World's Fair"; Noble 505; and Schaff 303. For Far Away Moses as a "worthy old Hebrew" and "Holy Moses," see Bell and Montbard 48, and Bates 257, respectively.

11. On the image of Ottoman Jews as beggars, see Cohen, *Becoming Ottomans* 23–24. For the poverty of Istanbul's Jews in particular, see Baudin; Cyrus Adler, diary entry 29 Jan. 1891; and Rosenspitz.

12. "Photographs" 118. For other recommendations of the Abdullah Frères studio, see "Pera, or Bey Oghloo" 64; "Shops" 647; "Photographers" 651; "Photographs" 640.

13. Not all observers were equally taken with Far Away Moses and his much-vaunted honesty. For an early skeptical account, see Audenreid 482.

14. Montgomery viii, with the note "'Far-Away Moses' (from photograph)." The author also mentioned his encounter with Far Away Moses, "a guide and dragoman known to all modern travellers" (372).

15. For the long and complex European associations of Jews and the "East," see Kalmar and Penslar, and Brunotte, Ludewig, and Stähler.

16. For the exoticizing effect of using objects as the background of ethnographic representations, see Gaudio.

17. For other sources recommending Far Away Moses's services during this period, see Radcliffe 721; Swift 424; and Murray, *Handbook*, 1871, 18.

18. Technically, Cox was not a consul but the "Envoy Extraordinary and Minister Plenipotentiary to the Ottoman Empire." There was, as of yet, no official ambassador stationed in Istanbul.

19. An American commentator, in turn, suggested that Far Away Moses's attire surpassed the attempts of master authors to depict oriental costume: "Neither Irving nor Booth ever conceived so fine and fitting a costume as this old man wears every day in and out of the bazaar" (Smith).

20. Hyde 377. See also Bell and Montbard 48, which simply suggests that Far Away Moses had been "so named by some facetious American—title duly registered in a guide-book, and accepted by the worthy old Hebrew in a large board over his stall."

21. A note of the parodical, which infused *Innocents Abroad*, comes through in Twain's portrayal here: "Far Away Moses" was clearly an English rather than a foreign name, after all, and one that no American traveler could possibly have had difficulty pronouncing.

22. Another faux Moses is described in Barton 103.

23. In one observer's words, this allowed Far Away Moses to become "attached, as a sort of advertisement" to the company that bore his name (Adler, *I Have Considered the Days* 86). For more on Elia Souhami, the firm's Jewish partner, see Cohen, *Becoming Ottomans* 62–63; for more on Sadullah Bey, the firm's Muslim partner, see Wayne 15; "Queer Sign Manuals"; Adler, *I Have Considered the Days* 139; Maruzat; "Sadullah Talip Bey" 498–99; Bali; and Berry.

24. Notably, neither this nor any of the subsequent ads made explicit Far Away Moses's Jewishness. Borrowing from Twain's description, they referred to him only as the American author's "Turkish guide."

25. "Wanamaker's," *Philadelphia Times*, 3 Dec. 1891; "Wanamaker's," *Bucks County (PA) Gazette*; "Wanamaker's," *Denton (Md.) Journal*. Wanamaker was known to accuse his competitors of dishonest business practices; see Whitaker 8.

26. For Wanamaker's involvement with the Centennial Exposition, see Gibbons 1.153–60.

27. Over a decade later another American department store chain—Chamberlain, Johnson, Dubose, of Atlanta—ran a smear campaign that invoked Far Away Moses's name to similar ends ("Chamberlain, Johnson, Dubose Co. Furniture").

28. This interpretation appears to be confirmed by the fact that, by the 1890s, the company made increasingly infrequent use of the name and image of Far Away Moses in their advertisements and commercial listings.

29. On "Oriental Curiosities" as a rubric for advertisers in late Ottoman Istanbul, see, for example, "Curiosités Orientales (Marchands de)," 1880, 436–37; "Curiosités Orientales (March. de)," 1881, 302; "Curiosités Orientales (Marchands de)," 1889–90, 436; "Curiosités Orientales," 1891, 503. A commercial directory of late Ottoman Izmir and Anatolia also featured antiquities dealers who registered themselves as vendors of "Oriental Curiosities" (Nalpas 72, 146, 270; de Andria 50). Elia Souhami Sadullah & Company (later Sadullah, Levy, and Vve. Souhami & Company; Sadullah, Levy & Company; and—finally—Sadullah, Levy, and Mandil) advertised in each of these commercial directories under the rubric of "Oriental Curiosities"

through the 1920s and in material published abroad. See "Curiosités Orientales," 1899, 1371; *Meyers Reisebücher* 267.

30. For the company's new international branches, see *L'Indicateur Ottoman*, 1881, 88, and 1885, 345. For reports of Far Away Moses in Cairo during different periods, see E. S. P., "Letter from Egypt"; Bell and Montbard 48; and Stoddard 280. For the company's nearly six hundred employees, see Lecomte 104. Advertisements the company ran during the 1890s announced a two-story shop made up of seven consecutive rooms, up from the four rooms mentioned in ads from the 1880s. For the shop's expansion see also Willard 194, and Berry 48, which describes a three-story shop with an enclosed central courtyard by the 1920s.

31. For Jews and department stores in Germany, see Lerner. For department stores in the Middle East, see Stein, *Making Jews Modern*, especially 175–201, and Kupferschmidt.

32. The same description was later reprinted in the 1907 edition of the handbook.

33. This photograph is misidentified in the book as representing the shop of "Maisons Abdullah et Cie." That it is actually a picture of the premises of Elia Souhami Sadullah & Company is evidenced by the presence of Far Away Moses and other recognizable employees of the company as well as the faint white writing in the bottom left corner of the photograph, which reads "Maison Sadullah," an abbreviated name sometimes employed to refer to the firm.

34. For how he came to be appointed in this capacity, see Adler, *I Have Considered the Days* 72–75.

35. Straus recommended Levy to others as well. In a letter to his brother Isidor, he wrote that Levy had more "snap and sense" than any merchant he knew and suggested that the two meet; Straus, Letter to Isidor Straus, 21 Mar. 1889.

36. The contract was also published in "Malumat-ı Dahiliye-Şikago Sergisi" 3.

37. Robert Levy represented his firm in Chicago, whereas two Ottoman civil officials— İbrahim Hakkı Bey and A. Fahri Bey—were appointed to serve as commissioner and assistant commissioner of the empire at the exposition.

38. This was not the only source to describe Levy as a Turk. See also Bates 257; *Chicago Times Portfolio*; Potuoğlu-Cook; Cohen, "Oriental by Design"; and Cohen, *Becoming Ottomans*.

39. Of the dozens of references and images I have found of Far Away Moses, I have found only one mention of his wearing anything else. See "'Far Away' Moses and His Pets." For further discussion of the many outfits Robert Levy and others donned at different moments, see my discussion of the phenomenon I've labeled "clothes-switching" in Cohen, "Oriental by Design."

40. In at least one respect the advertisement was accurate: during his stay in Chicago, Robert Levy was inducted into a local Shriner branch. See "Turkish Village Dedicated."

41. For Far Away Moses as an oriental, see "Dr. Henshall at the World's Fair." Knox (177–78), described Far Away Moses as "a dignified oriental with a Jewish cast of

features," who (despite his apparent Jewish distinctiveness) might easily be replaced by "some English-speaking Turk, Jew, or Christian who affectionately inquires after Mark Twain and hopes he is well and happy." For Far Away Moses as an Eastern magician, see "Far-Away Moses: The Girls Visit an Eastern Bazar."

42. Paine 180, told how, upon his travels to Istanbul during the early twentieth century, he and his travel companions had "called at the bazaar of Far-away Moses" only to find that he had died and "gone to that wonderful grand bazaar of delight which the Mohammedan has selected as his heaven."

43. For references to Far Away Moses as a Turk, see Twain, *Innocents Abroad* 381; "Troubles of Far-Away Moses"; Bates 257; and "Personal"; for Far Away Moses as an Egyptian, see *Chicago Times Portfolio*; for his Persian incarnation, see Wister 352; for a description of Far Away Moses as Algerian, see Buel n.p. Most recently, Nance, *How the Arabian Nights*, cross-referenced Far Away Moses in her index with the entry "Peddlers, Syrian." A different type of confusion about Far Away Moses's nationality has resulted from a misreading of the company's business contract (in Ottoman Turkish); Wayne 16, and, following him, Kirshenblatt-Gimblett, "Place in the World" 72, have suggested that Far Away Moses was the American-born Harry Mandil, who eventually became a partner in the company in the early twentieth century. This assumption is undermined by the great disparity in age between the two men, by a comparison of their photographs, and by the evidence Wayne used to make the link: he understood the word "mösyö" next to Mandil's name to have meant Moses, an unfortunate misreading of the Turkish word for "monsieur." On this see also Bali 61–62.

44. The image is nearly identical to another illustration of Far Away Moses published during the exposition in Smith 698. See also the reference to Far Away Moses as "graybeard" at the fair; "Finishing the Fair."

45. Roosevelt had traveled to the Ottoman capital in 1873 with his family; see Kohn 22.

46. On the concept of the repertoire in performance studies, see Taylor.

47. For attempts to foster imperial identification among Ottomans of all backgrounds, see, for example, Kayalı; Rahme; Frierson, "Mirrors Out, Mirrors In"; Frierson, "Gender, Consumption and Patriotism; Blumi; Makdisi; Petrov; Anagnostopoulou and Kappler; Özbek; Campos; Hartmann; Bashkin; Philliou; Levy; Ueno; Cohen, *Becoming Ottomans*; and Kechriotis.

48. For transactions with the Vanderbilts, see Brendel-Pandich and Dodds 306; Berry 73; and Receipts from Sadullah, Levy and Vve Souhami. For those with the Smithsonian and the Victoria and Albert Museum, respectively, see *Report of the U.S. National Museum*, and MA/1/S2606.

49. Rare and contradictory references to Far Away Moses's other possible names do exist. See Buckham 381, which refers to him as Samuel Moses. A man by that name was registered (although without any indication that he was Far Away Moses) in "Guide and Interpreter" 638. Whether he was the same man listed in *L'Indicateur*

Ottoman, 1880, 169, as "Samuel Mozas" is unclear, as is the possibility that this Mozas was Far Away Moses, since the same page on which Mozas's name appears includes a separate entry for "Sadoullah Faraway (Moses et Cie)" and lists the two at separate addresses. A later source suggests that Far Away Moses's last name may have been Guerson, as a Jewish merchant active in Istanbul in the mid-twentieth century and bearing that name claimed to be Far Away Moses's grandson (though without noting whether the connection was maternal or paternal) (McLemore). Still other contemporaries, who claimed that he had a familial relationship to Robert Levy, introduced the possibility that Far Away Moses's surname may have been Levy; see Wood 566.

50. For one writer's skepticism about the company's Jewishness, see Snider 373.

51. Straus, Letter to his family; Adler, Letter to Sarah Sulzberger Adler, 24 Dec. 1890; Adler, Letter to Sarah Sulzberger Adler, 26 Dec. 1890; Adler, Letter to Sarah Sulzberger Adler, 6 Feb. 1891; Adler, *I Have Considered the Days* 86. When Oscar Straus's brother Isidor came to the Ottoman capital a few years later, Robert Levy also toured him around the city; "Se. Izidor Straus."

52. On the cup and saucer in Levy's possession, see the diary entry for 6 June 1915. It is likely that Straus chose the gift from the porcelain collections of his family business, L. Straus & Sons, which specialized in glassware, china, and porcelain products—including cups and saucers. On this, see Hower, and Henderson.

Works Cited

Adler, Cyrus. Diary entry 29 Jan. 1891. Diary of a trip to the Near East, 1891, Cyrus Adler Papers, Box 17, Jewish Theological Seminary Archives, New York.

———. *I Have Considered the Days.* Jewish Publication Society of America, 1941.

———. Letter to Sarah Sulzberger Adler. 24 Dec. 1890. Cyrus Adler Papers, Box 14, Folder 3, Jewish Theological Seminary Archives, New York.

———. Letter to Sarah Sulzburger Adler. 26 Dec. 1890. Cyrus Adler Papers, Box 14, Folder 3, Jewish Theological Seminary Archives, New York.

———. Letter to Sarah Sulzberger Adler. 6 Feb. 1891. Cyrus Adler Papers, Box 14, Folder 4, Jewish Theological Seminary Archives, New York.

"The Age of Bric-a-Brac." *New York Times,* 2 Jan. 1879, p. 4.

"America's Trade in Oriental Rugs." *Upholsterer and Interior Decorator,* Feb. 1920, p. 54.

Anagnostopoulou, Sia, and Matthias Kappler. "*Zito Zito o Sultanos/Bin Yaşa Padişahımız*: The *Millet-i Rum* Singing the Praises of the Sultan in the Framework of Helleno-Ottomanism." *Archivum Ottomanicum,* vol. 23, 2005–2006, pp. 47–78.

Andria, Jacob de. *Indicateur des Professions Commerciales et Industrielles de Smyrne, de l'Anatolie, des Côtes, des Îles, Etc.* Izmir, 1896.

Angel, Marc. *La America: The Sephardic Experience in the United States.* Jewish Publication Society, 1982.

Aslanian, Sebouh. *From the Indian Ocean to the Mediterranean: The Global Trade Networks of Armenian Merchants from New Julfa.* Univ. of California, 2011.

Audenreid, J. C. "General Sherman in Europe and the East." *Harper's Magazine,* vol. 47, Sept. 1873, pp. 225–42, 481–95, 652–71.

Auslander, Leora. "The Boundaries of Jewishness, or When Is a Cultural Practice Jewish?" *Journal of Modern Jewish Studies,* vol. 8, no. 1, 2009, pp. 47–64.

———. "'Jewish Taste'? Jews and the Aesthetics of Everyday Life in Paris and Berlin, 1933–1942." *Histories of Leisure,* edited by Rudy Koshar, Bloomsbury, 2002, pp. 299–318.

Baker, James. *Turkey in Europe.* London, 1877.

Bali, Rıfat. *Anadolu'dan Yeni Dünya'ya: Amerika'ya I<do>lk Göç Eden Türklerin Yaşam Öyküleri.* Iletisim Yayincilik, 2004.

Bancroft, Hubert How. *The Book of the Fair,* vol. 5. Chicago, 1893. 5 vols.

Bar-Yosef, Eitan. *The Holy Land in English Culture, 1799–1917: Palestine and the Question of Orientalism.* Clarendon, 2005.

Barber, Julia Langdon. "Lunch with Far-Away Moses." *Mediterranean Mosaics: Or, the Cruise of the Yacht Sapphire, 1893–1894.* N.p., 1895, 126–29.

Barton, William Eleazer. *The Old World in the New Century: Being the Narrative of a Tour of the Mediterranean, Egypt and the Holy Land, with Some Information about the Voyage and Places Visited.* Pilgrim, 1902.

Bashkin, Orit. "'Religious Hatred Shall Disappear from the Land': Iraqi Jews as Ottoman Subjects, 1864–1913." *International Journal of Contemporary Iraqi Studies*, vol. 4, no. 3., 2010, pp. 305–23.

Bates, J. H. *Notes of Foreign Travel.* New York, 1891.

Baudin, P. *Les Israélites de Constantinople: Étude Historique.* 1873. Isis, 1989.

Beaugé et al., Gilbert. *Images d'empire: Aux origines de la photographie en Turquie.* İnstitut d'études françaises d'Istanbul, 1993.

Bell, Charles Frederic Moberly, and Georges Montbard. *From Pharoah to Fella.* London, 1888.

Ben-Ur, Aviva. *Sephardic Jews in America: A Diasporic History.* New York Univ., 2009.

Berry, Burton Yost. *Out of the Past: The Istanbul Grand Bazaar.* Arco, 1977.

Bilski, Emily D. *Berlin Metropolis: Jews and the New Culture, 1890–1918.* Univ. of California, 1999.

Bishop, Randa. "Re: Getting Back in Touch." Received by Julia Phillips Cohen, 23 Feb. 2013.

———. "Re: Book!" Received by Julia Phillips Cohen, 5 June 2014.

———. "Re: Valensi Souhami Family Items." Received by Julia Phillips Cohen, 24 Oct. 2014.

Bleichmar, Daniela, and Peter C. Mancall. *Collecting across Cultures: Material Exchanges in the Early Modern Atlantic World.* Univ. of Pennsylvania, 2011.

Blumi, Isa. "Teaching Loyalty in the Late Ottoman Balkans: Educational Reform in the Vilayets of Manastir and Yanya, 1878–1912." *Comparative Studies of South Asia, Africa and the Middle East*, vol. 21, no. 1–2, 2001, pp. 15–23.

Brendel-Pandich, Susanne, and Dennis R. Dodds. "George W. Vanderbilt's Collection of Oriental Rugs at Biltmore Estate, Asheville, North Carolina, Part I: Formation of the Collection." *Hali*, vol. 3, no. 4, 1981, p. 306.

Brunotte, Ulrike, Anna-Dorothea Ludewig, and Axel Stähler, editors. *Orientalism, Gender, and the Jews.* De Gruyter, 2015.

Buckham, George. *Notes from the Journal of a Tourist: Egypt, the Holy Land, Syria, Turkey, Austria, Switzerland.* New York, 1890. 2 vols.

Buel, James William. *The Magic City.* 1894. Arno, 1974.

"Calls from Foreign Representatives." *Chicago Daily Tribune*, 28 April 1893, p. 10.

Campos, Michelle U. *Ottoman Brothers: Muslims, Christians, and Jews in Early Twentieth-Century Palestine.* Stanford Univ., 2010.

Carathéodory Effendi, Etienne. Letter to Said Pasha. 1 June 1886. Hariciye Nezareti Evrakı Mütenevvia (HR.MTV) 363/14, Prime Ministry's Ottoman Archives, Istanbul, Turkey.

Çelik, Zeynep. *Displaying the Orient: Architecture of Islam at Nineteenth-Century World's Fairs.* Univ. of California, 1993.

Cervati, Raphael C. "Grand Bazar d'Orient." *Annuaire Oriental du Commerce*, vol. 14, 1895, p. 1179.

"Chamberlain, Johnson, Dubose Co. Furniture." *Atlanta Constitution*, 24 Sept. 1904, p. 5.

Chicago Times Portfolio of the Midway Types, Part 6: Cairo Street Number. Chicago, 1893.

Chiswick, Carmel. *Judaism in Transition: How Economic Choices Shape Religious Tradition.* Stanford Economics and Finance, 2014.

Chiswick, Carmel, Tikva Lecker, and Nava Kahana, editors. *Jewish Society and Culture: An Economic Perspective.* Bar-Ilan Univ., 2007.

Cohen, Julia Phillips. *Becoming Ottomans: Sephardi Jews and Imperial Citizenship in the Modern Era.* New York: Oxford Univ., 2014.

———. "Oriental by Design: Ottoman Jews, Imperial Style, and the Performance of Heritage." *American Historical Review*, vol. 119, no. 2, 2014, pp. 364–98.

Cook's Continental Time Tables and Tourists' Hand Book. London, 1892.

Corneli, René, and Pierre Mussely. *Anvers et l'Exposition Universelle 1885.* Brussels, 1886.

Coufopoulos, Demetrius. *A Guide to Constantinople.* London, 1895.

Cox, Samuel Sullivan. *The Isles of the Princes: Or, the Pleasures of Prinkipo.* New York, 1887.

———. *Orient Sunbeams: Or, from the Porte to the Pyramids by Way of Palestine.* New York, 1882.

"Curiosités Orientales (Marchands de)." *L'Indicateur Ottoman: Annuaire-Almanach du Commerce*, vol. 2, 1880, pp. 436–37.

"Curiosités Orientales (March. de)." *L'Indicateur Ottoman: Annuaire-Almanach du Commerce*, vol. 3, 1881, p. 302.

"Curiosités Orientales (Marchands de)." *Annuaire Oriental du Commerce*, vol. 9, 1889–1890, 436.

"Curiosités Orientales." *Annuaire Oriental du Commerce*, vol. 10, 1891, p. 503.

"Curiosités Orientales." *Annuaire-Almanach du Commerce de l'Industrie de la Magistrature et de l'Administration ou Almanach des 1,500,000 Adresses de Paris, des Departements, des Colonies et des Pays Étrangers Didot-Bottin: 101e année de la publication, 1898: Troisième Partie, Colonies Françaises et Pays de Protectorats.* Étranger, 1899.

Daston, Lorraine J., and Katharine Park. *Wonders and the Order of Nature, 1150–1750.* Zone, 2001.

Davenne, Christine. *Cabinets of Wonder.* Abrams, 2012.

Davis, John. *The Landscape of Belief: Encountering the Holy Land in Nineteenth-Century Art and Culture.* Princeton Univ., 1996.

Davis, Marni. *Jews and Booze: Becoming American in the Age of Prohibition.* New York Univ., 2012.

Diner, Hasia R. *Roads Taken: The Great Jewish Migrations to the New World and the Peddlers Who Forged the Way.* Yale Univ., 2015.

Donlon, Thomas James. "Getting Wise in the Rug Business." *Saturday Evening Post*, 31 July 1915, p. 14.

"Dr. Henshall at the World's Fair." *Forest and Stream*, June 1921, p. 267.

Dynner, Glenn. *Yankel's Tavern: Jews, Liquor, and Life in the Kingdom of Poland*. Oxford Univ., 2014.

"El Sabah." *El Tiempo*, 2 Nov. 1891, p. 2.

E. S. P. "Letter from Egypt." *Daily Alta California*, 13 Mar. 1871, p. 1.

"Europe and the Holy Land." From online exhibit, "Mark Twain at Large: His Travels Here and Abroad." Mark Twain Project, University of California, Berkeley, http://bancroft.berkeley.edu/Exhibits/MTP/europe.html. Accessed 2 May 2014.

Exposition universelle d'Anvers: Le tour de l'exposition; Seul guide pratique avec plans de la ville et de l'Exposition universelle d'Anvers. Brussels, 1885.

"Faithful Subjects of the Sultan Celebrate Ottoman Empire Day." *Chicago Daily Tribune*, 1 Sept. 1893, p. 2.

Far Away Moses. Letter written his behalf to Samuel Cox. 19 Nov. 1886. UCLC39417, Mark Twain Project Archive.

"Far Away Moses." *Chicago Daily Tribune*, 15 Dec. 1888, p. 8.

"'Far Away' Moses and His Pets." *Chicago Times Portfolio of the Midway Types*, n.p.

"Far-Away Moses: The Girls Visit an Eastern Bazar." *Harper's Weekly*, 28 Apr. 1877, p. 329.

"Far Away Moses—Grand Collection of Rare Rugs, Antique Carpets, Portieres." *Chicago Daily Tribune*, 14. Dec. 1888, p. 8.

"Far-Away Moses—He's Back in Turkey." *Chicago Daily Tribune*, 6 Oct. 1880, p. 1.

"Far-Away-Moses: Jew." *Portrait Types of the Midway Plaisance*, by F. W. Putnam. St. Louis, 1894.

"Faraway Moses, Mark Twain's Famous Guide." *Sandusky Star-Journal*, 30 June 1903, p. 7.

"Finishing the Fair." *San Francisco Chronicle*, 19 April 1893, p. 1.

Fischer, Stefanie. *Ökonomisches Vertrauen und antisemitische Gewalt: Jüdische Viehhändler in Mittelfranken, 1919–1939*. Wallstein, 2014.

Frierson, Elizabeth B. "Gender, Consumption and Patriotism: The Emergence of an Ottoman Public Sphere." *Public Islam and the Common Good*, edited by Armando Salvatore and Dale F. Eickelman, Brill, 2004, pp. 99–125.

———. "Mirrors Out, Mirrors In: Domestication and Rejection of the Foreign in Late-Ottoman Women's Magazines (1875–1908)." *Women, Patronage and Self-Representation in Islamic Societies*, edited by D. Fairchild Ruggles, State Univ. of New York, 2000, pp. 177–204.

Gabler, Neal. *An Empire of Their Own: How the Jews Invented Hollywood*. Anchor, 1989.

Gaudio, Michael. *Engraving the Savage: The New World and Techniques of Civilization*. Univ. of Minnesota, 2008.

Gibbons, Herbert Adams. *John Wanamaker*. Harper, 1926. 2 vols.

Glazebrook, Philip. *Journey to Kars*. Penguin, 1985.

Godley, Andrew. *Jewish Immigrant Entrepreneurship in New York and London, 1880–1914*. Palgrave, 2001.

"Grand choix varié de tapis orientaux." *Le Moniteur Oriental*, 4 Jan. 1886.

Greenblatt, Stephen. *Marvelous Possessions: The Wonder of the New World.* Univ. of Chicago, 1992.

Grossman, Grace Cohen, and Richard Eighme Ahlborn. *Judaica at the Smithsonian: Cultural Politics as Cultural Model.* Smithsonian, 1997.

"Guide and Interpreter." *Bradshaw's Continental Railway,* vol. 482, 1887, p. 638.

Guttstadt, Corry. *Die Türkei, die Juden und der Holocaust.* Assoziation A, 2008.

Hartmann, Elke. "The 'Loyal Nation' and Its Deputies." *The First Ottoman Parliament: Perception, Significance and Prosopography,* edited by Christoph Herzog and Malek Sharif, Ergon, 2010, pp. 187–222.

Heinze, Andrew R. *Adapting to Abundance: Jewish Immigrants, Mass Consumption, and the Search for American Identity.* Columbia Univ., 1990.

Henderson, James. D. *Royal Austria Porcelain: History and Catalog of Wares.* Schiffer, 2008.

Hoganson, Kristin. *Consumers' Imperium: The Global Production of American Domesticity, 1865–1920.* Univ. of North Carolina, 2007.

———. "Cosmopolitan Domesticity: Importing the American Dream, 1865–1920." *American Historical Review,* vol. 107, no. 1, 2002, pp. 55–83;

Hooper-Greenhill, Eilean. *Museums and the Interpretation of Visual Culture.* Routledge, 2000.

Hower, Ralph M. *History of Macy's of New York, 1858–1919: Chapters in the Evolution of the Department Store.* Harvard Univ., 1946.

Hutton, Laurence. *A Boy I Knew: Four Dogs, and Some More Dogs.* New York, 1900.

Hyde, James N. "The Yankee Editor Abroad." *Lakeside Monthly,* vols. 10–11, 1873, p. 377.

Impey, Oliver, and Arthur MacGregor. *The Origins of Museums: The Cabinet of Curiosities in Sixteenth- and Seventeenth-Century Europe.* House of Stratus, 2001.

Jacob, Robert Urie. *A Trip to the Orient: The Story of a Mediterranean Cruise.* Winston, 1907.

Jenkins-Madina, Marilyn. "Collecting the 'Orient' at the Met: Early Tastemakers in America." *Ars Orientalis,* vol. 30, 2000, pp. 69–89.

Joselit, Jenna Weissman. *The Wonders of America: Reinventing Jewish Culture, 1880–1950.* Hill & Wang, 1994.

Kalmar, Ivan Davidson, and Derek Penslar, editors. *Orientalism and the Jews.* Brandeis Univ., 2004.

Karp, Jonathan. "Blacks, Jews, and the Business of Race Music, 1945–1955." *Chosen Capital: The Jewish Encounter with American Capitalism,* edited by Rebecca Kobrin, Rutgers Univ., 2012, pp. 141–67.

———. *The Politics of Jewish Commerce: Economic Thought and Emancipation in Europe, 1638–1848.* Cambridge Univ., 2008.

Kayalı, Hasan. *Arabs and Young Turks: Ottomanism, Arabism and Islamism in the Ottoman Empire, 1908–1918.* Univ. of California, 1997.

Kechriotis, Vangelis. "Ottomanism with a Greek Face: Karamanlı Greek Orthodox Diaspora at the End of the Ottoman Empire." *Mediterranean Diasporas: Politics and*

Ideas in the Long 19th Century, edited by Maurizio Isabella and Konstantina Zanou, Bloomsbury, 2015, pp. 189–204.

"Kirk's American Family Soap." *Chicago Daily Tribune*, 29 April 1893, p. 7.

Kirshenblatt-Gimblett, Barbara. "A Place in the World: Jews and the Holy Land at World's Fairs." *Encounters with the "Holy Land": Place, Past and Future in American Jewish Culture*, edited by Jeffrey Shandler and Beth Wenger, National Museum of American Jewish History; Univ. of Pennsylvania, 1997, pp. 60–82.

———. *Destination Culture: Tourism, Museums, and Heritage*. Univ. of California, 1998.

Knox, Thomas W. *Backsheesh! Or Life and Adventures in the Orient*. Hartford, 1875.

Kobrin, Rebecca, editor. *Chosen Capital: The Jewish Encounter with American Capitalism*. Rutgers Univ., 2012.

Kobrin, Rebecca, and Adam Teller, editors. *Purchasing Power: The Economics of Modern Jewish History*. Univ. of Pennsylvania, 2015.

Kohn, Edward P. "Pride and Prejudice: Theodore Roosevelt's Boyhood Contact with Europe." *America's Transatlantic Turn: Theodore Roosevelt and the "Discovery" of Europe*, edited by Hans Krabbendam and John M. Thompson, Palgrave, 2012, pp. 15–29.

Kupferschmidt, Uri. "Who Needed Department Stores in Egypt? From Orosdi-Back to Omar Effendi." *Middle Eastern Studies*, vol. 43, no. 2, 2007, pp. 175–92.

"La Ekspozision de Shikago." *El Tiempo*, 11 Jan. 1892, p. 2.

"Large and Choice Selection of Eastern Carpets." *Oriental Advertiser*, 5 Jan. 1886.

Leach, William R. *Land of Desire: Merchants, Power, and the Rise of a New American Culture*. Vintage, 1993.

Lecomte, Prétextat. *Les Arts et métiers de la Turquie et de l'Orient*. Société d'Éditions scientifiques, 1902.

Lederhendler, Eli. *Jewish Immigrants and American Capitalism, 1880–1920*. Cambridge Univ., 2009.

Leech, Harry Harewood. *Letters of a Sentimental Idler, from Greece, Turkey, Egypt, Nubia, and the Holy Land*. New York, 1869.

Lerner, Paul. *The Consuming Temple: Jews, Department Stores, and the Consumer Revolution in Germany, 1880–1940*. Cornell Univ., 2015.

Levy, Lital. "Partitioned Pasts: Arab Jewish Intellectuals and the Case of Esther Azhari Moyal (1873–1948)." *The Making of the Arab Intellectual: Empire, Public Sphere and the Colonial Coordinates of Selfhood*, edited by Dyala Hamzah, Routledge, 2013, pp. 128–63.

Levy, Robert. Diary entry 6 June 1915. *United States Diplomacy on the Bosphorus: The Diaries of Ambassador Morgenthau, 1913–1916*, by Henry Morgenthau, Taderon, 2004, p. 248.

"L'Exposition de Chicago." *Stamboul*, 26 Jan. 1892, p. 1.

L'Indicateur Ottoman, vol. 2, 1880, p. 169.

L'Indicateur Ottoman, vol. 3, 1881, p. 88.

L'Indicateur Ottoman, vol. 7, 1885, p. 345.

Long, Burke O. *Imagining the Holy Land: Maps, Models, and Fantasy Travels.* Indiana Univ., 2002.

"M. Elia Souhami." *Jewish Chronicle*, 19 May 1893, p. 9.

MA/1/S2606. Nominal file: Elia Souhami Sadullah & Company, Victoria and Albert Museum Archive, London, England.

MacGregor, Arthur. *Curiosity and Enlightenment: Collectors and Collections from the Sixteenth to the Nineteenth Century.* Yale Univ., 2007.

Makdisi, Ussama. "After 1860: Debating Religion, Reform, and Nationalism in the Ottoman Empire." *International Journal of Middle East Studies*, vol. 34, no. 4, 2002, pp. 601–17.

"Malumat-ı Dahiliye-Şikago Sergisi." *Tercüman-ı Hakikat*, 28 June 1892, p. 3.

Maruzat, Yıldız Resmi. (Y. A. RES) 95/24, 15 Cemaziyelevvel 1316, 3 Aug. 1898, Başbakanlık Osmanlı Arşivi (Prime Ministry's Ottoman Archives), Istanbul, Turkey.

Mauriès, Patrick. *Cabinets of Curiosities.* Thames & Hudson, 2002.

McLemore, Henry. "Hankerings." *Odessa American*, 30 July 1956, p. 12.

Memorial of John Eliot Bowen. Brooklyn, 1890.

Mendelsohn, Adam. *The Rag Race: How Jews Sewed Their Way to Success in America and the British Empire.* New York Univ., 2014.

Meriwether, Lee. *A Tramp Trip: How to See Europe on Fifty Cents a Day.* New York, 1887.

Meyers Reisebücher: Türkei, Rumänien, Serbien, Bulgarien. Leipzig, 1902.

Miller, Michael B. *The Bon Marché: Bourgeois Culture and the Department Store, 1869–1920.* Princeton Univ., 1994.

Mirak, Robert. *Torn between Two Lands: Armenians in America, 1890 to World War I.* Harvard Univ., 1984.

Molineux, Catherine. *Faces of Perfect Ebony: Encountering Atlantic Slavery in Imperial Britain.* Harvard Univ., 2012.

Montgomery, James Eglinton. *Our Admiral's Flag Abroad: The Cruise of Admiral D. G. Farragut, Commanding the European Squadron in 1867–68, in the Flag-Ship Franklin.* New York, 1869.

Morris, Caspar. *Letters of Travel of Caspar Morris, M.D., 1871–1872.* Philadelphia, 1896. 2 vols.

Muller, Jerry Z. *Capitalism and the Jews.* Princeton Univ., 2010.

Murray, John. *Handbook for Travellers in Constantinople: The Bosphorus, Dardanelles, Brousa and Plain of Troy.* London, 1871.

———. *Handbook for Travellers in Constantinople, Brusa, and the Troad, with Maps and Plans.* London, 1893.

Nalpas, Joseph. *Annuaire des Commerçants de Smyrne et de l'Anatolie.* Izmir, 1893.

Nance, Susan. "A Facilitated Access Model and Ottoman Empire Tourism." *Annals of Tourism Research*, vol. 34, no. 4, 2007, pp. 1056–77.

———. *How the Arabian Nights Inspired the American Dream, 1790–1935.* Univ. of North Carolina, 2009.

"Never Ending Stream of People." *Chicago Daily Tribune*, 9 Dec. 1892, p. 2.

"No Laggards Here." *Chicago Daily Tribune*, 17 Dec. 1888, p. 6.

Noble, Annette L. "Scheveningen, Holland." *Christian Work Weekly: Continuing the Christian at Work*, vol. 63, no. 1597, 1897, p. 505.

Obenzinger, Hilton. *American Palestine: Melville, Twain, and the Holy Land Mania.* Princeton Univ., 1999.

"Orient at the Fair—Subject of the Sultan Tells of the Turkish Exhibit." *Chicago Daily Tribune*, 12 April 1893, p. 9.

Ottoman Ministry of Trade and Public Works and Elia Souhami Sadullah & Company. Y. A. RES 58/33, 25 S<du>evval 1309, 24 May 1892, Prime Ministry's Ottoman Archives, Istanbul, Turkey.

Özbek, Nadir. "Philanthropic Activity, Ottoman Patriotism and the Hamidian Regime, 1876–1909." *International Journal of Middle East Studies*, vol. 37, 2005, pp. 59–81.

Paine, Albert Bigelow. *The Ship-Dwellers: A Story of a Happy Cruise.* 1910. Dossier, 1937.

Papo, Joseph M. *Sephardim in Twentieth Century America: In Search of Unity.* Pele Yoetz, 1987.

Penslar, Derek. *Shylock's Children: Economics and Jewish Identity in Modern Europe.* Univ. of California, 2001.

"Pera, or Bey Oghloo." *Handbook for Travellers in Turkey in Asia, including Constantinople.* London, 1878, p. 64.

"Personal." *Troy Daily Times*, 26 Dec. 1894, p. 3.

Petrov, Milen. "Everyday Forms of Compliance: Subaltern Commentaries on Ottoman Reform, 1864–1868." *Comparative Studies in Society and History*, vol. 46, no. 4, 2004, pp. 730–59.

Philliou, Christine. *Biography of an Empire: Governing Ottomans in an Age of Revolution.* Univ. of California, 2010.

"Photographs." *Bradshaw's Continental Railway, Steam Transit, and General Guide for Travellers through Europe.* London, 1887.

"Photographers." *Bradshaw's Continental Railway, Steam Transit, and General Guide for Travellers through Europe.* London, 1880.

Picturesque Chicago and Guide to the World's Fair. Hartford, 1893.

Pierce, James Wilson. "Mr. Faraway Moses." *Photographic History of the World's Fair and Sketch of the City of Chicago*, by James Wilson Pierce. Baltimore, 1893, p. 363.

Pitman, Marie J. *European Breezes.* Boston, 1882.

Pomian, Krzysztof. *Collectors and Curiosities.* Polity, 1990.

Potuoğlu-Cook, Öykü. "Night Shifts: Moral, Economic, and Cultural Politics of Turkish Belly Dance across the Fins-de-Siècle." Dissertation, Northwestern University, 2008.

Putnam, S. B. "The Shop of Far-Away Moses." *Decorator and Furnisher*, vol. 19, no. 6, 1892, 206.

Quataert, Donald. "Clothing Laws, State, and Society in the Ottoman Empire, 1720–1829." *International Journal of Middle East Studies*, vol. 29, no. 3, 1997, pp. 403–25.

————. *Ottoman Manufacturing in the Age of the Industrial Revolution*. Cambridge Univ., 2002.

"Queer Sign Manuals." *Chicago Daily Tribune*, 11 June 1893, p. 11.

"Race Types at the World's Fair." *Chicago Daily Tribune*, 30 July 1893, p. 25.

Radcliffe, J. N. "Scutari-March, 1863." *Journal of Psychological Medicine*, vol. 16, 1863, p. 721.

Rappaport, Erika. *Shopping for Pleasure: Women in the Making of London's West End*. Princeton Univ., 2001.

"Rare Turkish Embroideries." *Chicago Daily Tribune*, 4 Dec. 1892, p. 26.

Receipts from Sadullah, Levy and Vve Souhami, 3 May, 6 May, and 28 Aug. 1895. Vanderbilt Family Furniture Receipt Collection, Box 1, Folder 14, Biltmore Estate Archive, Asheville, North Carolina.

Report of the U.S. National Museum under the Direction of the Smithsonian Institution for the Year Ending June 30, 1893. Appendix 6, p. 256.

Reuveni, Gideon, and Nils Roemer, editors. *Longing, Belonging, and the Making of Jewish Consumer Culture*. Brill, 2010.

Reuveni, Gideon, and Sarah Wobick-Segev, editors. *The Economy in Jewish History: New Perspectives on the Interrelationship between Ethnicity and Economic Life*. Berghahn, 2011.

Rahme, Joseph G. "Namık Kemal's Constitutional Ottomanism and Non-Muslims." *Islam and Christian-Muslim Relations*, vol. 10, no. 1, 1999, pp. 23–39.

Rogers, Stephanie Stidham. *Inventing the Holy Land: American Protestant Pilgrimage to Palestine, 1865-1941*. Lexington, 2011.

Rosenspitz, Sándor. "Jeruzsálemtől Rómáig II." *Magyar Zsidó Szemle*, vol. 10, 1890, pp. 608–21.

Roxburgh, David. "Au Bonheur des Amateurs: Collecting and Exhibiting Islamic Art, ca. 1880-1910." *Ars Orientalis*, vol. 30, 2000, pp. 9–38.

"Rugs at Auction." *Chicago Daily Tribune*, 28 Dec. 1878, p. 8.

"Sadula i Robert Levi." *El Luzero*, 4 July 1905, p. 4.

"Sadullah Talip Bey." *Türkiye Teracimi Ahval Ansiklopedesi/Encylopédie biographie de Turquie*, Istanbul, 1928-1932, pp. 498–99.

Schaff, David Schley. *The Life of Philip Schaff: In Part Autobiographical*. New York, 1897.

Schroeter, Daniel. *The Sultan's Jew: Morocco and the Sephardi World*. Stanford Univ., 2002.

"Se. Izidor Straus." *El Tiempo*, 7 Feb. 1898, p. 3.

Shandler, Jeffrey. "Sanctification of the Brand Name: The Marketing of Cantor Yossele Rosenblatt." *Chosen Capital: The Jewish Encounter with American Capitalism*, edited by Rebecca Kobrin, Rutgers Univ., 2012, pp. 255–71.

"Shops." *Bradshaw's Continental Railway, Steam Transit, and General Guide for Travellers through Europe*. London, 1880.

Slezkine, Yuri. *The Jewish Century*. Princeton Univ., 2004.

Smith, F. Hopkinson. "The Picturesque Side." *Scribner's Magazine*, vol. 14, 1893, p. 606.

Snider, Denton J. *World's Fair Studies*. Chicago, 1895.

Spooner, Brian. "Weavers and Dealers." *The Social Life of Things: Commodities in Cultural Perspective*, edited by Arjun Appadurai, Cambridge Univ., 1986, pp. 195–235.

Stein, Sarah Abrevaya. *Making Jews Modern: The Yiddish and Ladino Press in the Russian and Ottoman Empires*. Indiana Univ., 2004.

———. *Plumes: Ostrich Feathers, Jews, and a Lost World of Global Commerce*. Yale Univ., 2008.

Stevens, Charles McClellan. *The Adventures of Uncle Jeremiah and Family at the Great Fair: Their Observations and Triumphs*. Chicago, 1893.

Stoddard, Charles Warren. *A Cruise under the Crescent: From Suez to San Marco*. Chicago, 1898.

Straus, Oscar. Letter to his family. 28 Jan. 1888. Archives of the Straus Historical Society, Smithtown, New York.

_____. Letter to Isidor Straus. 21 Mar. 1889. Archives of the Straus Historical Society, Smithtown, New York.

_____. Letter to Isidor Straus. 28 Mar. 1889. Archives of the Straus Historical Society, Smithtown, New York.

_____. Letter to Isidor Straus. 11 Apr. 1889. Archives of the Straus Historical Society, Smithtown, New York.

_____. Letter to Isidor Straus. [?] May 1889. Archives of the Straus Historical Society, Smithtown, New York.

_____. Letter to Isidor Straus. 28 May 1889. Archives of the Straus Historical Society, Smithtown, New York.

Swift, John Franklin. *Going to Jericho: Or, Sketches of Travel in Spain and the East*. New York, 1868.

Taylor, Diana. *The Archive and Repertoire: Performing Cultural Memory in the Americas*. Duke Univ., 2003.

Teller, Adam. *Kesef, koah ve-hashpa'ah: Ha-Yehudim be-ahuzot Beit Radzivil be-Lita ba-meah ha-18*. Jerusalem, 2005.

Thacher, S. O. "Palestine Letter No. 30." *Lawrence Daily Journal*, 11 July 1891, p. 2.

Trivellato, Francesca. *The Familiarity of Strangers: The Sephardic Diaspora, Livorno, and Cross-Cultural Trade in the Early Modern Period*. Yale Univ., 2009.

"The Troubles of 'Far-Away Moses.'" *New York Times*, 6 Nov. 1877, p. 8.

"Turkey Holds the Key." *Chicago Daily Tribune*, 13 Sept. 1891, p. 10.

"Turkish Village Dedicated." *Davenport Democrat and Leader*, 30 Apr. 1893, p. 16.

Twain, Mark. *The Innocents Abroad, or the New Pilgrim's Progress*. Hartford, 1869.

———. Letter to Elisha Bliss Jr. 11 Aug. 1870. *Mark Twain's Letters to His Publishers, 1867–1894*, edited by Hamlin Lewis Hill, Univ. of California, 1967, p. 38.

Ueno, Masayuki. "'For the Fatherland and the State': Armenians Negotiate the Tanzimat Reforms." *International Journal of Middle East Studies*, vol. 45, 2013, pp. 93–109.

Valensi, Jean-Paul. "Re: Greetings!" Received by Julia Phillips Cohen, 25 Feb. 2013.

———. "Turkish Carpets." Received by Julia Phillips Cohen, 20 Mar. 2014.

Wadsworth, Wedworth. "In the Land of the Fez." *Brooklyn Daily Eagle*, 5 May 1895, p. 11.

"Wanamaker's." *Philadelphia Times*, 17 Sept. 1891, p. 6.

"Wanamaker's." *Philadelphia Times*, 3 Dec. 1891, p. 6.

"Wanamaker's." *Philadelphia Times*, 6 April 1892, p. 8.

"Wanamaker's." *Bucks County (PA) Gazette*, 10 Dec. 1891, p. 2.

"Wanamaker's." *Denton (Md.) Journal*, 12 Dec. 1891, p. 2.

Wayne, John. "Constantinople to Chicago: In the Footsteps of Far-Away Moses." *Library of Congress Information Bulletin*, 13 Jan. 1992, pp. 14–16, 18–21.

Wharton, Annabel Jane. *Selling Jerusalem: Relics, Replicas, Theme Parks*. Univ. of Chicago, 2006.

Whitaker, Jan. *Service and Style: How the American Department Store Fashioned the Middle Class*. Macmillan, 2006.

Willard, Mary Frances. *Along Mediterranean Shores*. Silver, Burdett, 1914.

Wister, Jones. *Jones Wister's Reminiscences*. Lippincott, 1920.

Wood, Casey A. "A Winter Cruise to the Orient." *Montreal Medical Journal*, vol. 37, no. 8, 1908, p. 549–86.

Yıldız Perakende (Y. R. PRK) 27/43, Prime Ministry's Ottoman Archives, Istanbul, Turkey.

CHAPTER 5

The Roots of Jewish Concentration in the American Popular Music Business, 1890–1945

by Jonathan Karp

T hat Jews have played a conspicuous role in the creation of American popular music will come as no surprise. The Jewish tunesmiths of Tin Pan Alley in the 1910s, of Broadway popular song in succeeding decades, and even of many of the hits of the early rock 'n' roll era—as epitomized by the "Brill Building" phenomenon—have been widely heralded (Melnick; Most; Emerson; Sidran). To a lesser extent, too, the Jewish role in the business side of American popular music has been explored, particularly in the post-World War II era. This chapter, however, aims to map the key routes through which Jews came to music business prominence in an earlier period—essentially the first half of the twentieth century—and argues that tracing these "roots" is essential to understanding how Jews would later help organize the American popular music industry as something approaching an ethnic business niche.

The American popular music business evolved in the interstices of the entertainment, arts and media industries and cannot be adequately understood separately from them. Music was performed on the stage, in radio studios, and on the screen. Sheet music publishing companies were scooped up during the 1920s by major Hollywood movie studios. Musicians were booked in all these venues and media by booking agents, while record companies had strong ties to radio stations, movie production companies and even television stations.

Thus, coherently assessing the role of Jews in music simultaneously requires the delicate tightrope act of both situating the music business in and abstracting it from this wider context.

Equally challenging is the effort to highlight the role of Jews in a field where they represented at best a highly disproportionate ethnic element—only sometimes the dominant one—that constantly interacted with non-Jews without a consistently clear ethnic division of labor. One might even question the value of such an undertaking. Was the music business culturally "Jewish"? Was there a singular or clear Jewish agenda at work? And finally, what if anything constituted the Jewishness of its participants beyond the mere fact of ethnic origins? These questions are themselves understandably problematic and threaten to provide fodder for hoary anti-Semitic tropes. Nevertheless, if we wish to understand some of the important ways in which Jews operated within the world of American business and economy we need to address and refine questions like these. Patterns of group behavior require explanation, perhaps especially in domains where business and culture are so tightly intertwined.

The goal of this essay is to trace the broad historical contours of Jewish involvement in the business side of American popular music from the late nineteenth to the mid-twentieth centuries, seeking to highlight certain demographic and functional patterns that characterized much of this activity even as it took disparate forms. While the history of Jews in the popular music industry is by no means synonymous with that of the industries themselves, looking at Jews' roles provides valuable insight into how entertainment capitalism offered a powerful vehicle for ethnic subgroups to Americanize and at the same time put their particular stamp on the character of American business and culture. Other ethnic groups, it is true, made signal contributions to American entertainment, above all African Americans. As popular entertainment pioneers, the Irish were perhaps preeminent in the second half of the nineteenth century, from the blackface minstrel Dan Rice to the vaudeville giant George M. Cohan.[1] German immigrants too were prominent, particularly in the early evolution of popular music publishing. But what distinguished the Jews from these and others was their combined contribution to *both* the performance and business wings of popular entertainment, including music. It is precisely this duality—and the fruitful interplay between the two—which makes the Jewish role stand out.

The roots of Jewish participation in the popular music industry lie in the nineteenth-century settlement patterns of European Jewish immigrants. While Jews are often viewed stereotypically as a quintessential urban population, many of the Jews who migrated to the United States between 1830 and 1880 settled in medium-sized and small towns across the Midwest, in California, and to a limited extent in the American South. These "small-town Jews" typically created retail businesses and established commercial networks that would eventually prove crucial to Jewish involvement in the entertainment industries (Morawska; Weissbach). Jewish mass settlement in New York City and other major centers (Baltimore, Boston, Chicago, Cincinnati, Cleveland, Los Angeles, Philadelphia, and San Francisco, especially) in the last two decades of the nineteenth and the first two of the twentieth centuries set up a dynamic between hubs and hinterlands that would prove vital to Jewish penetration into popular entertainment businesses, one that still remains little understood. Jewish general stores and dry goods shops, evolving out of earlier peddling activity, placed Jewish small businessmen in a position to shift readily into theater ownership, sheet music publishing, and later the sale and distribution of musical recordings (records).[2] More impressionistically, the "insider-outsider" status of American Jews, their familiarity with local cultures while remaining self-consciously distinct—and their commercial dependency on reading and anticipating local consumer tastes—must have served them well when it came to marketing entertainment. Similarly, Jewish involvement in brokering and adapting black musical styles gave them a leg up in an industry which became increasingly if intermittently linked to the merchandizing of African American genres over the course of the twentieth century (J. P. Melnick; Karp, "Of Maestros and Minstrels"; idem., "Blacks, Jews"; idem., "Brokering a Rock 'n' Roll International").

But the story of Jewish entrance into American popular music really begins with the field of theater ownership and management. Jews appear increasingly prominent as local theater managers in the medium-sized cities of upstate New York, Pennsylvania, Ohio and regions further west by the 1870s and 1880s. By the turn of the century we find Jews remarkably conspicuous in the two principal types of evolving American theatrical entertainment: vaudeville and "legitimate" theater. Vaudeville was the culmination of an extended process in the development of nineteenth-century American entertainment genres. It was the inheritor of such genres as the minstrel show, the concert saloon, the circus museum (à la P. T. Barnum), the burlesque show, and variety, which the producers of vaudeville aspired to regiment and make respectable for more middle-class audiences, including women, and thereby convert into a mass entertainment commodity. At the same time, a realignment was taking place in the structure of the field of legitimate theater, as the "stock company" (a group of actors contracted to perform a repertoire of plays over the course of a season at a single theater), which had dominated American theater during the first half of the century, gave way by the 1870s to the "combination system," a traveling troupe, usually put together in New York or San Francisco, that toured a region of the country performing a single play. Both developments came about as part of a rationalization of entertainment. They lent themselves to the consolidation and centralization of bookings and therefore to the creation of not just regional (and eventually national) theatrical circuits but of chains of theaters under the control of single owners or partnerships.[3]

This rationalization occurred first in the domain of "legitimate" (as opposed to vaudeville or variety) theater, under the auspices of a small group of theater owners known as the American Theatrical Syndicate. Of the six partners—Abraham Erlanger, Marc Klaw, Charles Frohman, Al Hayman, Samuel Nixon and Fred Zimmerman—four were Jews (Erlanger, Frohman, Hayman, and Nixon). Erlanger, who became the Syndicate's dominant figure, represented a type that we will meet repeatedly in this account, the mogul drawn into the entertainment field largely by chance, or rather as a serendipitous consequence of entrepreneurial enterprise rather than through a clear affinity for the arts. Born in 1860, Abraham Lincoln Erlanger was the son of German-speaking Jewish immigrants who first settled in Albany (where Abraham was born) but soon moved to Cleveland. He received little in the way of education, as a youth working at various jobs, including delivering coal and serving as an errand boy in a dry goods shop, before finding employment in the cloak room and opera glass stand at the Cleveland Academy of Music. Impressing employers with his intelligence and industry, he was later kept on as business manager when the Academy was acquired by the Republican politician Mark Hanna. As his *New York Times* obituary describes, "Backed by Hanna's millions, young Erlanger inaugurated a new era in Cleveland theatrical affairs. Within less than a month Hanna placed him in absolute control" ("A. L. Erlanger Dies after Long Illness").

In fact, Erlanger's rise was not so sudden; it was preceded by years as an "advance man," drumming up local interest in towns throughout the Midwest by publicizing the arrival of a theater company a week or two in advance of the show, duties which Erlanger performed with ingenuity and meticulous attention to detail. It was in this capacity that he met a counterpart, the Kentuckian Marc Klaw, who had extensive legal knowledge and would become his most important partner. Their time on the road managing tours made them realize that the most urgent need was for a regularization of the booking process. For example, the same traveling troupe performing a given play might be booked into two venues on the same date; or actors might find themselves stranded on the road with no means home. Company tours were inadequately planned, transportation was haphazard, and local theater managers were forced to travel to New York during each summer at considerable expense to arrange bookings for their venues. In 1894 Klaw and Erlanger purchased Taylor's Theatrical Agency in New York and searched for their competitive advantage by addressing these and similar problems. As their reputation spread, they were approached by Al Hayman, owner of a chain of theaters in the Midwest and West, with the proposal to establish a national booking syndicate that would unite various regional chains under a single booking policy. Born Raphael Hayman in Wheeling, West Virginia, as a young man he had come under the influence of Michael B. Leavitt, a pioneering American theater impresario based in San Francisco and New York who mentored many Jews into the theatrical business during the late nineteenth century, not least of all David Belasco and Leavitt's distant relative and fellow Silesian immigrant William Morris (born Zelman Moses). Indeed, Leavitt claimed to have originated the concept of the national booking system which came to Klaw and Erlanger via his disciple Hayman.[4] Of the other future Syndicate members, Nixon and Zimmerman had formed their partnership in Philadelphia in the 1860s. Born in Fort Wayne, Indiana in 1848 as Samuel Nidlinger, Nixon had Americanized his name when he moved from his father's clothing business into theater management, while Zimmerman had been an advance man like Klaw and Erlanger. In typical pattern the pair shifted between leasing or (where possible) buying theaters and booking tours. Of the founders of the Syndicate only Charles Frohman (b. 1856 in Sandusky, Ohio) had been principally a theatrical producer rather than a booker or advance man, although he also moved into theater ownership.

In fact, the key to the syndicate's success was not theater chain ownership but rather control of the booking function within the "combination" chain. The model the Syndicate established, which would be followed again and again in the history of the American popular entertainment industry, was to try to create monopoly control over acts, productions, and talent. Owning numbers of theaters vastly simplified this process but wasn't its essence. If a local theater manager could only import a given play or act by utilizing the services of the Syndicate and paying the required fees, then the organization effectively exerted control. And, to ensure this outcome, ruthless tactics were employed where necessary: the Syndicate, for instance, did not hesitate to blacklist managers and performers who bucked their system, even building—

or sometimes merely threatening to build—a new theater in a given locale, thus pressuring an uncooperative owner or manager to accept its terms or risk going out of business.

The emergence of the Syndicate reflects the growing salience of Jews in the entertainment business and compounded it. This is not to say that the Syndicate's Jewish majority promoted a policy of ethnic group advancement; the only agenda its members pursued was one of monopolistic domination and enrichment. Yet the efforts of the Syndicate inspired competition and compounded Jewish prominence in the entertainment business, as exemplified by Syracuse's Shubert brothers. The Shuberts had been part of the Syndicate, even as they plotted to subvert it. In doing so they had the backing of other Jewish theater magnates: Marcus Heiman in upstate New York, Julius Cahn and Abram Spitz in New England, and Moses Reis in Pennsylvania-Ohio. All started off under the Syndicate's umbrella and—through varying means—came to challenge it (*Variety*; *New York Times*, 9 April 1910; on Reis, see Leeson 387, 404; *New York Times*, 25 Oct. 1937).

In the realm of vaudeville, a similar situation emerged. It is tempting to suggest that Jews were typically aligned with the innovators or the new guard challenging the old. The reality is that Jews were heavily represented among both new and old. The Syndicate's model was self-consciously followed in vaudeville by two of the most powerful monopolists in the history of American popular entertainment: Benjamin Franklin Keith and Edward Franklin Albee, both New Englanders, one Catholic and the other Protestant, but each emerging out of the circus world shaped by P. T. Barnum and his successors. Keith and Albee weren't really partners—Albee was Keith's employee—but they constituted a team of likeminded business magnates who strived with single-minded determination to control all of the vaudeville circuits east of the Mississippi and beyond. Starting with Keith's New York Dime Museum on Boston's Washington Street in 1883, Keith had become the dominant force in all of American vaudeville by 1905 at the latest. Two years later he and Albee established the United Booking Offices of America (UBO), which created package—that is entire multi-part vaudeville—shows that, emanating from Keith and Albee's New York command and control center, moved through various regions of the country like blood through the body's arteries. Any theater that refused their terms (including the full set of acts, the booking fees and commissions) would be blacklisted. The pair relentlessly set out to ruin—or at least subordinate—all rivals, that is, independent booking agencies like William Morris (Wertheim). The "Vaudeville Wars" often seemed to pit these puritan Midases against the Jewish upstarts who repeatedly sought to topple them: Morris, the Shuberts, Marcus Loew, *Variety* magazine's founder and editor Sime Silverman—even Abraham Erlanger himself. But the reality is that the Keith-Albee empire included many prominent Jews; not just former subordinates like Julius Cahn but also their own junior partners who created a parallel monopoly booking system west of the Mississippi.

The Orpheum circuit was controlled by the team of Morris Meyerfeld, a Westphalia-born Jewish liquor distributor who bailed out and inherited a failing San Francisco theater chain, and Martin Beck, whose family had emigrated from Slovakia and settled in Chicago where Meyerfeld employed him to run the Orpheum's booking office in 1898. Beck later married Meyerfeld's niece, Louise Heims. The Orpheum circuit extended from California through the western states, even penetrating the American South, though eventually headquartered in Chicago. While Keith and Albee had sometimes butted heads with the Orpheum, by 1907 the two pairs joined forces to create the Combine, a national syndicate every bit as extensive and powerful as the one Erlanger and Hayman had created in legitimate theater a decade earlier. In fact, Keith's fortress proved far more impregnable than Erlanger's, enduring well past Keith's death in 1914 and nearly to the end of Albee's life in 1930. Whereas the Shuberts overtook the syndicate by the onset of World War I, Keith and Albee outlived the partnership of Meyerfeld and Beck, whose Western Vaudeville Managers Association (WVMA) was eventually taken over by Marcus Heiman, later a lieutenant in the vast Shubert empire (*Vaudeville News*).[5]

While there was frequent overlap between the legitimate and vaudeville domains, as seen in the case of Heiman, the popular entertainment landscape became further complicated by the advent of new media, motion pictures and radio. From the earliest days of the Combine film shorts had been employed as filler or novelty items between live acts. But as motion pictures moved beyond the nickelodeon storefronts, they dictated the creation of new venues for their display—often converted vaudeville houses and theaters. Even before the advent of talkies—in fact, especially before their emergence—silent picture houses needed live music, both as entertainment prior to the projection and as the soundtrack to it. Movie theater chains established by Jewish entrepreneurs like William Fox and Marcus Loew in New York and Los Angeles, Jacob Fabian in New Jersey, and Abraham Joseph Balaban in Chicago thereby became venues for the performance of live music.[6] But whereas Albee saw movies merely as a component of vaudeville, exhibitors like Fox, Loew and Balaban recognized them as the main event. Thus, by the 1920s, with vaudeville on the wane, the Shuberts firmly in control of legitimate theater, and movie houses springing up across the nation, Jewish businessmen were now exercising increasing preeminence in a wide range of entertainment venues.

With the loosening of the Keith-Albee stronghold, independent booking agencies like William Morris finally came into their own, representing not only actors and comedians but also singers and musicians performing in live theater, nightclubs, and, after 1927's *The Jazz Singer*, in Hollywood talkies and musicals as well. Indeed, the late 1920s and 1930s was also the period when Hollywood studios began to purchase entire Tin Pan Alley sheet music publishing houses. In this sense, too, however innovative, Hollywood was also the inheritor of a body of preceding entertainment industries in which Jews had become prominent. This included the sheet music publishing business, which since the 1880s had been headquartered near New York's Union Square, known as the Rialto. While there existed a demand from the general public for sheet music to popular songs (elementary musical literacy being more widespread then than now), the songs became popular largely through performance in variety and vaudeville theaters (and after 1910 increasingly in Broadway shows). For this reason, the music publishing business tended to creep uptown along the path of the slowly migrating theater district, reaching 28th Street west of Broadway by 1890 (See generally, Suisman; still valuable is Goldberg; Fricke 270, 296–300).

By the late nineteenth century, music publishing was on the verge of a major commercial breakthrough. Much of the sheet music sold to that point consisted of imports of European classical or light classical and quasi-operatic ballads. Prior to 1886, when the Berne Convention for the Protection of Literary and Artistic Works mandated copyright protections, pirating foreign creations was a relatively simple matter. The gradual enforcement of copyrights proved a powerful impetus to the growth of a "native" American commercial sheet music industry. This new premium on popular songwriting coincided with the large-scale immigration of Jews to New York, but as with the case of theater and vaudeville, the focus on New York City can be misleading. Charles Kassell Harris, one of the founders of the modern American popular music business, was one of ten children born to a Jewish fur merchant who moved his family from Poughkeepsie, New York to Saginaw, Michigan and eventually to Cleveland. Harris's sentimental ballad "After the Ball" ushered in the sheet music revolution, selling an unheard of five million copies after it was performed by John Phillips Sousa at the 1893 World Columbian Exposition in Chicago. Harris was truly a Tin Pan Alley tunesmith, even before he shifted operations to New York City in 1895, custom producing songs to the customer's order, and publishing and marketing them himself, even designing the sheet music covers (Harris, *After the Ball*).

Theater and vaudeville impresarios were rarely without any personal experience of the stage; even Sam Shubert and Abe Erlanger made brief childhood forays "treading the boards." Similarly, music publishers as often as not themselves dabbled in songwriting, an activity for which no technical musical knowledge was required, or even necessarily much in the way of talent. Harris certainly possessed an abundance of the latter, but the point is that music publishing was a business in which the practitioner could also be the entrepreneur and the producer could be the broker as well. Harry Von Tilzer, born Aaron Gumbinsky in Detroit, was the eldest of five children. His father opened a shoe store when the family moved to Indianapolis (and shortened the name to Gumm), the room above which was rented to a theatrical company. Aaron—now Harry—traveled with circuses, vaudeville companies, and medicine shows before settling in New York as a songwriter. He and his lyricist partner, Andrew B. Sterling, wrote numerous numbers for vaudeville performers though few were published before their 1898 breakthrough hit, "My Old New Hampshire Home," which brought him into partnership with the music publisher Maurice Shapiro (a firm Shapiro had opened with his brother-in-law, Louis, a New York City realtor). Tilzer's 1900 "A Bird in a Gilded Cage" (in this case with lyrics by Arthur J. Lamb) fully justified Shapiro's offer, selling two million copies, the year's top seller (*Shapiro Bernstein*). In 1902, Von Tilzer broke away from Shapiro-Bernstein to form his own publishing company, the Harry Von Tilzer Musical Publishing Company, whose success lasted into the 1920s. Like many of the most skilled and savvy Tin Pan Alley composers, Von Tilzer wrote in the widest array of styles; though his specialty was the sentimental ballad, his songs covered all of the contemporary popular genres: coon and plantation songs, patriotic anthems, holiday songs, ethnic simulations (particularly Irish and German), and later ragtime styled songs.

This versatility reflects the character of Tin Pan Alley as equal measure craft and hackery. It was grounded in fashion, capitalizing on recent trends, while gambling on new ones. The product was viewed as occasional, not eternal. One of the earliest Jewish sheet music publishers, M. Witmark and Sons, started off as a greeting card publisher. Von Tilzer, like many of the successful tunesmiths, was highly attuned to marketing and salesmanship. While Charles Harris designed his own attractive sheet music covers, Von Tilzer sought the services of the finest commercial artists available, particularly Gene Buck (also a song lyricist). Von Tilzer also "plugged" his songs by performing them in

music halls, restaurants, and sheet music stores. With his vaudeville and theater connections he had little difficulty persuading performers to "interpolate"
his songs into their acts, a standard practice that often entailed payoffs of one
or another kind (the prototype of later radio disc jockey "payola"). Indeed, the
traffic between publishers and performers ran in both directions, placing their
products in a performer's or show's repertoire while also hunting out freshly
performed material for their own copyrights.

Just as in theatrical bookings, in music publishing profit was rooted in
control of the product, in this case copyright. With pirating rampant and royalties haphazard, music publishers sought to secure the kinds of protections
that theater and vaudeville had won through strict if informal control of the
booking process. The Copyright Act of 1909, the first major revision of eighteenth-century American copyright statute (relevant provisions of the Berne
Convention had only been applied piecemeal to earlier law), proved crucial to
this effort. It provided for 28-year copyright protection for all published works
with attached notice of copyright. It also applied copyright protections to me-
chanical reproductions (initially piano rolls but later record and film recordings) which had not been included in previous statutes. Aligned with this, the
American Society of Composers, Authors and Publishers (ASCAP), founded
in 1914, in effect required and collected royalties for the performance of published music (Sanjek 7–19).

While Jewish music composers and publishers had not been the drivers
of these two developments, they were among the leading beneficiaries, given
the remarkable numerical increase in Jews on Tin Pan Alley. Music historian
Edward Pessen, after examining the membership records of ASCAP, concluded
that Jews wrote the music to around 50% of the three hundred "great" and
three hundred "good" songs of the 1920s and 1930s (determined by their success and general aesthetic merit) and to a whopping 75% of the lyrics (Pessen
184–85). Something similar can be said of the sheet music publishers after
1910. Although some scholars have argued that Jews never comprised a majority of the owners, managers, and executives of Tin Pan Alley publishing, they
unquestionably dominated the field, controlling the great proportion of large
firms. M. Witmark and Sons; Shapiro-Bernstein; Marks and Stern; Leo Feist;
Snyder and Waterhouse (later Snyder, Waterhouse, and Berlin); T. B. Harms
(by 1900 controlled by Max Dreyfus); Chas. K. Harris; Harry Von Tilzer; and
Jerome Remick were the most important in this period.[7]

It is a widespread misimpression that Tin Pan Alley, that is, the music
publishing industry, went into rapid decline by the late 1920s, with the advent

of such media as 78 rpm recordings, radio, and talking pictures. But exactly to the contrary, in the long run, these new technologies proved an enormous boon to music publishing and gave it several new leases on life. First, as noted, during the 1920s and early 1930s several Hollywood studios purchased some of the principal Tin Pan Alley firms (or rather, their copyrights and song catalogues), capturing control of ASCAP along the way. After the success of *The Jazz Singer* (1927), not only did Warner Bros.' profits multiply, but the company became newly attractive for massive Wall Street investment. Suddenly cash rich, Warner Bros. determined to invest in music publishing firms, including M. Witmark, T. B. Harms, and Dreyfus (Chappell-Harms). Not to be outdone, MGM purchased Robbins Music Corp., and Paramount acquired Spier-Coslow. Now, instead of paying royalties the studios were earning them; hence their focus on the grand movie musicals of the 1930s (Messinger 20–24). But even if ownership of some of the classic Tin Pan Alley publishers now resided in Hollywood (or rather still New York, where the studios' business headquarters were located), the transition was a boon to sheet music sales, since movies could promote songs to millions as no mere vaudeville act could.

In the wake of the complex struggles over performance rights and royalties that took place during the early 1940s—struggles waged at various times between ASCAP, film studios, national radio broadcast stations, the musicians' unions, the record companies, and even the wartime US government—the great songbook catalogues of the Tin Pan Alley houses proved suddenly inaccessible to radio broadcasters, through bans or exorbitant costs. To fill the gap, some broadcasters and film companies began to turn to music that wasn't covered by ASCAP rules, namely, more vernacular forms of popular music, such as "race music" (rhythm and blues) and hillbilly (country) music. Broadcasters' Music International (BMI) was formed in 1940 as a parallel performance rights organization that would collect royalties on types of music that had been ignored or excluded from ASCAP. While this did not result in an initial explosion in the mainstream popularity of indigenous, hitherto marginalized music, by the mid-1950s it helped bring about a full-scale revolution in American popular music (Garofalo 113–17; Sanjek 32–42; Karp, "Jews and the Business of Race Music"). This transformation has been understood mostly in terms of recorded music popularized through radio and juke boxes, but music publishers also benefited enormously, including the old Tin Pan Alley houses that defied ASCAP and went over to BMI, like E. B. Marks and Max Dreyfus. They were soon joined by a host of new music publishing concerns—Jean and Julian Aberbach, Howard Richmond, and Freddy and Miriam Bienstock. Many of them Jewish emigres from interwar Europe, these figures were not only attuned to the new sounds emanating from Memphis and Nashville in the 1950s, but also recognized the profit-making potential of holding publishing copyrights on hit records.[8]

If music publishing provides one pillar of the foundational period of Jewish prominence in the popular entertainment and the music industry, booking and talent agencies is surely another. First in prestige, if not in profits, was the William Morris Agency, whose roots go back to the vaudeville wars of the early twentieth century and whose fortunes fluctuated wildly, with the agency surviving several near-death experiences before finally shifting to a steady upward trajectory by the 1920s, and whose personnel remained consistently, overwhelmingly ethnically Jewish, at least through the 1960s. It would be simpler to pick out the non-Jews than the other way around, and while ostensibly the agency eschewed hiring the relatives of its agents, in practice it was populated by brothers, in-laws, nephews, fathers and sons. The founder's only child, Bill, Jr., was nominally the successor, in truth William Morris's surrogate son, Abe Lastfogel, guided the agency through its most prosperous decades.[9] The WMA's roots lay in vaudeville, which certainly included musicians, but especially singers or singing actor-comedians like Al Jolson, Harry Lauder, Sophie Tucker, Fannie Brice, Eddie Cantor, and Georgie Jessel. As vaudeville fragmented, never quite disappearing but morphing into radio (Burns and Allen, Amos and Andy), movie comedy (e.g., the Marx Brothers), and later television (Milton Berle, Sid Caesar, *Rowan & Martin's Laugh-In*), Lastfogel smoothly navigated the transition (Rose).

Only a part of the WMA's sprawling business focused on popular music per se, including a handful of prominent African American jazz musicians: Count Basie, Cab Calaway, and Duke Ellington. The Agency handled Frank Sinatra and even Elvis Presley too, but principally in their dealings with the movie rather than the recording industry. Instead, it was WMA's alter ego, the dark-suited agents of the Music Corporation of America (MCA) that would thoroughly dominate musician bookings throughout the United States from the late 1920s through the 1940s, when it shifted its focus to Hollywood and soon to TV. Its founder, Jules Stein, was born in South Bend, Indiana in 1896, the son of Lithuanian immigrants, his father a peddler who eventually opened a dry goods store. This stereotypical tale of American Jewish upward mobility took an odd turn when Jules, pursuing post-graduate education at the University of Chicago, and even a degree in ophthalmology from the University of Vienna, jettisoned his medical career to start a band booking business. In fact, this remarkable young man was also a skilled musician but above all an avid and ruthless businessman who had begun booking activities as a sideline while still in high school.[10] When he established MCA in 1924, just as the Jazz Age band craze was sweeping the nation, he quickly turned to the head of the Chicago local of the American Federation of Musicians (AFM), James Caesar Petrillo, to negotiate a waiver for MCA acts allowing them to tour outside their home territories.[11] It was the beginning of a long and mutually profitable relationship not just with Petrillo but with other tough Italian and Jewish Chicagoans associated with the mob "Outfit." Stein employed the monopolistic booking tactics of Abe Erlanger and Edward Albee, backed by union and mob muscle, combined with meticulous planning and reconnoitering, to create regional and national touring circuits that effectively transformed the nature of live musical performance in America. MCA had a formidable presence not just in bookings but in nightclub ownership and liquor supply (in these fields clearly in partnership with the mob) as well as in sheet music publishing. In the 1930s Stein had also helped develop the concept of the entertainment "package," supplying not just band bookings but entire shows—production, promotion, sponsorships, etc.—to theaters and hotel ballrooms as well as to radio broadcast networks. By the 1940s the company had been become so dominant and ubiquitous it was labeled "the octopus" in a famous Saturday Evening Post exposé (Wittels). But if MCA's intimidating image and monopolistic modus operandi were the antithesis of William Morris's projection of paternal solicitude ("our small act of today is our big act of tomorrow"), its personnel were no less thoroughly Semitic.

The same was true of the several smaller agencies that specialized in black musical bookings from the 1920s through the Second World War. This was clearly a niche field compared with the capacious reach of WMA and MCA. But it was likewise a field dominated by Jews, most outstandingly in this period Irving Mills and Joe Glaser. Mills (born Hyman Minsky in 1895) was the son of a hat maker from Odessa who settled in New York's Lower East Side. A competent and perceptive musician, he became a song plugger for Tin Pan Alley publisher Leo Feist's Philadelphia operation and with his brother Jack (Jacob) formed Mills Music, Inc. in 1919. This was the period of jazz's inception in northern cities; in fact, Mills was among a small group of whites and northern blacks to early glean the significance and promise of the new music. His principal association was with Duke Ellington (before the Duke left for William Morris in the late 1930s). Mills' management of Ellington was highly intrusive, at times definitely exploitative, and his role remains controversial today among Ellington biographers. But there is no doubt that the Duke himself regarded Mills not just as a business manager and agent, but as a legitimate creative and even musical force, helping to shape the orchestra's repertoire and forge Ellington's public image as a sophisticated black musical artist, rather than a primitive force, as black musicians tended to be depicted at the time. As Ellington recalled in *Music is My Mistress*, written long after he had broken with his former manager, "Irving Mills came to me one day with an original idea. He was always reaching toward a higher plateau for our music" (82). In fact, Mills's contribution was probably less musical than professional, meaning that his ambition to continuously augment Ellington's artistic stature helped drive the composer to greater heights.

Ellington was singular among Mills's clients (as well as in the history of American music) but he wasn't uniquely the object of Mills's ambition to win respectability for black musicians in the 1930s. In a 1931 story, the *Pittsburgh Courier*, a black newspaper, lauded Mills's "effort to build high class attractions with colored talent which hitherto has not developed because of the mishandling or a lack of proper opportunity" (quoted in Cohen 86). Glaser, it would appear, was entirely different. He was born in Chicago and like Jules Stein was reputed to have cultivated lifelong connections with the mob. Not a doctor like Stein but the son of a prominent physician, Glaser took on the persona of a ruffian, insinuating himself with the very mobsters whose social company Stein increasingly took pains to avoid. While MCA had very little to do with black acts, Stein's monopolizing tendencies caused him to form a subsidiary for black musicians, Consolidated Booking, headed by Glaser. Glaser had already demonstrated an affinity for the world of black music and sports, becoming the manager of Louis Armstrong almost from the moment of his initial arrival in Chicago from New Orleans, and of black and white boxers as well. When in the face of an antitrust suit Stein was forced to sell Consolidated, Glaser shifted to New York and created his own Associated Booking in 1931 (*New York Times*, 8 June 1969). He managed Ella Fitzgerald, Billy Holiday and many other luminaries, but his lifelong relationship with Armstrong proved extraordinarily intense, at once fatherly and oedipal, dictated by love, opportunism, and an inescapable reliance on the mob.[12]

The labors of Mills and Glaser as Jewish managers and booking agents specializing in black music were matched by the prominent role played by Jewish owners and managers of venues presenting black entertainment. This was notably the case in New York, although parallels can be found in other cities throughout the Northeast, Midwest and West. Of the major black music venues in pre-World War II Harlem, the Alhambra (owned by Milton

Gosdorfer) and the Savoy ballrooms (founded and owned by Moe Gale) were Jewish owned, as was the Apollo Theater on 125th St. (initially owned by Sidney S. Cohen and later by Frank Schiffman), the Lafayette Theater at 132nd St. (owned by Schiffman after 1923), and Connie's Inn on 131st St. (owned by Connie and George Immerman), an important showcase for early black jazz that rivalled the more famous Cotton Club (which itself, although owned by the Irish mobster Ownie Madden, was managed by the Jewish Herman Stark). The Roseland Ballroom on W. 51st St., established in 1924 by Louis J. Brecker, presented both black and white jazz big bands (it was among the first showcases for the Fletcher Henderson Orchestra, which pioneered Big Band swing), although like the Cotton Club and Connie's Inn, the Roseland admitted only whites as patrons. Rather more liberal were the many nightclubs on or near 52nd St. during the 1940s, a true jazz mecca and veritable birthplace for the new style of Be-Bop. A majority of these clubs were Jewish-owned or managed, including Birdland, Kelly's Stable, the Hickory House, and the Royal Roost.[13] Of a different character altogether was the Sheridan Square nightclub Café Society opened by the leftist activist and former New Jersey shoe salesman Barney Josephson. Dubbed "the right place for the wrong people," Josephson actively sought out black patrons and showcased black artists with a distinctly protest message (Billie Holiday debuted the anti-lynching song "Strange Fruit" there).[14]

The disparate backgrounds and ideological orientations of these Jewish impresarios were matched by those of the founders of the "little labels" that first emerged in the early 1940s and that would provide the seedbeds for the postwar blossoming of Rhythm and Blues and later Rock 'n' Roll. These included labels like King in Cincinnati, Savoy in Newark, Apollo, Old Time, and Atlantic in New York, Chess in Chicago, King in Cincinnati, and Specialty, Aladdin, and Modern in Los Angeles, as well as many others of lesser stature and duration. While some of the Jewish label founders had musical backgrounds, more typical was their previous business experience in such fields as liquor and cigarette distribution, used furniture, small manufacturing and retail sales. Only a handful, like Milt Gabler, Norman Granz, and Moe Asch were committed leftists and black music aficionados, along the lines of Barney Josephson, but many, like Chicago's famous Chess brothers and Specialty Records founder Art Rupe in Los Angeles, were simply restless and hungry young businessmen and women in search of an angle (Karp, "Jews and the Business of Race Music"). The fact that these entrepreneurs stemmed from all areas of the US attests not only to the increasingly local and regional character of the popular record industry (mirroring the emergence of local radio broadcast stations and affiliates largely shaping their own programming to suit community and niche markets). It also reflects an older factor, one emphasized at the start of this chapter: the diffusion of Jews in a wide range of major American cities as well as smaller hinterland communities continued to afford them—even by the middle of the twentieth century—a distinct ethnic business advantage. What distinguished indie (independent) record labels from so-called major ones was the former's need to patch together their own distribution networks—a crucial condition for success. These networks were comprised of local retailers, and while they have not yet been adequately studied, the preponderance of Jews among the lists of indie distributors suggests that local Jewish-owned retail shops (many of which sold small appliances and vinyl records) and their supply networks comprised the vertebrae of these distribution systems (see Broven Appendix B).

Typically, the story of the indie labels is usually told as one of spontaneous generation, without links to the vast body of prior entertainment and music business activity that has been sketched here. But clearly if we focus on patterns of function rather than specific media, on the effort to consolidate, modernize, refine and mass produce, we see that the revolution in popular music which made it a billion dollar business by the 1960s is firmly rooted in earlier practices and tendencies, ones in which Jews, often from unrelated family business backgrounds and centered in far flung regions of the United States, played a conspicuous and influential role.

Notes

1. Robert Cherry is currently completing a book that explores the comparison between Irish and Jews in American entertainment in great detail.

2. On peddlers, see Diner, *Roads Taken*. Diner points out that while Jewish women often peddled in Old World Europe, they rarely did so in America (73). Throughout this examination we encounter few businesswomen. That doesn't mean they didn't exist, but more likely that their contributions remained hidden behind those of their husbands, fathers, and brothers. It is only in the post-World War II era that we find independent Jewish businesswomen prominently operating as small-label record entrepreneurs and occasionally as agents and managers.

3. The classic work is Bernheim, *The Business of the Theate*. See also Leavitt, *Fifty Years in Theatrical Management*.

4. "I may mention here that Klaw and Erlanger began purely and simply as a booking agency, and later on Al Hayman, who had been connected with me, and observed the policy which I had originated, of forming theatrical circuits for the West and noted its success, went to Klaw and Erlanger and gave them the idea, which they seized upon" (Leavitt 266). On Hayman's Jewish business affiliations in San Francisco, and the antisemitism sometimes leveled against them, see Rosenbaum (80).

5. Like the Shuberts, Heiman hailed from Syracuse, NY and got his entrée into show business distributing programs in a local Shubert theater. Astonishingly, the Jewish movie theater mogul Sam Katz (later of the partnership Balaban and Katz) was also a Syracuse native. See Provol (32).

6. The burgeoning film industry recognized the vital importance of live music, as attested, for instance, by a conference of film exhibitors held at the De Witt Clinton Hall in New York City on 23 Jan. 1921. Keynoted by Samuel "Roxy" Rothafel, the German-born Jewish immigrant movie palace entrepreneur and impresario, who, like so many of those surveyed here, was reared in the hinterlands (Stillwater, Minnesota), the entire conference was devoted to the uses of live music in film presentation. The program is published in *Motion Picture News*. *New York TImes*, 18 Aug. 1970. On Rothafel, see R. Melnick.

7. Close to half of the forty-six publishers listed as ASCAP members in December, 1923 were Jewish owned or co-owned. See the *Exhibitors Trade Review*.

8. Jewish music business emigres and refugees from interwar Continental Europe didn't just come to the US but to Britain too, where they helped broker the importation of 1950s American Rock 'n' Roll to the UK and in the following decade the first "British Invasion." On this story see Karp, "Brokering a Rock 'n' Roll International; Biszick-Lockwood.

9. This conspicuously male orientation belies the fact that Lastfogel's wife, the vaudevillian Frances Arms, consulted in almost every important decision her husband made in guiding WMA to success.

10. There is no full-scale biography of Stein. A biographical portrait of him can be found in Pye's *Moguls* 15-74, and the two major biographies of his disciple and successor, Lew Wasserman, provide abundant material on Stein. McDougal, esp. 9–44, and Bruck, esp. 3–89.

11. Bruck (27–44), is especially strong in detailing Stein's (invariably denied) ties with the underworld.

12. For a powerful, thinly fictionalized depiction by an Armstrong biographer, see the play by Teachout, *Satchmo at the Waldorf.*

13. Of the twenty-one most important midtown jazz clubs, fourteen were Jewish-owned or managed.

14. As we have seen throughout, family ties proved crucial to the expansion of Jewish business networks. Roseland Ballroom owner Louis J. Brecker (Philadelphian son of an Austrian Jewish immigrant) was the brother-in-law of Isadore "Jay" Faggen, co-owner of the Savoy Ballroom (with Moe Gale), the Roseland's hipper uptown cousin. Faggen also owned and managed black dance ballrooms in Brooklyn and Chicago. A remarkable nine of the major jazz clubs on or just off 52nd St. were owned by members of a single extended family.

Works Cited

"A. L. Erlanger Dies after Long Illness." *New York Times*, 8 Mar. 1930, pp. 1, 10.

Bernheim, Alfred L. *The Business of the Theater: An Economic History of the American Theater, 1750–1932*. Bloom, 1932; reprint 1964.

Biszick-Lockwood, Bar. *Restless Giant: The Life and Times of Jean Aberbach and Hill and Range Songs*. Univ. of Illinois, 2010.

Broven, John. *Record Makers and Breakers: Voices of the Independent Rock 'n' Roll Pioneers*. Univ. of Illinois, 2010.

Bruck, Connie. *When Hollywood Had a King: The Reign of Lew Wasserman, Who Leveraged Talent into Power and Influence*. Random House, 2003.

Cohen, Harvey G. *Duke Ellington's America*. Univ. of Chicago, 2010.

Diner, Hasia. *Roads Taken: The Great Jewish Migrations to the New World and the Peddlers Who Forged the Way*. Yale Univ., 2015.

Ellington, Duke. *Duke Ellington: Music is My Mistress*. Doubleday, 1973.

Emerson, Ken. *Always Magic in the Air: The Bomp and Brilliance of the Brill Building Era*. Viking, 2005.

Exhibitors Trade Review, Dec. 1923–Feb. 1924, public notice.

Fricke, Jr., John Warren. "The Rialto: A Study of Union Square, the Center of New York's First Theater District, 1870–1900." Dissertation, New York University, 1983.

Garofalo, Reebee. "Crossing Over: From Black Rhythm & Blues to White Rock 'n'Roll." *Rhythm & Business: The Political Economy of Black Music*, edited by Norman Kelley, Akashic, 2002, pp. 113–17.

Goldberg, Isaac. *Tin Pan Alley: A Chronicle of Popular Music*. Unger, 1961.

Harris, Charles K. "After the Ball." 1891.

———. *After the Ball, Forty Years of Melody, an Autobiography*. Frank-Maurice, 1926.

Holliday, Billie. "Strange Fruit." Composed by Abel Meeropol. Commodore, 1939.

The Jazz Singer. Directed by Alan Crosland, performances by Al Jolson, May McAvoy, and Warner Oland, Warner Bros., 1927.

Karp, Jonathan. "Blacks, Jews, and the Business of Race Music, 1945–1955." *Chosen Capital: The Jewish Encounter with American Capitalism*, edited by Rebecca Kobrin, Rutgers Univ., 2012, pp. 141–67.

———. "Brokering a Rock 'n' Roll International: Jewish Record Men in America and Britain." *Purchasing Power: The Economics of Modern Jewish History*, edited by Rebecca Kobrin and Adam Teller, Univ. of Pennsylvania, 2015, pp. 125–52.

———. "Jews and the Business of Race Music." *Chosen Capital: The Jewish Encounter with American Capitalism*, edited by Rebecca Kobrin, Rutgers Univ., 2012, pp. 141–65.

———. "Of Maestros and Minstrels: American-Jewish Composers between Black Vernacular European Art Music." *The Art of Being Jewish in Modern Times*, edited by Barbara Kirshenblatt-Gimblett and Jonathan Karp, Univ. of Pennsylvania, 2008, pp. 57–78.

Rowan & Martin's Laugh-In. Created by Digby Wolfe, performances by Dan Rowen and Dick Martin, NBC, 1967–1973.

Leavitt, M. B. *Fifty Years in Theatrical Management.* Broadway, 1912.

Leeson, M. A. *History of the Counties of McKean, Elk, and Forest, Pennsylvania, with Biographical Selections.* Chicago: J. H. Beers, 1890.

McDougal, Dennis. *The Last Mogul: Lew Wasserman, MCA, and the Hidden History of Hollywood.* Crown, 1998.

Melnick, Jeffrey Paul. *A Right to Sing the Blues: African Americans, Jews, and American Popular Song.* Harvard Univ., 1999.

Melnick, Ross. *American Showman: Samuel 'Roxy' Rothafel and the Birth of the Entertainment Industry.* Columbia Univ., 2012.

Messinger, Cory Luke Joseph. "Calling the Tune: Hollywood and the Business of Music." Dissertation, Griffith University, 2010.

Morawska, Ewa. *Insecure Prosperity: Small-Town Jews in Industrial America, 1890–1940.* Princeton Univ., 1996.

Most, Andrea. *Making Americans: Jews and the Broadway Musical.* Harvard Univ., 2004.

Motion Picture News, Feb. 1921, p. 1070.

New York Times, 9 April 1910, p. 11.

New York Times, 25 Oct. 1937, p. 28.

New York Times, 8 June 1969, p. 92.

New York Times, 18 Aug. 1970, p. 36.

Pessen, Edward. "The Great Songwriters of Tin Pan Alley's Golden Age: A Social, Occupational, and Aesthetic Inquiry." *A Celebration of American Music: Words and Music in Honor of H. Wiley Hitchcock*, edited by Richard Crawford, R. Allen Lott, and Carol Oja, Univ. of Michigan, 1990, pp. 184–85.

Pittsburgh Courier, 1931.

Provol, William Lee. *The Pack Peddler.* Winston, 1937.

Pye, Michael. *Moguls: Inside the Business of Show Business.* Holt, Rinehart and Winston, 1980.

Rose, Frank. *The Agency: William Morris and the Hidden History of Show Business.* Harper, 1995.

Rosenbaum, Fred. *Cosmopolitans: A Social and Cultural History of the Jews of the San Francisco Bay Area.* Univ. of California, 2009.

Sanjek, Russel. *From Print to Plastic: Publishing and Promoting America's Popular Music (1900–1980).* Brooklyn College of CUNY, 1983.

Shapiro Bernstein. Www.shapirobernstein.com/about-us. Accessed 27 July 2018.

Sidran, Ben. *There Was a Fire: Jews, Music, and the American Dream.* 3rd ed., Unlimited Media, 2014.

Suisman, David. *Selling Sounds: The Commercial Revolution in Popular Music.* Harvard Univ., 2009.

Teachout, Terry, playwrite. *Satchmo at the Waldorf.* Dramatists Play Service, 2015.

Variety, Jan. 1909, p. 2.

Vaudeville News, 23 Mar. 1923, p. 12.

Von Tilzer, Harry, and Arthur J. Lamb. "A Bird in a Gilded Cage." 1900.

Von Tilzer, Harry, and Andrew B. Sterling. "My Old New Hampshire Home." 1898.

Weissbach, Lee Shai. *Jewish Life in Small-Town America.* Yale Univ., 2005.

Wertheim, Arthur Frank. *Vaudeville Wars: How the Keith-Albee and Orpheum Circuits Controlled the Big-Time and Its Performers.* Palgrave, 2006.

Wittels, David G. "Star-Spangled Octopus." *Saturday Evening Post,* vol. 219, nos. 6–9, 10 Aug., 17 Aug, 24 Aug., 31 Aug. 1946.

CHAPTER 6

"Sometimes It Is Like I Am Sitting on a Volcano": Retailers, Diplomats, and the Refugee Crisis, 1933–1945[1]

by Niki C. Lefebvre

"The Jewish tragedy opened by the rise of Hitler to power hit him like a heavy personal blow. Like so many others he had blood relatives caught in the clutches of Nazi barbarism; time and again he, too, said, "There but for the grace of God go I." But his pain went far deeper than that, far deeper than any sense of personal fear and outrage . . . Kirstein gave of his heart and his substance to Jewish relief."

—Benjamin Selekman, tribute to Louis E. Kirstein

*I*NTRODUCTION

In late April 1938 Nazi storm troopers burst into the Vienna trade office of the Associated Merchandising Corporation (AMC), an international cooperative buying firm for a network of department stores based in the United States.[2] The notorious brown shirts ransacked the desk of the AMC's longtime merchandise buyer Kurt Schwartz, a former German citizen and a Jew, before arresting him.[3] Schwartz was one of twenty thousand Jews arrested in the immediate aftermath of the German-Austrian *Anschluss* in March. In the course of a few terrifying months Austrian Jews were stripped of their citizenship, deprived of nearly all their legal and civil rights, and more or less banned from public life. In late March thousands of Austrians cheered at a political rally in Vienna when German Field Marshall Herrmann Goering threatened the city's Jewish population. "Vienna must become German again," Goering inveighed. "The Jew must know we do not care to live with him. He must go." During the two weeks following Goering's address, more than thirty thousand Jews, Kurt Schwartz likely among them, crowded the US Consulate in Vienna seeking visa applications and information about immigration.[4] Around the same time Schwartz sent a cable to a friend in the United States regarding an affidavit he needed to secure a US travel visa.[5] Nazi authorities intercepted the cable and, upon further investigation, reported that Schwartz was illegally manipulating currency exchange rates to keep up with the excessive taxes levied on Jewish-owned properties in the Third Reich.[6] Nazi storm troopers arrested Schwartz at the AMC's Vienna trade office soon after the investigation and even visited Schwartz's home to warn his mother that any attempt to seek American counsel would only bring harm to her son.

Louis Kirstein, Chairmen of the AMC's foreign offices, learned of Schwartz's arrest on May 17, 1938, when he received an urgent telegram at his office in Boston, where he also served as Vice President of Filene's department store. The telegram came from the AMC trade office in Paris, where two American merchandise buyers had just returned from a trip to the AMC trade office in Vienna and brought news of Schwartz's arrest. Hanns Streicher, an Austrian native and head of the AMC offices in Berlin and Vienna, did not send word directly from Vienna to Kirstein in Boston because he feared that any communication from his office to the United States would make things worse for Schwartz. And although Streicher made several trips to see Schwartz's mother, he found her unwilling to cooperate with him because of his ties to the United States. Streicher later wrote that he felt "powerless" to help Schwartz, but he and other AMC executives and buyers in Europe suspected that, if anyone could help, it would be Louis Kirstein. They were right. In a burst of transatlantic telegrams and letters, Kirstein called on retailers and diplomats stationed in Vienna, Berlin, Paris, New York, and Washington, D.C., facilitating Schwartz's release in less than one week. Though Schwartz was one among hundreds of thousands of Jews terrorized by the expanding Nazi regime in the spring of 1938, he was fortunate to become one of the comparatively few who made it to the United States before the end of the year.[7] More remarkable still, by October, Kurt Schwartz was gainfully employed in New York City at Bloomingdale's, a longtime member of the AMC network of department stores.

Historians have long charged Americans, especially leading American Jews and government officials, particularly those serving in the U.S. State

Department, of inaction and ambivalence in the face of violent Nazi persecution. More recently, studies have acknowledged the extent to which a rising tide of virulent anti-Semitism and a political climate hostile to any interventions abroad crippled American responses to the refugee crisis.[8] These studies, however, have tended not to emphasize relief and rescue efforts undertaken by influential Americans working outside traditional channels—that is to say, efforts beyond the field of traditional government action or formal relief and rescue initiatives. And while many historians have acknowledged the herculean efforts of Ira Hirschmann, an executive at Bloomingdale's who forced his way onto the War Refugee Board before it was officially formed, none has explored how his position as a leading retail executive might have helped him forge such an extraordinary path.[9] To be sure, Hirschmann was a man of unusual courage and conviction, and he possessed the kind of exemplary negotiation skills that eventually led to the release of tens of thousands of prisoners from concentration camps in Romania. Still, Hirschmann's connections in the American retail industry were not incidental to his outstanding interventions in Europe's refugee crisis. For many executives and buyers, connections and opportunities formed through the retail trade were integral to their efforts to oppose Nazism and aid European Jews. That seems especially so for retail leaders in the AMC network.

No field of American commerce was as deeply shaken by the rise of Nazism in Europe as the retail industry, in part because retailers were not dependent on third-party news reports or unknown intermediaries for information. Through regular communication with their trade offices abroad, retailers were reliably informed about the dangers wrought by Adolf Hitler's violent anti-Semitism from the very beginning. Equally important, the leaders of the American retail industry, including those in the AMC network, were overwhelmingly Jewish. In 1937 American Jews owned two thirds of the wholesale and retail establishments in New York City, the nation's commercial capital, including the largest and most influential firm, R. H. Macy's. Studies have also shown that similar patterns of Jewish leadership in the retail and wholesale fields emerged in other major cities across the country (Feingold, *Bearing Witness* 209–10). Retail executives were acutely aware of the realities facing Europe's Jews not only because of their professional connections in the capital cities of the Third Reich but also because of their familial and social ties to countless men and women victimized by Nazi anti-Jewish policies.

Although the individual department stores mentioned in this study will be familiar to readers, the AMC network is likely not. Established by Louis Kirstein, Lincoln Filene, and others in the aftermath of the First World War, the AMC network included twenty-two department stores located in twenty cities across thirteen states by the late 1930s. On the eve of the *Anschluss*, AMC member stores maintained large, cooperative trade offices in London, Paris, Berlin, Vienna, Brussels, and Florence, and six smaller offices stationed throughout China and Japan.[10] The firm also managed export accounts for department stores based in Canada, England, Scotland, Holland, Sweden, France, South Africa, and Australia. Scores of cooperative buying firms based in New York City operated trade offices in Europe by the mid-thirties, but the AMC had three times the buying power of any one of them. In addition, the AMC had developed more than two hundred lines of its own branded merchandise, such as Barbara Lee women's wear or Baby Crest infant goods, which were sold in department stores around the world. Without question, it was the largest and most innovative retail corporation in the United States during the interwar period. And, equally important to this study, nearly all of the leading executives at the stores that formed the core membership in the AMC, from Abraham & Straus in Brooklyn to Bullock's in Los Angeles, were Jewish.[11]

This study will focus on executives and buyers in the AMC network who, under the leadership of Louis Kirstein, went to great lengths to undermine the influences of Nazism on their trade offices abroad and to intervene in Europe's refugee crisis after 1933. If Ira Hirschmann's well-documented leadership as the first special attaché to the War Refugee Board can be considered the culmination of these efforts, then Louis Kirstein's efforts to shield his relations, friends, and colleagues in Germany and Austria from Nazi persecution must be considered the foundation. This study will reveal how Kirstein, a towering figure in the retail industry and well beyond it, cultivated professional and social connections that granted him privileged insights into the terrible conditions facing Europe's Jews—and, in some cases, the ability to make successful interventions. Between 1933 and the closing of German borders in 1941, Kirstein supported a growing number of relations and friends with the help of his intermediary, Hanns Streicher. After the German invasion of Austria in March 1938, Kirstein and Streicher relied on their contacts in the U.S. State Department, especially Assistant Secretary of State George S. Messersmith, to help a few dozen refugees make their way out of the Third Reich to safety in the United States, England, and even Cuba. Although these efforts were not always successful and affected only a small and select group of refugees, they nonetheless bring to light how influential businessmen and diplomats collaborated privately to resist Nazi persecution and aid individuals suffering under the anti-Jewish policies of the Third Reich.

AMC retail executives were well positioned to respond to the refugee crisis—in ways both large and small—because of their connections within the borders of the Third Reich and the contacts they had cultivated in Washington and with diplomats stationed abroad. That so many retail executives were themselves Jewish was also paramount. AMC executives confronted the dangers of Nazism long before most other Americans because of their extensive familial, social, and professional ties to Jews living in Germany and Austria. And although Jewish retailers like Kirstein and Hirschmann did not always agree on the answers to critical questions facing American Jewry about how to respond to the threat of Nazism, in one vital respect they shared some common ground—a calling to leverage their powerful transatlantic resources and contacts in the US State Department to respond meaningfully to the greatest humanitarian crisis of the twentieth century.[12]

ANTI-NAZIS AND THE AMC: NETWORKS BETWEEN WASHINGTON AND BERLIN, 1933–1938

Hanns Streicher had been in charge of the AMC trade office in Berlin for less than a year when he received an ominous knock on the door. It was October 1933 and a uniformed Nazi officer presented an order for Streicher and his staff to decorate the exterior of the AMC building with swastika flags. AMC executives had purchased the building that housed its foreign trade office on Berlin's Lindenstrasse in 1921, when the street was at the heart of the city's export district. In 1933, however, the Nazi Party chose Lindenstrasse as a central thoroughfare for political parades.[13] Much to the surprise of the Nazi officer, Streicher boldly refused to comply with the order. "If all businesses are going to be decorated," he calmly explained, "we shall do likewise and put out the American flag and the German black-white-red flag." The officer insisted under the threat of force, but Streicher was resolute. He later learned that, by German law, no foreign firm could be forced to display the swastika flags. Regardless, Streicher's refusal was no small act of courage. Nazi thugs had already beaten enough foreigners in the streets for refusing to appropriately honor party symbols that US Ambassador William Dodd had requested a personal meeting with Chancellor Hitler to demand state intervention ("Stern Nazi Orders Protect Americans"; "Another American Beaten by a Nazi"; "Dodd to See Hitler Today on Assaults; also see Stiller 44–45). Streicher wrote at length about the episode with the Nazi officer in a letter to Louis Kirstein at Filene's in Boston. "Sometimes," Streicher confessed with an eerie prescience, "it is like I am sitting on a volcano."[14]

In order to defend his relations, friends, and colleagues against the impact of Nazism, Kirstein, as early as 1933, cultivated the close support and friendship of many influential people, but two men in particular stand out: Hanns Streicher, a leather goods buyer from Gmunden, Austria, and George S. Messersmith. While Streicher's name is all but lost to history, and the details of his life are scant, Messersmith is well known to historians, particularly for his rigid adherence to restrictive immigration policies that kept thousands of would-be immigrants out of the United States. Messersmith was arguably the best-informed official in the State Department as to the crisis facing Europe because of the critically important posts he held over the course of the 1930s: first as Consul General in Berlin (1930–1934), then as Minister to Austria (1934–1937), and finally as Assistant Secretary of State (1937–1940). Although Messersmith is by far the better known of these two important figures in Kirstein's circle of contacts, Streicher's role ought not be overshadowed. It was through Streicher's visits to the US Consulate in Berlin that Kirstein learned first-hand of the extent of Messersmith's anti-Nazi feelings, setting the stage for their collaboration in the rescue of several German and Austrian Jews. More importantly, Streicher himself was Kirstein's most intimate ally in a quiet campaign to aid and rescue people suffering under Nazi anti-Jewish policies, personally attending to the needs of Kirstein's relations and friends in Germany and Austria. In 1933 and 1934 Kirstein promoted Streicher to manager of the AMC offices in both Berlin and Vienna and entrusted him with dispensing aid to his relations in Germany. Over the same period, both Kirstein and Streicher developed connections to Messersmith that would prove indispensable after the German invasion of Austria in 1938. A close look at these overlapping professional, political, social circles reveals how Kirstein established a private network of anti-Nazi retailers and diplomats who would provide vital assistance to his relations and friends, especially after 1938.

Louis Kirstein was the son of a Jewish lens grinder, Edward Kirstein, who fled Leipzig in the wake of the revolutionary uprisings in 1848.[15] He was born in Rochester, New York, in 1867 and, after a youth checkered with failed business ventures, married Rose Stein, daughter of the successful owner of the men's clothing company, Stein-Bloch. Eventually Kirstein found his way to Filene's in Boston and rapidly ascended the executive ladder to become a partial owner in the business by 1911. Though he was never a religious man, Kirstein was deeply committed to his social and civic obligations as a Jew and as an American.[16] During the First World War he joined important Democratic Party circles while serving as Chairman of the Board of Control for Labor Standards, and in the 1920s he became a leading figure in several Jewish organizations, especially the elite American Jewish Committee (AJCOMM). By the mid-thirties, Kirstein had become a giant in the American retail industry, was regularly elected to the executive board of the AJCOMM, and Franklin Roosevelt appointed him to serve as an administrator on the Industrial Advisory Board. Kirstein was widely celebrated for his fairness, modesty, and generosity. At his seventy-fifth birthday celebration, he was called "Boston's first Jewish citizen," and it was said that he had given away "practically his entire income for philanthropic causes." Thus, during the period that Adolf Hitler rose to power in Germany, Kirstein commanded a vast network of social and professional contacts that were rooted in the country's leading Jewish organizations and retail corporations but also extended deep into the inner circles of Washington and as far as the foreign offices of the AMC.

Although Kirstein was meticulous in his oversight of all the foreign offices in the AMC, he took special care to ensure that the right person took charge of the Berlin office in the spring of 1932. When AMC executives had voted to purchase a building in Berlin in 1921, they agreed to place their head representative in Central Europe, a former Harrods' buyer and Englishman named Roger Day, in charge of the new trade office. Day successfully developed the AMC's German trade through the 1920s, but by the early 1930s the global depression and a surge of popular economic nationalism in both the United States and Britain decimated sales in the region. The AMC's offices in Berlin and Vienna experienced a tremendous drop in sales volumes.[17] During the spring of 1932, as AMC executives debated how to cut costs and consolidate their buying operations in Central Europe, Adolf Hitler established himself as a major force in German politics by earning more than one third of the vote in the presidential elections. Roger Day wrote to Kirstein from the trade office in Berlin with some optimistic reflections on Hitler's triumph: "The majority of serious thinking people here cannot help but welcome the fact that the sword has now fallen," Day conceded. "It is now up to Hitler to fulfill the many promises he has made." Less than three weeks later Kirstein wrote to Day with the support of the AMC's executive committee to ask for his resignation (Day, Letter to Kirstein; Kirstein, Letter to Day). In turn, executives agreed to promote a relative newcomer to the organization to serve as the head of operations in both Berlin and Vienna: Hanns Streicher.

While there is very little information on Streicher's personal background in the archival records of the AMC, enough of his correspondence
with Louis Kirstein and other AMC executives survives to provide a glimpse
into his politics, which were avowedly anti-Nazi, and his character. A native
of Gmunden, Austria, Streicher was a top leather goods buyer for the popular
Vienna firm Max Grab & Co., which represented the AMC's buying interests in
that region for most of the 1920s. When the founder of that firm died in 1930,
the AMC purchased the business, made it their own, and placed Streicher in
charge (Reilly, Letter to Fischer; also see documents in "Establishment of Vienna
Office"; "Vienna Office is Reopened by the AMC"). Within two years Streicher
was promoted over Day to serve as the head of operations for the AMC in both
Berlin and Vienna. When he first arrived in Berlin, Streicher expressed his disdain for Nazi political propaganda in letters to Kirstein. "I saw on a poster four
words, 'Hitler . . . our last hope,'" Streicher lamented in August 1932. "Surely a
country must have reached the bottom when such words can appear on post-
ers" (Streicher, Letter to Kirstein, 3 Aug 1932). During his first year in Berlin,
Streicher became devoted to "curing the whole office of Nazi spirit." His efforts
included the delicate task of discharging an employee, a German citizen named
Mr. Klippel, who had become an official member of the Nazi Party. In order
to manage Klippel's dismissal responsibly and legally, Streicher appealed to the
US consulate in Berlin for guidance. Fortunately for Streicher, who had as yet
spent little time in Berlin, a friend of his in the American embassy in Vienna
granted him a personal introduction to the most influential consular official in
Germany, Consul General George S. Messersmith.[18]

Messersmith's connection to Streicher, and later to Kirstein, offers a rare
insight into the private actions of an influential diplomat whose legacy has long
confounded historians. Messersmith's principal biographer argued that, in the
context of the anti-Semitism that gripped the United States in the 1930s, the
diplomat's record on "Jewish matters" was relatively good, but "by any ethical
standard, it was not good enough. He failed the persecuted when they most
needed him" (Stiller 50–51). For a brief period in the mid 1930s, a number of
influential American Jews, Justice Louis D. Brandeis and Rabbi Stephen Wise
among them, considered Messersmith their best ally in the State Department,
but, as historians have noted, this fact says more about the attitudes of the
State Department than it does about Messersmith. Born in rural Pennsylvania
in 1883, Messersmith trained as a secondary school teacher and worked as a
school principal before finding his way to a career in the State Department.
He was twice counseled against pursuing the diplomatic branch of the Foreign

Service because he lacked the financial resources, educational background, and social connections to succeed on that track.[19] Instead, Messersmith entered the consular service in 1914 and spent his first years at an inconsequential consulate in Fort Eerie, Canada. Fifteen years later, however, as consul general at Berlin, Messersmith witnessed the rise of Adolf Hitler and supplied Washington with the best daily analyses of German affairs. No one in the State Department was better informed as to the threat Hitler posed to Europe and to Jews, and none was more openly critical of the Nazi regime. Yet Messersmith neither put forth any proposals for asylum in response the refugee crisis nor did he yield in his unbending commitment to upholding restrictive immigration policies. As late as 1936 Messersmith insisted that the State Department guide for consular officials include a reminder that they should not aim "to maintain the United States as an asylum or refuge for dissatisfied and oppressed people in other parts of the world" (Ami-Zucker 156). At a time when US immigration procedures made no official exceptions from the usual visa requirements for refugees, Messersmith's rigid adherence to restrictive policies sealed the fates of thousands of Jews trapped in the Third Reich.[20]

While it is not surprising that Streicher found Messersmith to be a wellspring of advice on how to cure the AMC's Berlin office of the Nazi spirit, it is surprising that he also found the counsul general willing to aid two Jews who aspired to immigrate to the United States. In the early 1930s, US consular officials in Germany issued visas at a rate far below the annual quotas (sometimes up to 75–80% below). Due to the widespread influence of restrictionist immigration attitudes in Washington, consular offices were also woefully understaffed and many officials adhered to financial requirements so high that few would-be immigrants could meet them.[21] In 1934, Alan Steyne, a young consular official and Louis Kirstein's nephew, described his work at the consulate in Hamburg as "exciting, but too busy . . . at times I feel like a one-armed paper hanger" (Steyne, Letter to Kirstein). In this harried climate, Messersmith, the top-ranking consular official in Germany, made time for several meetings with Streicher in which he offered guidance on how to discharge the AMC employee who had joined the Nazi Party. Moreover, Messersmith was "most obliging" in his acceptance of visa applications that Streicher had completed on behalf of two men whom he had never met: the German Jewish nephews of Julius Baer, a longtime friend of Kirstein and founder of the AMC member store Stix, Baer & Fuller in St. Louis, Missouri (Streicher, Letter to Kirstein, 10 Oct. 1933). As the nephews of a wealthy American retailer, the Baers would have had no trouble meeting the financial requirements for immigration to the

United States, however, direct access to Messersmith through Streicher allowed them to circumvent a lengthy screening process by which consular officials could reject applicants on the grounds of physical, mental, or moral defects, or for political and economic reasons (Ami-Zucker). In a letter to Kirstein, Streicher marveled over Messersmith, who had "really gone out of his way to help in every respect" (Streicher, Letter to Kirstein, 10 Oct. 1933). Streicher and Messersmith remained friendly and met for occasional dinners even after the latter received his appointment as Minister to Vienna.[22]

In December 1933 Kirstein acknowledged that he was "anxious" to meet Messersmith, but so too was the diplomat eager to meet Kirstein. Through his nephew at the consulate in Hamburg, Kirstein learned that Messersmith was looking for introductions to Supreme Court Justices Louis D. Brandeis and Benjamin N. Cardozo (the first and second Jewish Supreme Court justices, respectively). While it is possible that Messersmith was seeking the social connections that might help him advance into the Foreign Service, it is also likely that he wanted to confer with leading American Jews who shared his concerns over the rise of Hitler in Germany (Shafir 35–36; also see Stiller). In January 1934 Messersmith and Kirstein met for the first time at a dinner in New York City given by Dr. Jacob Billikopf, a vocal advocate for Jewish civil rights who was especially concerned with the plight of refugees. Kirstein described the event as a "Jewish who's who" of the country, with the exception of Messersmith and James G. McDonald, a fellow diplomat who would later become chairman of the President's Advisory Committee on Refugees.[23] Several weeks after that dinner, Messersmith accepted an invitation to visit Kirstein at his home in Boston. Over the course of an afternoon, Messersmith imparted what Kirstein called "valuable information and suggestions" regarding the "German situation." Thereafter, the two men met whenever they could, either in Washington or Boston, and Kirstein introduced Messersmith to several influential friends and acquaintances, including the two Supreme Court justices, Felix Frankfurter (then founder of the American Civil Liberties Union and future Supreme Court judge), Senator Robert F. Wagner (D-NY), and the influential journalist Walter Lippman.[24] In turn, Kirstein's nephew at the Hamburg consulate received a rare double promotion and Messersmith's own troubled nephew was offered a job at R. H. White's department store in Boston where Kirstein was a partial owner (Messersmith, Letters to Kirstein, 4 Aug. 4 & 15 Sept. 1936, 8 Mar. 1939). Increasingly, Messersmith and Kirstein also made social engagements that included their wives. In early 1937 the two couples even planned to meet in Vienna during one of Kirstein's trips to the AMC foreign offices, but the gathering never took place because Messersmith was called back to Washington to serve as assistant secretary of state (Messersmith, Letter to Kirstein, 1 July 1937). Instead, Kirstein and his wife spent several days touring Austria with Streicher and his extended family (Streicher, Letter to Kirstein, 1 July 1937; Kirstein, Letter to Streicher, 20 Aug. 1937).

In 1934, however, while Kirstein was still building his connection to Messersmith, Streicher traveled to the United States, where, among other business, he held an important private meeting with Kirstein. Due to the rise of consumer-driven anti-Nazi boycotts, Streicher's trade office in Berlin had fared the worst of all the AMC's foreign offices during the lowest point of the Great Depression (1933–1934). Regardless, AMC executives had selected Streicher as the sole representative from the foreign offices to travel to the United States carrying merchandise samples from all the European sales regions. Streicher spent most of his time traveling the country to visit the flagships of AMC member stores, but he also attended the annual meeting of AMC executives. At some point during that meeting, Kirstein met privately with Streicher and asked him to take on more responsibility providing financial support to his relations living in Berlin, whose suffering under Nazi anti-Jewish policies was growing more severe. While there are no records of the words exchanged in this conversation, it is clear that Streicher obliged. When Streicher returned to Berlin from his American trip he received a visit from Kirstein's cousin, Rosi Bohm, and her husband, who had become seriously ill. The couple learned that, due to the effects of anti-Jewish policies on the medical profession in Germany, they would have to leave the country to secure appropriate medical care, but they had neither the financial means nor the ability to make such arrangements.[25] Without hesitation, Streicher helped the Bohms make travel arrangements to Denmark and he set up a draft account through the AMC that they could access once they left country. To be sure, Kirstein reimbursed the firm for the Bohms's expenses, but such a transaction could not have taken place so readily without the AMC office in Berlin—or without Streicher's support. In reflecting on Streicher's handling of the Bohms's circumstances, Kirstein wrote, "I am sure that their lives are a good deal brighter because they realize there is someone who understands their situation and has some sympathy for them" (Kirstein, Letter to Streicher, 5 Mar. 1934; Kirstein, Letter to Streicher, 16 Oct. 1934; Streicher, Letter to Kirstein, 3 Oct. 1934).

Over the course of the decade Streicher would become a vital intermediary between Kirstein and a growing number of distant cousins, nieces, and nephews living under the Nazi regime. Kirstein had first become acquainted with these family members in Germany during a trip to Europe on government business after the First World War (see chapter three). Following that trip, Kirstein and his two siblings began sending occasional financial aid, clothing, and even foodstuffs to their cousin Ida Maria Zachart, who had lost her husband in the war, and her grown daughter, Ilse Sternberg, who had left an abusive husband and cared for their children on her own. Around 1925 Kirstein began transferring occasional funds to Zachart and Sternberg through the AMC office in Berlin rather than directly to their homes, at least in part because the two women moved often (see all letters in the file "Germany Correspondance," but especially: Zachart, Letter to Kirstein). However, after a series of decrees in 1933–1935 stripped Jews of their citizenship and expelled them from nearly all forms of professional labor, many more families found themselves in need of financial assistance. Kirstein responded by providing regular monthly allowances, and any other support as needed, to at least five families connected to him through blood or marriage. Streicher facilitated the distribution of these allowances by using AMC merchandise receipts to record "orders" to family members and forwarding these receipts directly to Kirstein's secretary at Filene's department store, who paid for the orders through Filene's accounts. Kirstein then reimbursed Filene's from his personal funds, to which his sister and brother also contributed.[26] Above and beyond these transactions, Streicher became an important personal friend to several of Kirstein's relations, especially to Dr. Heymann and his extended family. Although Heymann was pushed out of his teaching position in 1933, he was offered another post as long as he agreed to teach in the "nationalistic spirit." At his new school, Heymann was forced to begin every morning with a salute to Hitler and attend Nazi parades. While at dinner with Streicher one evening, Heymann exclaimed hopelessly, "You can put me in a concentration camp tomorrow. . . . " (Streicher, Letter to Kirstein, 10 Oct 1933). Streicher kept up his friendship with Dr. Heymann and regularly updated Kirstein on the professor's wellbeing.

On the eve of the German invasion of Austria in March 1938 Kirstein had developed connections to Streicher and Messersmith that extended well beyond business concerns. Streicher was closely intertwined with Kirstein's private efforts to support his relations with financial assistance and checked in with them monthly. Messsersmith had become valued friend and returned from Europe to serve as assistant secretary of state in Washington, DC, a post he held over the critical period between 1937 and 1940. While both Streicher and Kirstein lamented Messersmith's removal from Europe, in fact, the position granted him even greater influence over consular officials stationed in Berlin and Vienna. It also provided more opportunities for Kirstein and Messersmith to meet personally in Washington to discuss what they called the "German situation." Despite Messersmith's official opposition to changing immigration policies for refugees, he worked with Kirstein to expedite visas on behalf of several people after the *Anschluss*. And despite Streicher's citizenship in the Third Reich, he continued to act as Kirstein's intermediary in Berlin and Vienna on behalf of people whose suffering he had come to know so well.

RETAILERS, DIPLOMATS AND REFUGEES AFTER THE ANSCHLUSS

The American diplomat John C. Wiley arrived in Vienna to begin his new post as consul general shortly before the German invasion of Austria in March 1938. In the aftermath of the invasion, he received a missive from George Messersmith, then serving as assistant secretary of state, instructing him to make no changes to any immigration policies at the consulate. There was, at the time, considerable apprehension as to the status of US diplomats in Austria given the dissolution of the government there. Over the next few months, however, the anti-Jewish measures that had evolved over a five-year period in Germany went into effect rapidly across Austria. Reporters estimated that across the country nearly 80,000 Jews had been dismissed from their jobs, and not a single Jew in Vienna was permitted to retain an automobile. Nazi fanatics regularly picketed, vandalized, and looted Jewish owned shops and businesses, and gangs of Nazi thugs publicly humiliated and injured Jews with little to no repercussions from the government or police (see N 4; also see Wyman 28–30; Beller 231–36). In June, as tens of thousands of Austrian Jews rushed the foreign consulates desperate to emigrate, consul general Wiley wrote to Messersmith to express concern about the "constantly increasing" dimensions of the catastrophe. He characterized Nazi policies as "utterly lunatic" and lamented that consular officials in Vienna were immersed in "heartrending misery." Although Wiley reiterated his agreement that the State Department ought to remain "aloof" from such matters, he confided in Messersmith that the "instinct to do something for everybody is overwhelming." Private organizations, Wiley concluded, or "a private person with tact and energy might be able to alleviate matters with the Austrian authorities" (Messersmith, Letter to Wiley; Wiley).

Kirstein was indeed a private person with both tact and energy who tried to improve the circumstances of a select group of people living in Austria and

Germany after March 1938, but he did not manage it alone. On behalf of his relations, a handful of friends, and some AMC employees, Kirstein called on all of his contacts in the State Department and in the retail industry to intervene where he could. In some cases, most notably in the case of Kurt Schwartz, who, as described in the introduction to this study, was arrested in the aftermath of the *Anschluss*, the results were dramatic. Most other cases, however, involved a complicated exchange of paperwork and considerable financial commitments. When Kirstein feared legal complications or other delays at the consulates might prevent the emigration of people dearest to him, he wrote to Messersmith, who tried in some cases to expedite the visa approval process. Messersmith also met with Kirstein frequently to offer privileged insights into conditions in Germany and Austria and to help connect the retailer with people who might aid broader public rescue and relief efforts.[27] In the archives that hold Kirstein's personal and business files at Harvard's Baker Library, there are well over one thousand documents detailing the retailer's efforts to help individual refugees, mostly between 1938 and 1941.[28] This section will highlight a handful of cases in which Kirstein intervened, sometimes successfully, to aid the escape of Jewish relations, friends, and colleagues from the Third Reich after the *Anschluss*. While several cases reveal the depth of Kirstein's influence in retail and diplomatic circles, others expose the limits that confronted a "private person" working against the tremendous forces of bureaucracy in the State Department and the violence of the Nazi regime. However, that Kirstein had the contacts, resources, and support to intervene at all underscores the influence and empathy that guided the AMC network as Nazism took root across Europe.

Just a few weeks after the *Anschluss*, in April 1938, Kirstein began receiving urgent requests from Austrian Jews eager to leave the country, some of whom he had never met. One woman named Lisolette Chiger, who described herself as the daughter of a manufacturer in Vienna with whom the AMC had contracted for years, wrote to Kirstein begging him to sign an affidavit to sponsor her family for an American visa. Applicants were required by most consular officials in Austria and Germany to provide affidavits proving that a friend or relative in the United States could provide for them financially in the event that they could not find work. For many would-be immigrants, this requirement proved a major barrier to entry in the United States.[29] Chiger begged Kirstein: "The situation is so earnest," she wrote, "that we must ask you to treat this as an SOS service." Kirstein immediately wired Chiger for more information and wrote to his lawyer to draw up the appropriate papers. Fearful that his tenuous connection to Chiger would undermine the entire process and cause delays,

Kirstein called his lawyer directly. "Do you think it would help any to send the whole thing to Messersmith?" Kirstein asked. His lawyer advised against contacting Messersmith in the Chiger case, but it is not surprising that Kirstein asked. Messersmith had already expedited at least three visa applications on behalf of people connected to the AMC.[30]

Although Messersmith took care never to disclose anything of consequence in writing, after 1938 his correspondence with Kirstein makes clear that he shared privileged insights and connections that might help Jewish refugees. More often than not, Messersmith filled his letters with broad impressions of his opinions: "Far be it for me to be a pessimist," he wrote of Europe in May 1938, "but I am not at all satisfied that things are going for the better" (Messersmith, Letter to Kirstein, 11 May 1938). Some letters do, however, offer clearer insights into the content of their personal meetings. In 1939, for example, Messersmith alluded to a recent conversation he had with the former German chancellor Joseph Wirth, who had been exiled in 1933 for his opposition to the Nazi Party. The diplomat explained that Wirth was "extremely useful in matters connected with Germany, the refugee problem, et. Cetera," and added that Wirth wished to meet Kirstein. "I have some interesting things in this connection to tell you," Messersmith explained, "which I would rather not put in writing" (Messersmith, Letter to Kirstein, 8 Mar. 1939). Kirstein traveled to Washington, DC for a private meeting with Messersmith less than one week later (Messersmith, Letter Kirstein, 8 & 13 Mar. 1939, Kirstein, Letter to Messersmith, 11Mar. 1939). In correspondence with his nephew, Kirstein often mentioned his dinners with Messersmith, and sometimes expressed surprise at how "freely and frankly" the Assistant Secretary of State talked with him on matters in Germany.[31] Equally important, however, Messersmith provided Kirstein with personal introductions to ambassadors and consuls general in Berlin, Vienna, Paris, London, and any other location that Kirstein requested. While Kirstein, in some cases, was already acquainted with the leading diplomats in these cities through the AMC offices, his endorsements from Messersmith ensured the cooperation of these officials with Kirstein's requests.[32]

In no case were these diplomatic connections more vital than in that of Kurt Schwartz. Although the circumstances surrounding Schwartz's arrest were described above, the details of his rescue reveal more precisely how retailers and diplomats came together, under Kirstein's direction, to facilitate Schwartz's release.[33] When two merchandise buyers arrived at the AMC's Paris office with news of Schwartz's arrest, they enlisted the help of not only the longtime manager of the AMC's Paris office, Edouard Léon, but also Charles

D. Hutzler, owner of the AMC member store Hutzler Brothers of Baltimore.[34] Hutzler had a good sense of Kirstein's far-reaching influence and immediately wired him about Schwartz. Upon receipt of Hutzler's telegram, Kirstein sent urgent messages to officials at the US Embassy in Paris and to Wiley at the US consulate in Vienna. He also wrote directly to Streicher in Berlin and asked him to personally visit the consulate in Vienna to inform consul general Wiley that, if he could not facilitate Schwartz's release, Kirstein would call on Messersmith to intervene.

Meanwhile, Hutzler and Léon followed up with the U.S. ambassador's secretary in Paris who, they reported, had "dropped everything" when he learned of Kirstein's personal interest in the case.[35] After a series of coded communications were exchanged between the embassy in Paris and Wiley in Vienna, US consular officials successfully pressured Nazi authorities to release Schwartz on the condition that he leave Austria within the week. Wiley immediately arranged a US visa for Schwartz while another AMC manager in London set up a temporary travel visa to England for Schwartz's mother.[36] In advance of Schwartz's arrival in the United States, Kirstein worked with fellow AMC executives at Bloomingdale's to ensure that Schwartz would have a job waiting for him in New York City.[37] This, too, was no easy feat. The American economy had taken another downturn in 1938 and rumors circulated that Jewish retailers intended to dismiss large numbers of cash-strapped American workers and replace them with refugees. No one denied these rumors as loudly as the President of Bloomingdale's, Michael Schapp, who publicly testified that he had only hired eleven "possible" Jewish refugees. Schwartz was one of those eleven ("Stores Here Deny Refugee Rumor"; Wyman 6). "I am convinced," wrote a grateful friend of Schwartz in a letter to Kirstein, "that no one but yourself, through your friends in the diplomatic service could have accomplished this" (Marss, Letter to Kirstein). That was probably true, and Schwartz was not the only AMC employee who benefitted from Kirstein's friends in the State Department.

Although Schwartz's case was an outlier among those that crossed Kirstein's desk, archival records indicate that the AMC transferred at least three other Jewish employees from the offices in Berlin and Vienna to AMC member stores and affiliates in the United States and England.[38] Messersmith intervened in at least one of these cases, on behalf of Eva Lustig who had worked for thirteen years as a guide for American retail buyers visiting the German markets. In 1935 AMC executives had managed to create a position for Lustig's brother at the firm's headquarters in New York. When Kirstein began to "take steps" on Lustig's behalf, he wrote to Messersmith, who assured him that the case would receive "very careful and sympathetic attention." From his post in Washington, Messersmith wrote to the consul general in Berlin with a request to expedite Lustig's application. Although the consul general quickly agreed to Messersmith's request, when he looked further into the case he found that Lustig had never completed a proper visa application, even though she had supplied all the supporting materials. The consul general wrote directly to Kirstein to explain that, without an application, he could do nothing for Lustig. Streicher, however, stepped in not only to help Lustig secure a temporary travel visa to England, but also to connect her personally to retailers in London. By mid-1939 Lustig was on her way to England with a scheduled interview at the London trade office of an AMC-affiliated department store based in Australia, Myer's Emporium.[39]

Kirstein also reached out to Messersmith in April 1938 on behalf of a dear friend of his, Julius Marx of Vienna. For years the AMC Vienna office had contracted with Marx, who owned a large shoe factory just outside the city. In the mid-1930s Kirstein and Marx had taken several trips together to the spas in Bad Gastein, Austria, where Kirstein had often encouraged Marx to leave the region—but he refused. Several weeks after the *Anschluss*, however, Marx departed to a sanatorium in Zurich, from which he cabled Kirstein that he would "not return anymore to Vienna." Marx requested Kirstein's help getting to the United States, at least for a few weeks, to determine what he might do next. Kirstein immediately appealed to Messersmith on Marx's behalf. As was characteristic of Messersmith's replies, the assistant secretary of state cautioned Kirstein that he had no direct authority over the decisions of consular officials. Regardless, Messersmith sent a personal telegram to the consul general in Zurich attesting to Marx's character and urging the quick issue of a U.S. travel visa. Despite the fact that Marx had not yet submitted a visa application, the consul general immediately issued a visa for him upon receipt of Messersmith's telegram. Less than two weeks later, Marx was on a steamship bound for the United States (correspondence and telegrams in "G-A Refugees, J Marx"). After consulting with Kirstein in Boston, Marx determined to apply for American citizenship and hired a lawyer in Zurich to obtain the appropriate documents for him in Vienna, including a birth certificate. Tragically, after spending several days in pursuit of the birth certificate, Marx's lawyer informed him that the document could not be secured. Moreover, the lawyer advised Marx against pursuing the case any further for fear of reprisals from Nazi authorities against friends and relatives still living in the Third Reich. Doubtful of his prospects for securing American citizenship, Marx departed for Tel Aviv with a personal introduction from Kirstein to a chancellor at Hebrew University who would help him get settled. In December 1938, Kirstein wrote to Marx reflecting on the year's events: "A halt must be called sooner or later," Kirstein surmised, "or all civilization will be destroyed."[40]

In order to help his family members escape Germany and Austria, Kirstein relied not only on Messersmith's interventions but also on the managers at the AMC foreign offices across Europe, especially Streicher. When the violence subsided following the two days of terror in November 1938 known as *Kristallnacht*, or the Night of the Broken Glass, Streicher trekked past the shattered windows of the capital city to visit the families he had supported for years with the monthly allowances from Kirstein. While Streicher found all the women and their children shaken but uninjured, he learned that at least two men, including Dr. Heymann, had been taken under "protective arrest," and no one had seen or heard from them. Nor, at least as far as archival records indicate, would they ever see or hear from them again. After *Kristallnacht*, Streicher dared not communicate important details about the Kirstein relations by mail or telegram to the United States. Instead, he increasingly relied on the manager of the AMC Paris office to relay messages to Kirstein or merely included vague references to visiting the family and finding them well.[41] While several of Kirstein's relations had filed applications for US or British travel visas before *Kristallnacht* and Streicher continued to follow up personally on these applications, some were reluctant to leave their homes. Rosi Bohm, for example, had lost her husband to illness and did not want to leave his possessions and memories behind (Streicher, Letter to Kirstein, 2 June 1937). In stark contrast to Bohm, another relation of Kirstein, a young man named Fritz Levi living in Vienna, fled the Third Reich on foot without so much as a hat or a coat. Remarkably, Léon of the AMC Paris office tracked down Levi in Bordeaux weeks later and supplied him with clothing and money from Kirstein's funds. He also helped the young Levi and his parents, still in Vienna, begin the visa application process from consulates in France and the former Austria.[42]

Between 1938 and 1940, Kirstein intervened in ways both large and small on behalf of refugees whom he knew personally or who were connected to friends or fellow retailers. With the help of another personal note from Messersmith, Kirstein aided the emigration of Dr. Heymann's wife, mother-in-law, and two daughters, who settled permanently in Los Angeles (see correspondence and memos in "Heymann"). And with the help of Streicher, his staff in Vienna, and Léon in Paris, Kirstein also located and passed along information to friends in Boston eager to learn about the circumstances of relations with whom they had lost touch. In one case, Streicher sent a trusted merchandise buyer out to interview a cousin of Dr. Paul Sachs of Harvard University and relayed news that the family's photography business in Vienna had been placed under the control of a Nazi commissar and that the patriarch was facing trial for misusing his passport. For Sachs, the information was vital and enabled him to begin the work of passing financial and legal aid on to his cousin (see correspondence and memos in "Sachs/Schostal"). Kirstein also found a position at the AMC headquarters in New York City for the last employee classified as a "non-Aryan" still working at one of Berlin's most successful Jewish-owned department stores, Wertheim's (see correspondence and memos in "Weigart/ Wertheim"). Kirstein helped, if he could, in smaller, but meaningful ways on behalf of refugees who arrived in Boston, as in the case of a skilled leather glove maker whom he personally introduced to a Filene's glove buyer (Bergas, Letter to Kirstein; Kirstein, Letter to Dr. Blumgart; Dr. Blumgart, Letter to Kirstein). After 1940, however, it became much harder to for Kirstein to intervene personally in cases that involved emigration from Germany.

In 1941 widespread fears about the presence of fifth columnists among the ranks of refugees entering the United States prompted the State Department to pass more restrictive guidelines for visa approvals. At the age of seventy-three, Kirstein was deemed too old to sign affidavits to sponsor immigrant visas (Wyman 191–205). In the midst of these policy changes, Ilse Sternberg, whom Kirstein had supported financially through the AMC office in Berlin for more than a decade, decided at last that she was ready to leave her home in Germany. "We still love our Fatherland," she wrote to Kirstein, "but we want to live and see what the future has in store for us." Sternberg specifically requested a temporary pass that would allow her to return to Germany "at will." Kirstein again appealed to Messersmith who had by then left Washington to serve as the US Ambassador to Cuba in Havana. Although Sternberg's case was too complicated, and the backup at the US consuls in Germany too overwhelming, to arrange a US visa, Messersmith used his influence to secure permits for Sternberg to travel to Cuba—but it was too late. Germany's borders closed to emigration before Sternberg could secure passage aboard a steamship. Thirty-five years later, in 1974, Dr. Heymann's daughter, who became a US citizen, filed a report with the Council of Post-War Jewish Organizations in her adopted hometown of Los Angeles. According to Ms. Heymann's report, Sternberg was deported to an unknown concentration camp sometime in 1942, shortly after the German borders closed.[43]

When Germany declared war on the United States in December 1941, the AMC cut all ties with its trade office in Berlin, the last point of access Kirstein had into the Third Reich. AMC executives had voted to close the Vienna office in early 1939, and one year later the Paris office was disbanded, following the German invasion of France. Although the AMC managed to bring Léon from the Paris office to the United States in 1941, all contact with Streicher, who became an enemy alien almost overnight, was lost.[44] Messersmith's ascent in the Foreign Service took him further and further from the European theater after 1940, and he spent the rest of his career in Central and South America. Kirstein continued to advocate for refugees by contributing substantial funds and leadership to major Jewish organizations immersed in addressing the refugee crisis. In 1942 Kirstein's health began to fail and, at the age of seventy-five, he succumbed to pneumonia. In a tribute published in the *Boston Globe,* Kirstein's longtime friend Supreme Court Justice Felix Frankfurter remarked that with his passing "a deep well of rare goodness has suddenly dried" ("Louis Kirstein Dead"). It was a fact well known to many who knew Kirstein, and especially to those whom he tried to shield from the terror of the Third Reich.

CONCLUSION: BEYOND LOUIS KIRSTEIN

Within the AMC network, Kirstein's spirit and commitment to aiding refugees transcended his passing in 1942, in part through the work of Ira Hirschmann. It was Kirstein, after all, who had brought Hirschmann into the fold of the AMC during the summer of 1938. The son of A. B. Hirschmann, a Latvian Jewish immigrant and a prosperous merchant and banker in Baltimore, Hirschmann had first met Kirstein when he was an ambitious young executive at Bamberger's (then an AMC member store that was later bought by R.H. Macy's) (Hirschmann, *Caution to the Winds* 8). He went on to spend most of the 1930s as an executive at stores outside the AMC network, namely Lord & Taylor and Saks. Over the course of that decade, Hirschmann became a vocal proponent of the anti-Nazi boycotts, helped plan a national retail campaign in response to the depression, and began making annual trips to work at the European offices of Lord & Taylor and Saks.[45] Hirschmann also became involved with the establishment of the University in Exile, which brought dozens of scholar refugees and their families to safety in the United States, and contributed to a widely respected volume, *Nazism: An Assault on Civilization,* in which his writing appeared alongside essays by Dorothy Thompson, Senator Robert F. Wagner, and rabbi Stephen Wise.[46] When Kirstein met Hirschmann again in Paris in 1938, the latter was no longer a brash, young publicity manager—his reputation as a leading retailer and active opponent of Nazism were well known.

The chance encounter between the two retailers occurred shortly after the *Anschluss* during one of Hirschmann's annual trips to Saks' Paris office. In his memoir Hirschmann describes their conversation as focused almost entirely on the troubles facing Bloomingdale's, an AMC member store that Kirstein believed was not living up to its potential.[47] As Hirschmann remembered it, Kirstein offered him a new position as director of advertising and publicity at Bloomingdale's before they left Paris. Indeed, Hirschmann's abrupt resignation seemed to surprise the president of Saks, who had not yet chosen a replacement by the time reporters caught wind of the news ("Hirschmann resigns from Saks Fifth Avenue"; "Store Official Resigns"). A few weeks later, Hirschmann became a vice president at Bloomingdale's and began working under the supervision of Michael Schaap, the same executive who found a position for Kurt Schwartz after Kirstein facilitated his release from a Nazi prison in Vienna ("Hirschmann Bloomingdale Ad").

It is hard to imagine that Kirstin and Hirschmann did not discuss the growing refugee crisis when they met in Paris in 1938. After all, part of Kirstein's purpose in Paris was to work with Hanns Streicher on a plan to close the AMC's Vienna trade office. Before arriving in Paris, Hirschmann had spent time at the Vienna consulate where he worked furiously to help as many Jews as he could leave the city. Though the two retail leaders had disagreed on how to approach the anti-Nazi boycott, they shared a commitment to aiding refugees.[48] During their short time together as AMC executives, Kirstein created a number of opportunities for Hirschmann to travel abroad to meet with consular officials and to make connections in Washington, DC. In 1942, for example, Kirstein helped Hirschmann receive an appointment to serve as special investigator to the newly formed National War Labor Board. While in Washington, Hirschmann made and strengthened many relationships with State Department officials who would later help support his path to the War Refugee Board. In an interview he gave decades later, Hirschmann recalled that when he was first denied the opportunity to work as a special envoy helping refugees, he began contacting his "friends in the administration around Roosevelt" and "started pushing" (Ira Hisrchmann interview in Medoff 85). One of Hirschmann's most important "friends" in Washington was, in fact, a dear and longtime friend of Kirstein's, Felix Frankfurter.[49]

Hirschmann's work as the first special attaché to the War Refugee Board in 1944 would be impressive if he were a career diplomat; that he was not is one of reasons why at least one historian has labeled his efforts "superhuman" (Diner, *We Remember* 297). During his two missions to Ankara, Hirschmann negotiated a series of agreements that brought nearly 7,000 Jews out of danger in the Balkans, through Turkey, and on to safety in Palestine. In March 1944, he also helped implement safeguards for Jews still living in Bulgaria and Romania, and he played a critical role in the infamous Joel Brand affair, one of the Nazis' desperate attempts to trade the release of one million Jews for ten thousand Allied trucks.[50] His most impressive achievement, though, came through his negotiations with a Romanian Minister in 1944, which ensured the release and protection of 48,000 Jews imprisoned in concentration camps in that country. In every published recollection of his tireless efforts to convince State Department officials that they should allow him to serve as a special envoy for refugees in Ankara, Hirschmann recalls his best argument: "Sometimes a non-professional in a new situation may be able to pry open a window or a door which others have found hopelessly barred" (Hirschmann, *Caution to the Winds* 130–32; Hirschmann, *Life Line To A Promised Land* 16–18; also Long, Letter to Hirschmann).

Though several studies have covered Ira Hirschmann's refugee work in extensive detail, his status as a retailer has only merited passing mention and a handful of amusing anecdotes.[51] However, as this study has shown, for Kirstein, Hirschmann, and others, retailing provided privileged access to trade centers in Europe and connections to a great many influential people in Washington and well beyond. Far from incidental to their interventions in the refugee crisis, for many retailers the industry itself provided a critical platform for developing the connections and opportunities that made their efforts possible. That was especially true for executives in the AMC stores network, the most influential retailing organization in the country. And it cannot be forgotten that the retail industry at large, and the AMC in particular, was so shaken by Nazism in part because so many retailers themselves were Jewish with extensive familial, social, and professional ties to Jews living in Germany and Austria. For all of these reasons, the retail industry was an important hub of opposition to Nazism and aid for refugees between 1933 and 1945. Just as Hirschmann imagined, some American retailers did "pry open doors and windows" where others could not and, for a great many people, that made all the difference.

Notes

1. The author would like to thank Hasia Diner for her encouragement and the invitation to contribute to this volume. For their invaluable guidance in developing this project at Boston University I would also like to thank Brooke Blower, Marilyn Halter, Casey Riley, and Bruce Schulman.

2. The details of Schwartz's case are taken from dozens of letters and telegrams included in "Schwartz"; Streicher, Letter to Reilly, 30 May 1938; Streicher, Letter to Reilly, 3 June 1938.

3. Although Streicher refers to Schwartz as a German citizen in his letters, the Nazi Party stripped Schwartz of his citizenship with the enactment of the Nuremberg Laws in September 1935.

4. For a concise overview of Austria in the weeks following the *Anschluss*, see Beller 231–36; articles in the *Jewish Telegraphic Agency* and the *New York Times* offer a more detailed picture of Vienna after the *Anschluss*. I have cited a sample here: "30,000 Sought US Visas in Vienna in Two Weeks"; "Goering's Warning Sends Thousands to US, British Consulates in Rush for Visas"; "Hundreds Seek Visas to Quit Austria";"Hitler Proclaims Austria's Inclusion in Reich; Jews Lose Citizenship"; "500 Jews Seized in Austria As Nazi Purge Enters Third Day, Shops Looted, Wrecked"; "Suicides Mount, Austrian Jews Besiege Consulates as Terrorism, Sacking of Shops Rises"; "Vienna Jews Don Top Hats, War Medals to Clean Streets"; "Jewish Suicides in Austria Put at 2,000, Arrests 12,000 Since Anschluss"; "Organized Nazi Terrorism Goes On Secretly in Vienna"; "Goering Is Acclaimed in Vienna; Warns Jews Must Quit Austria."

5. With unemployment on the rise in 1930, the Hoover Administration sought to curb immigration by urging consuls abroad to deny visas to anyone who might become a public charge in the United States (this was a reinterpretation of the "Likely to Become a Public Charge" or LPC clause in the Immigration Act of 1917). Thereafter visa applicants were required to provide affidavits demonstrating that friends or relatives in the United States could provide for them in the event that they could not find work. Although the Roosevelt administration abandoned this policy following the *Anschluss*, the Visa Division failed to establish a new policy, leaving individual consuls to develop idiosyncratic and often unreasonable demands of refugees. See Wyman 4–5, 155–58.

6. During Schwartz's imprisonment there was no explanation given for his arrest. Later, when Schwartz was safely out of prison, Hanns Streicher sent a letter to Louis Kirstein to explain that these were the reasons for the arrest. See Streicher, Letter to Kirstein, 3 June 1938. For details regarding taxes and regulations imposed on Jewish-owned properties throughout the Reich in April 1938 see Wyman 6, 29.

7. Wyman estimates that perhaps thirty thousand Jews left Austria and Germany for the United States in 1938. See Wyman 37.

8. For less critical treatment of the response from leading American Jewish organizations and people, see Feingold, *Bearing Witness* 205–24; and Diner, *Jews of the United States* 210–17. For more critical treatment of the response from American Jews and government officials, see Morse; Wyman; Feingold, *The Politics of Rescue*; and Stuart. On anti-Semitism and the political climate in the United States during the 1930s–1940s, see Dinnerstein 105-127; Moore 78-86; Baldwin; Brinley; Blower; also see Wyman.

9. Hirschmann's work on the War Refugee Board appears in several scholarly studies, see Erbelding; King; Medoff; Breitman and Kraut 143; Favez 111. For his work as special envoy to the United Nations Relief and Rehabilitation Administration after the war, Hirschmann appears in: Diner, *We Remember* 150, 296. Hirschmann also wrote two books that touch on his experience on the WRB, see Hirschmann, *Caution to the Winds*; Hirschmann, *Life Line to A Promised Land*.

10. Although some of the stores in the AMC network publicly broke ties with Berlin following the rise of anti-Nazi boycotts, the work of the AMC Berlin trade office continued to source goods from throughout the region and sell them in regions of the United States where anti-Nazi sentiment was weak and to other countries. For a detailed account of how the AMC and other American department stores responded to the boycott, see Lefebvre.

11. The following stores were AMC members in 1939: Abraham & Straus of Brooklyn, L.S. Ayres & Company of Indianapolis, Bloomingdale's Inc. of New York, The Boston Store of Milwaukee, Bullock's of Los Angeles, Burdine's of Miami, The H.C. Capwell Company of Oakland, The Dayton Company of Minneapolis, The Emporium of San Francisco, William Filene's Sons Company of Boston, B. Forman Company of Rochester, Joseph Horne Company of Pittsburgh, The J. L. Hudson Company of Detroit, Hutzler Brothers of Baltimore, The F. & R. Lazarus & Co. of Columbus, The Rike-Kumler Company of Dayton, The John Shillito Company of Cincinnati, Stix, Baer & Fuller Company of St. Louis, Strawbridge & Clothier of Philadelphia, The William Taylor Son & Co. of Cleveland, Thalimer Brothers, Inc. of Richmond, R. H. White Company of Boston. All information on the formation of the AMC is gleaned from letters in Louis Kirstein's personal papers, and especially from Retail Research Association, *Story of the Retail Research Association*; Reilly, Letter to Kirstein.

12. Kirstein and Hirschmann disagreed over the anti-Nazi boycotts; the former was a vocal advocate and the latter was ideologically opposed. See Lefebvre 156–217.

13. Interestingly an AMC real estate report notes that in 1933 Lindenstrasse was also riddled with empty and deteriorated storefronts. The swastika flags would have obscured these symptoms of a depressed economy. See "Translation of Survey"; for a description of the Lindenstrasse district, see "Toys Largest Item Bought in German Market."

14. In his response to Streicher's letter, Kirstein wrote: "I think you showed a good deal of courage and certainly did the right thing in refusing as an American concern, to

display the swastika flag." See Kirstein, Letter to Streicher, 26 Oct. 1933; Streicher, Letter to Kirstein, 10 Oct 1933.

15. The details on Kirstein's life in this paragraph are taken from: Duberman; Berkley; Harris; Selekman; Arkin, and other tributes in "Death of Louis Kirstein." For more details on Kirstein's political appointments, see the Introduction and Chapter Two.

16. In many memorials published at Louis Kirstein's death, his equal devotion to being a patriotic American and an exemplary Jew is a constant theme. In his tribute, Benjamin Selekman reflected on witnessing the life of Kirstein: "There moves—every inch of him—an American and a Jew." See Selekman 36.

17. See Chapter Three for an early history of the Berlin Office. See Chapter Four for a discussion of the German trade, economic nationalism, and the depression.

18. Streicher, Letter to Kirstein, 10 Oct. 1933. Also, see Streicher's reference to Messersmith who "has been most helpful to me on many occasions," in: Streicher, Letter to Kirstein 16 Feb. 1934.

19. These recommendations to enter the consular service came despite the fact that Messersmith fared well enough on the Foreign Service exams to earn an appointment in 1914. See Stiller 6–7.

20. Refugees were granted a single exemption from the literacy test required for entrance to the United States, but this provided little benefit to German refugees who were reportedly 99% literate. See Ami-Zucker 157. For a sampling of historical accounts of George S. Messersmith, see Moss; Shafir; Ami-Zucker.

21. Restrictionist attitudes were so dominant that in 1931 the Senate would have passed, by a large majority, a bill to introduce ninety percent reductions in all the immigration quotas set in the National Origins Immigration Act of 1924. Fortunately, the legislative session ended before the vote could take place. See Wyman 4. See also Ami-Zucker.

22. Messersmith was also an advisor to Streicher as the AMC expanded its business in Vienna between 1935–1937. See Streicher, Letter to Reilly, 14 Nov. 1935.

23. Billikopf was President of the National Conference on Jewish Social Service. See Kirstein, Letter to Steyne, 23 Jan. 1934; "Future Held Dark for Exiled Jews." Also note that the two crossed paths before this, see Messersmith's recollections of Kirstein as "playing a major role" in the meeting of the International Chamber of Commerce in "Meetings of the International Chamber of Commerce in Europe." Also note that Kirstein's fellow executive at Filene's, Edward Filene, was a planner and co-organizer of the International Chamber of Commerce beginning in the late 1920s. See de Grazia 130–86.

24. With the exception of Wagner, all of Kirstein's introductions connected Messersmith with influential American Jews. It should be noted, however, that Wagner became one of the foremost advocates of refugees in Congress and collaborated on the Wagner-Rogers Bill to welcome twenty thousand Jewish children suffering in the Third Reich to the United States in 1938. The bill failed to pass. For the details

of these early meetings between Kirstein and Messersmith, see Kirstein, Letters to Steyne, 15 & 29 Dec. 1933, 23 Jan., 10 April 1934.

25. Shortly after Hitler came into power he passed series of decrees that cut Jews off from medical practice, which, in turn, made it difficult for Jews to secure medical care. Additionally, new tax regulations made it nearly impossible for Jews to take any capital out of Germany. Even if the Bohms had the money to pay for the treatments, Streicher noted, it would be impossible for them to leave the country with it. See Wyman 28; Streicher, Letter to Kirstein, 3 Oct. 1934.

26. Archival records indicate that Kirstein began transferring funds to a niece in Germany via Filene's for the first time in 1925. However, a brief survey of correspondence between Streicher and Kirstein reveals that they began transferring monthly allowances to a number of additional family members in 1933. See Secretary to Louis E. Kirstein, Letter to American Express Company; Ilse Sternberg Receipt. Also browse "Streicher Berlin" in Box 81 and the family files in Box 8, Louis Kirstein Papers, Baker Business Library, Harvard University.

27. Kirstein's involvement in and financial commitments to public relief operations are legion. They include the American Jewish Committee, Associated Jewish Philanthropies of Boston, the United Jewish Appeal, the Joint Distribution Committee, the Jewish Welfare Board, and the National Refugee Service, among others. See "National Refugee Service Launches Its First Drive for Funds"; Selekman; "Louis E. Kirstein Dies at 75"; Arkin.

28. Curiously the finding aid for Kirstein's papers gives this archival box a simple title, "Property," and lists only a few words in the description: "Beach Bluff, 1921, 1 envelope." Beach Bluff was the name of a property in Beverly, Massachusetts that Kirstein rented for several summers. While the box contains a small folder with several documents pertaining to Beach Bluff, there are also hundreds of documents tucked inside folders organized either by last names of refugees or, more generally as "G-A Refugees" or "G Financial." More documentation of Kirstein's efforts is sprinkled throughout files pertaining to Hanns Streicher, George Messersmith, Alan Steyne, and the AMC offices in Berlin and Vienna. See Boxes 8, 28, 54, 80, 81, 82, Louis Kirstein Papers, Baker Business Library, Harvard University. The Nazi government closed the German borders to emigration at the end of 1941. See Wyman 191–205.

29. See N 5 for a brief explanation of the affidavit requirement. Also see Ami-Zucker 154–56; Wyman 4–5, 155–58.

30. That figure includes the applications for the Baer nephews described on pp. ??, as well as Thea Marsi, an influential Viennese designer who contracted with the AMC (and whose brother was Streicher's second in command at the AMC's office in Vienna). See Streicher, Letter to Kirstein, 30 Dec 1935.

31. Kirstein often referenced confidential conversations with Messersmith in his letters to Alan Steyne, see Kirstein, Letter to Steyne, 15 Oct. 1938.

32. It is worth noting here that AMC foreign office managers worked regularly with consular officials to keep up to date with international trade policies, tax regulations, and currency exchanges among other things. However, high-ranking consular officials also relied on AMC managers to purchase gifts from local markets on their behalf and probably for additional insight into trade conditions. It is not hard to imagine all that a US diplomat might learn, for example, from the local managers of an American trade office that maintained contracts with dozens of manufacturers distributed throughout the region. And while it is unclear whether Messersmith used the AMC to purchase merchandise in Berlin, his predecessor in Vienna, Minister to Austria, George Howard Earl, did use the AMC. When Messersmith moved to Vienna, he, too, kept up with Streicher's second in command, Hanns Marss, who was permanently stationed at the AMC office there. See Streicher, Letter to Kirstein, 16 Feb. 1934; Messersmith, Letter to Kirstein18 Sept. 1934.

33. All details related to Schwartz's case in this and the following paragraph are taken from dozens of letters and telegrams included in "Schwartz," Box 81; and in Streicher, Letter to Reilly, 30 May 1938.

34. At the time, Charles Hutzler was on a tour of the foreign offices of the AMC. His brother, Albert, was then serving on the AMC's Board of Directors and Foreign Office Committee along with Louis Kirstein. See Reilly, *Story of the Retail Research Association*.

35. The official who responded in Paris was Carmel Offie. He was friendly with Louis Kirstein not only because Kirstein was personally acquainted (through Messersmith) with the Ambassador, but also because Offie was friendly with Kirstein's son, the prominent writer and artist, Lincoln Kirstein. For an example of friendly correspondence between Offie and Kirstein see Kirstein, Letter to Offie. For more information about Lincoln Kirstein, as well as some detailed biographical information about Louis Kirstein, see Duberman. For more about Offie, see Wilford 58–67.

36. Of interest to the larger study is the fact that Schwartz passed through Brussels on his way to the United States and spent time advising AMC buyers there on how to connect with Jewish manufacturers in Austria. See Léon, Letter to Kirstein, 7 Aug 1936. John C. Wiley was also personally acquainted with Kirstein, and a good friend of his nephew, Alan N. Steyne, who was then working in the American consular office in London. See Kirstein, Letter to Chiger. Also see Streicher, Letter to Reilly, 3 June 1938.

37. Michael Schaap, President of Bloomingdale's had been working to raise funds for the relocation of German Jews since 1934, and probably welcomed Schwartz with open arms. Moreover, Schaap and Kirstein were deeply connected in ways both professional and social. The two executives had enjoyed traveling through Europe together to visit the AMC foreign offices in 1934, and Schaap had happily employed

Kirstein's son George ever since. Kirstein also served on two executive boards that oversaw the business of Bloomingdale's: Federated Department Stores, Inc. and the AMC. Bloomingdale's was acquired by Federated Department Stores, Inc. in 1929 and joined the AMC in 1930. Kirstein joined the Board of Directors for the Federated Department Stores, Inc. in 1938. See "Federated Directors Re-elected"; *This is Federated* Stores, *Inc.* 1; Retail Research Association, *Story of the Retail Research Association* 2. On Michael Schaap: "M. Schaap to Head Businessmen's Body for Palestine Drive"; "Jewish Appeal Pays Tribute to Schaap"; "Schaap and Kirstein Sail Abroad, July 4."

38. In addition, the AMC created a position for a German Jewish executive at Wertheim's in Berlin at the personal request of the German retail magnate, Georg Wertheim. See "Weigart"; also see Streicher, Letters to Kirstein, 16 July & 2 Aug 1938. Also see "Former AMC Accountant Here."

39. I have yet to find any documents pertaining to Lustig's case after her departure for England. For details on Lustig's case, see "G-A Refugees AMC Lustig."

40. For details on Marx's case, see correspondence and telegrams in "Julius Marx"; also see Messersmith, Letter to Kirstein, 11 May 1938; Kirstein, Letter to Steyne, 27 April 1938.

41. William S. Sleap, manager of the AMC office in London remained in regular touch with both Kirstein and the London consulate to help relations and friends who preferred to go to England.

42. In all the correspondence Kirstein saved detailing the rescue and relief of his relations, I have not found any references to Dr. Heymann dated later than November 1938. Also see Miss Beverly, Letter to Mannheimer; Mannheimer, Letter to Miss Beverly; Léon, Letter to Kirstein, 16 Nov. 1938.

43. For details re: Ilse Sternberg's case, see references in "Hanns Streicher, 1938-42", but especially "Sternberg". Also see Ilse Sternberg Record; Wyman 191–205.

44. Hanns Streicher and his wife moved back to Austria and survived the war. Streicher returned to work for the AMC in 1947 and remained a manager of trade in Central Europe until he retired in 1964. See "Vienna Office is Reopened by the AMC"; "AMC Names Two Managers Abroad"; "Leon, Paris AMC Head Due June 1."

45. Hirschmann played a leading role in the planning of a national retail campaign to drive up retail sales during the worst years of the Great Depression. The purpose of the National Quality Movement, which had earned the endorsement of President Herbert Hoover in December 1932, was to convince shoppers that buying higher quality, higher priced merchandise offered better overall savings than buying only bargain basement goods at slashed prices. Hirschmann had begun speaking widely on this subject in 1932, see "'We Are Trading America Down'"; "Quality Campaign Gaining Headway"; "Hoover Endorses Quality Campaign"; "End of Shoddy Era Seen by Merchant." For more on Hirschmann's role in the anti-Nazi boycotts, see Lefebvre 156–217.

46. For a more detailed account of Hirschmann's work during the 1930s, see Lefebvre 217–79. Also see Van Paassen and Wise.

47. In addition to his executive role in the AMC, Kirstein was also on the board of directors for Bloomingdale's. Hirschmann describes his encounter with Kirstein in some detail in *Caution to the Winds* (107–08).

48. Among retailers, Hirschmann was the most outspoken advocate of the anti-Nazi boycott movement, but Kirstein was ideologically opposed. For details on retailers' positions relative to the anti-Nazi boycott movement, see Lefebvre 156–217.

49. For details on the relationship between Hirschmann and Kirstein, see Lefebvre 217–79.

50. In April 1944, Adolf Eichmann, one of the principal architects of the Holocaust offered Brand, a young Hungarian Jewish activist, a grotesque deal. Eichmann would release one million Jews if Brand could convince Allied leaders to give Germany ten thousand trucks and other needed supplies. After the British Foreign Office and the Colonial Office in Cairo detained Brand, the WRB sent Hirschmann to conduct preliminary interviews as a test of Brand's honesty. See Hirschmann, Report. See Breitman and Kraut 214–16.

51. See N 9 for a list of significant literature in which Ira Hirschmann plays a role. Charles King makes the most of Hirschmann's background as a retailer, but mostly to add levity to his text, referring to Hirschmann as a "Bloomie's exec" 324–29.

Works Cited

"500 Jews Seized in Austria As Nazi Purge Enters Third Day, Shops Looted, Wrecked." *Jewish Telegraphic Agency*, 17 Mar. 1938.

"30,000 Sought US Visas in Vienna in Two Weeks." *Jewish Telegraphic Agency*, 7 April 1938.

"AMC Names Two Managers Abroad." *Women's Wear Daily*, 27 July 1964, p. 3.

"AMC Story." Louis Kirstein Papers, Box 82, Baker Business Library, Harvard University.

Ami-Zucker, Bat. "American Refugee Policy in the 1930s." *Refugees from Nazi Germany and the Liberal European States*, edited by Frank Caestecker and Bob Moore, Berghahn Books, 2010, pp. 151–68.

Arkin, Leon. "The Most Prominent Jew in Boston in Now 75 Years Old." Louis Kirstein Papers, "Death of Louis Kirstein," Box 6, Baker Business Library, Harvard University.

Baldwin, Neil. *Henry Ford and the Jews: The Mass Production of Hate*. Public Affairs, 2001.

Beller, Steven. *A Concise History of Austria*. Cambridge Univ., 2006.

Bergas, Lottie. Letter to Louis Edward Kirstein. 8 Feb. 1939. Louis Kirstein Papers, "G-A Refugees, Miscellaneous," Box 8, Baker Business Library, Harvard University.

Berkley, George E. *The Filenes*. International Pocket Library, 1998.

Miss Beverly. Letter to Julia Mannheimer. 3 Dec. 1938. Louis Kirstein Papers, "G-A Refugees Miscellaneous," Box 8, Baker Business Library, Harvard University.

Blower, Brooke. "From Isolationism to Neutrality: A New Framework for Understanding American Political Culture." *Diplomatic History*, vol. 38, 2014, pp. 345–76.

Dr. Blumgart. Letter to Louis Edward Kirstein. 8 Feb. 1939. Louis Kirstein Papers, "G-A Refugees, Miscellaneous," Box 8, Baker Business Library, Harvard University.

Breitman, Richard, and Alan M. Kraut. *American Refugee Policy and European Jewry, 1933–1945*. Indiana Univ., 1987.

Brinley, Alan. *Voices of Protest: Huey Long, Father Coughlin, and the Great Depression*. Knopf, 1982.

Day, Roger. Letter to Louis Edward Kirstein. 26 April 1932. Louis Kirstein Papers, "Day, 1925–37," Box 80, Baker Business Library, Harvard University.

Diner, Hasia R. *Jews of the United States, 1654–2000*. Univ. of California, 2004.

———. *We Remember with Reverence and Love: American Jews and the Myth of Silence after the Holocaust, 1945–1962*. New York Univ., 2009.

Dinnerstein, Leonard. *Antisemitism in America*. New York: Oxford Univ., 1994.

Documents in Louis Kirstein Papers, "Vienna Office Grab Death." Box 82, Baker Business Library, Harvard University.

"Dodd to See Hitler Today on Assaults." Special to *New York Times*, 13 Oct. 1933, p. 15.

Duberman, Martin. *The Worlds of Lincoln Kirstein*. Knopf, 2007.

"End of Shoddy Era Seen by Merchant." *New York Times*, 21 June 1933, p. 33.

Erbelding, Rebecca L. "About Time: The History of the War Refugee Board." Dissertation, George Mason University, 2015.

"Establishment of Vienna Office." Louis Kirstein Papers, Box 81, Baker Business Library, Harvard University.

Favez, Jean-Claude. *The Red Cross and the Holocaust.* Edited and translated by John and Beryl Fletcher, Cambridge Univ., 1988.

"Federated Directors Re-elected." *New York Times,* 26 May 1936, p. 34.

Feingold, Henry L. *Bearing Witness: How America and Its Jews Responded to the Holocaust.* Syracuse Univ., 1995.

————. *The Politics of Rescue: The Roosevelt Administration and the Holocaust, 1938–1945.* Rutgers Univ., 1970.

"Former AMC Accountant Here." *Women's Wear Daily,* 27 Oct. 1938, p. 22.

"Future Held Dark for Exiled Jews." *New York Times,* 19 Nov. 1932, p. N6.

"G-A Refugees AMC Lustig." Louis Kirstein Papers, Box 8, Baker Business Library, Harvard University.

"Goering Is Acclaimed in Vienna; Warns Jews Must Quit Austria." *New York Times,* 27 Mar. 1938, p. 1.

"Goering's Warning Sends Thousands to US, British Consulates in Rush for Visas." *Jewish Telegraphic Agency,* 29 Mar. 1938.

de Grazia, Victoria. *Irresistible Empire: America's Advance through Twentieth Century Europe.* Belknap, 2005.

"Hanns Streicher, 1938–42," Louis Kirstein Papers, Box 81, Baker Business Library, Harvard University.

Harris, Leon. *Merchant Princes: An Intimate History of Jewish Families Who Built Great Department Stores.* Kondansha USA, 1994.

Hirschmann, Ira. *Caution to the Winds.* Mckay, 1962.

————. *Life Line to a Promised Land.* Vanguard, 1946.

"Hirschmann Bloomingdale Ad, Sales Head." *Women's Wear Daily,* 2 Nov. 1938, p. 1.

Hirschmann, Report, Ankara. 11 Sept. 1944. Ira Hirschmann Papers, "Preliminary Reports Re: Activities in Turkey, June 18, 1944–September 11, 1944," Box 2, Franklin D. Roosevelt Library.

"Hirschmann Resigns from Saks Fifth Avenue." *Women's Wear Daily,* 29 Sept. 1938, p. 1.

"Hitler Proclaims Austria's Inclusion in Reich; Jews Lose Citizenship." *Jewish Telegraphic Agency,* 16 March 1938.

"Hoover Endorses Quality Campaign." *New York Times,* 18 Dec. 1932, p. N6.

"Hundreds Seek Visas to Quit Austria." *Jewish Telegraphic Agency,* 15 Mar. 1938.

Ilse Sternberg Receipt. 18 Mar. 1930. Louis Kirstein Papers, "Germany Financial," Box 8, Baker Business Library, Harvard University.

Ilse Sternberg Record. "The Central Database of Shoah Victims' Names." *Yad Veshem,* yvng.yadvashem.org/nameDetails.html?language=en&itemId=1428674&ind=0. Accessed 12 Sept. 2018.

"Jewish Appeal Pays Tribute to Schaap." *New York Times,* 11 May 1944, p. 10.

"Jewish Suicides in Austria Put at 2,000, Arrests 12,000 Since Anschluss." *Jewish Telegraphic Agency*, 28 April 1938.

"Julius Marx." Louis Kirstein Papers, Box 28, Baker Business Library, Harvard University.

King, Charles. *Midnight at the Pera Palace: The Birth of Modern Istanbul.* Norton, 2014.

Kirstein, Louis Edward. Letter to Dr. Blumgart. 7 Feb. 1939. Louis Kirstein Papers, "G-A Refugees, Miscellaneous," Box 8, Baker Business Library, Harvard University.

———. Letter to Lisolette Chiger. 14 April 1938. Louis Kirstein Papers, "G-A Refugees," Box 8, Baker Business Library, Harvard University.

———. Letter to Roger Day. 21 May 1938. Louis Kirstein Papers, "Day, 1925–37," Box 80, Baker Business Library, Harvard University.

———. Letter to George Messersmith. 11 Mar. 1939. Louis Kirstein Papers, "Messersmith, GM," Box 28, Baker Business Library, Harvard University.

———. Letter to Carmel Offie. 27 May 1938. Louis Kirstein Papers, "Schwartz," Box 81, Baker Business Library, Harvard University.

———. Letters to Alan N. Steyne. 15 & 29 Dec. 1933, 23 Jan., 10 April 1934. Louis Kirstein Papers, "Alan Steyne, 1932–42," Box 54, Baker Business Library, Harvard University.

———. Letter to Alan N. Steyne. 23 Jan. 1934. Louis Kirstein Papers, "Alan Steyne, 1932–42," Box 54, Baker Business Library, Harvard University.

———. Letter to Alan Steyne. 27 April 1938. Louis Kirstein Papers, "Alan Steyne," Box 54, Baker Business Library, Harvard University.

———. Letter to Alan N. Steyne. 15 Oct. 1938. Louis Kirstein Papers, "Alan Steyne, 1932–42" Box 54, Baker Business Library, Harvard University.

———. Letter to Hanns Streicher. 5 Mar. 1934. Louis Kirstein Papers, "Streicher Berlin," Box 81, Baker Business Library, Harvard University.

———. Letter to Hanns Streicher. 26 Oct. 1933. Louis Kirstein Papers, "Streicher Berlin," Box 81, Baker Business Library, Harvard University.

———. Letter to Hanns Streicher. 16 Oct. 1934. Louis Kirstein Papers, "Streicher Berlin," Box 81, Baker Business Library, Harvard University.

———. Letter to Hanns Streicher. 20 Aug. 1937. Louis Kirstein Papers, "Streicher Berlin," Box 81, Baker Business Library, Harvard University.

———. Personal Files. Louis Kirstein Papers, Box 5, Baker Business Library, Harvard University.

Lefebvre, Niki C. "Beyond the Flagship: Politics and Transatlantic Trade in American Department Stores, 1900–1945." Dissertation, Boston University, 2016.

Léon, Edouard. Letter to Louis Edward Kirstein. 7 Aug. 1936. Louis Kirstein Papers, "G-A Refugees, Gotts Chalk," Box 8, Baker Business Library, Harvard University.

———. Letter to Louis Edward Kirstein. 16 Nov. 1938. Louis Kirstein Papers, "G Financial," Box 8, Baker Business Library, Harvard University.

"Leon, Paris AMC Head Due June 1." *Women's Wear Daily*, 21 May 1941, p. 2.

Long, Breckinridge. Letter to Ira Hirschmann. 23 Dec. 1943. Ira Hirschmann Papers, "Identity Certificate and Travel Authorizations," Box 2, Franklin D. Roosevelt Library.

"Louis E. Kirstein Dies at 75." *Jewish Telegraphic Agency*, 11 Dec. 1942.

"Louis Kirstein Dead." *Boston Evening Globe*, 10 Dec. 1942. Louis Kirstein Papers, "Death of Louis Kirstein," Box 6, Baker Business Library, Harvard University.

"M. Schaap to Head Businessmen's Body for Palestine Drive." *Jewish Daily Bulletin*, Monday, 29 Jan. 1934, p. 2.

Mannheimer, Julia. Letter to Miss Beverly. 29 Nov. 1938. Louis Kirstein Papers, "G-A Refugees Miscellaneous," Box 8, Baker Business Library, Harvard University.

Marss, Hanns. Letter to Louis Edward Kirstein. 30 May 1938. Louis Kirstein Papers, "Schwartz," Box 81, Baker Business Library, Harvard University.

Medoff, Rafael. *Blowing the Whistle on Genocide: Josiah E. Dubois, Jr. and the Struggle for a U. S. Response to the Holocaust.* Purdue Univ., 2009.

"Meetings of the International Chamber of Commerce in Europe." George S. Messersmith Papers, MSS109 2030, University of Delaware Library.

Messersmith, George. Letter to Louis Edward Kirstein. 18 Sept. 1934. Louis Kirstein Papers, "Messersmith, GM," Box 28, Baker Business Library, Harvard University.

———. Letter to Louis Edward Kirstein. 4 Aug. 1936. Louis Kirstein Papers, "Messersmith, GM," Box 28, Baker Business Library, Harvard University.

———. Letters to Louis Edward Kirstein. 15 Sept. 1936. Louis Kirstein Papers, "Messersmith, GM," Box 28, Baker Business Library, Harvard University.

———. Letter to Louis Edward Kirstein. 1 July 1937. Louis Kirstein Papers, "Messersmith, GM," Box 28, Baker Business Library, Harvard University.

———. Letter to Louis Edward Kirstein. 11 May 1938. Louis Kirstein Papers, "Messersmith, GM," Box 28, Baker Business Library, Harvard University.

———. Letter to Louis Edward Kirstein. 8 Mar. 1939. Louis Kirstein Papers, "Messersmith, GM," Box 28, Baker Business Library, Harvard University.

———. Letter to Louis Edward Kirstein. 13 Mar. 1939. Louis Kirstein Papers, "Messersmith, GM," Box 28, Baker Business Library, Harvard University.

———. Letter to John C. Wiley. 16 Mar. 1938. George S. Messersmith Papers, "109 1004," University of Delaware Library.

Moore, Michaela Hoenicke. *Know Your Enemy: The American Debate on Nazism, 1933–1945.* Cambridge Univ., 2010.

Morse, Arthur D. *While Six Million Died: A Chronicle of American Apathy.* Random House, 1968.

Moss, Kenneth. "George S. Messersmith and Nazi Germany: The Diplomacy Limits in Central Europe." *U. S. Diplomats in Europe, 1919–1941*, edited by Kenneth Paul Jones, ABC-Clio, 1981.

"National Refugee Service Launches Its First Drive for Funds." *Jewish Telegraphic Agency*, 20 Jan. 1941.

"Organized Nazi Terrorism Goes On Secretly in Vienna." *New York Times*, 23 May 1938, p. 1.

"Quality Campaign Gaining Headway." *New York Times*, 23 Oct. 1932, p. F9.

Reilly, Philip J. Letter to Mr. Paul Fischer. 28 Nov. 1932. Louis Kirstein Papers, "Streicher Berlin," Box 81, Baker Business Library, Harvard University.

———. Letter to Louis Edward Kirstein. 27 Dec. 1939. Louis Kirstein Papers, "AMC Story," Box 82, Baker Business Library, Harvard University.

Retail Research Association. *Story of the Retail Research Association and the Associated Merchandising Corporation, 1916–1939*. Associated Merchandising, 1939.

"Sachs/Schostal." Louis Kirstein Papers, Box 8, Baker Business Library, Harvard University.

"Schaap and Kirstein Sail Abroad, July 4." *Women's Wear Daily*, 25 June 1934, p. 24.

"Schwartz." Louis Kirstein Papers, Box 81, Baker Business Library, Harvard University.

Secretary to Louis E. Kirstein. Letter to American Express Company. 28 Sept. 1925. Louis Kirstein Papers, "G Financial," Box 8, Baker Business Library, Harvard University.

Selekman, Benjamin M. "Louis Edward Kirstein." *American Jewish Yearbook*, vol. 35, 1943–44, pp. 35–46.

Shafir, Shlomo. "George S. Messersmith: An Anti-Nazi Diplomat's View of the German Jewish Crisis." *Jewish Social Studies*, vol. 35, 1973, pp. 32–41.

"Stern Nazi Orders Protect Americans." *New York Times*, 23 Oct. 1933, p. 1.

"Sternberg." Louis Kirstein Papers, Box 8, Baker Business Library, Harvard University.

Steyne, Alan N. Letter to Louis Edward Kirstein. 7 Sept. 1934. Louis Kirstein Papers, "Alan Steyne, 1932–42," Box 54, Baker Business Library, Harvard University.

Stiller, Jesse H. *George S. Messersmith: Diplomat of Democracy*. Univ. of North Carolina, 1987.

"Store Official Resigns: I. A. Hirschmann Leaves Post at Saks Fifth Avenue." *New York Times*, 30 Sept. 1938, p. 39.

"Stores Here Deny Refugee Rumor." *New York Times*, 26 Nov. 1938, p. 4.

Streicher, Hanns. Letter to Louis Edward Kirstein. 3 Aug. 1932. Louis Kirstein Papers, "Streicher Berlin," Box 81, Baker Business Library, Harvard University.

———. Letter to Louis Edward Kirstein. 10 Oct. 1933. Louis Kirstein Papers, "Streicher Berlin," Box 81, Baker Business Library, Harvard University.

———. Letter to Louis Edward Kirstein. 16 Feb. 1934. Louis Kirstein Papers, "Streicher Berlin," Box 81, Baker Business Library, Harvard University.

———. Letter to Louis Edward Kirstein. 3 Oct. 1934. Louis Kirstein Papers, "Streicher Berlin," Box 81, Baker Business Library, Harvard University.

———. Letter to Louis Edward Kirstein. 30 Dec. 1935. Louis Kirstein Papers, "Streicher Berlin," Box 81, Baker Business Library, Harvard University.

———. Letter to Louis Edward Kirstein. 2 June 1937. Louis Kirstein Papers, "Streicher Berlin," Box 81, Baker Business Library, Harvard University.

———. Letter to Louis Edward Kirstein. 1 July 1937. Louis Kirstein Papers, "Streicher Berlin," Box 81, Baker Business Library, Harvard University.

————. Letter to Louis E. Kirstein. 3 June 1938, Louis Kirstein Papers, "Streicher Berlin 1938–1942," Box 81, Baker Business Library, Harvard University.

————. Letter to Louis Edward Kirstein. 16 July 1938. Louis Kirstein Papers, "Streicher Berlin, 1938–42," Box 81, Baker Business Library, Harvard University.

————. Letter to Louis Edward Kirstein. 2 Aug. 1938. Louis Kirstein Papers, "Streicher Berlin, 1938–42," Box 81, Baker Business Library, Harvard University.

————. Letter to Phillip J. Reilly. 14 Nov. 1935. Louis Kirstein Papers, "Streicher Berlin," Box 81, Baker Business Library, Harvard University.

————. Letter to Phillip J. Reilly. 30 May 1938. Louis Kirstein Papers, "Hanns Streicher, Vienna," Box 82, Baker Business Library, Harvard University.

————. Letter to Phillip J. Reilly, 3 June 1938. Louis Kirstein Papers, "Streicher, 1938–42," Box 81, Baker Business Library, Harvard University.

Stuart, Barbara M. *United States Government Policy on Refugees from Nazism, 1933–1940.* Garland, 1984.

"Suicides Mount, Austrian Jews Besiege Consulates as Terrorism, Sacking of Shops Rises." *Jewish Telegraphic Agency*, 18 Mar. 1938.

This is Federated Stores, Inc. Federated Dept. Stores, 1977.

"Toys Largest Item Bought in German Market." *Women's Wear Daily*, 14 June 1921.

"Translation of Survey Given by Messrs. ISR Schmidt Söhne." 16 Sept. 1933. Louis Kirstein Papers, "Streicher Berlin," Box 81, Baker Business Library, Harvard University.

Van Paassen, Pierre, and James Waterman Wise, eds. *Nazism: An Assault on Civilization.* Smith and Haas, 1934.

"Vienna Jews Don Top Hats, War Medals to Clean Streets." *Jewish Telegraphic Agency*, 25 Mar. 1938.

"Vienna Office is Reopened by the AMC." *Women's Wear Daily*, 9 June 1947, p. 2.

"'We Are Trading America Down', Asserts Ira Hirschmann." *Women's Wear Daily*, 20 April 1932, p. 1.

"Weigart." Louis Kirstein Papers, "German-Austrian Refugees," Box 8, Baker Business Library, Harvard University.

"Weigart/Wertheim." Louis Kirstein Papers, Box 8, Baker Business Library, Harvard University.

Wiley, John C. Letter to George Messersmith. 8 June 1938. George S. Messersmith Papers, "109 1004," University of Delaware Library.

Wilford, Hugh. *The Mighty Wurlizter: How the CIA Played America.* Harvard Univ., 2009.

Wyman, David S. *Paper Walls: America and the Refugee Crisis, 1938–1941.* Pantheon, 1985.

Zachart, Ida Maria. Letter to Louis Edward Kirstein. 10 Oct. 1919. Louis Kirstein Papers, "Germany Correspondence," Box 54, Baker Business Library, Harvard University.

CHAPTER 7

Max Moses Heller: Patron Saint of Greenville's Renaissance

by Diane Vecchio

O
n an August morning in 1938, Max Heller, a nineteen-year-old Austrian Jewish refugee stepped off a train in Greenville, South Carolina. He spoke no English and the only person he knew in Greenville was a young woman he had met briefly the year before.

Heller and a friend had been at an outdoor café in Vienna in 1937, when he caught sight of an American girl. He thought she was very attractive but he didn't have the nerve to approach her. She was with several other girls and a chaperone, all enjoying the Grand Tour of Europe. He and his friend rose to leave the café, but after they paid their bill, Heller decided to ask the girl to dance. He spoke no English and the girl spoke no German, but with motions and signs, the girl and her chaperone understood his intentions. They danced several times and the next day he called on her at the Hotel Imperial where she and the group were staying. She was from Greenville, South Carolina, and he worked for a merchandising firm in Vienna. He gave her a picture of himself. She gave him her address. They did not meet again in Vienna, but the contact probably saved his life (Dunn, "Heller 1: 'If You Remember At Me'"). The girl from Greenville was Mary Mills and she was ultimately responsible for helping Max Heller escape Nazi-occupied Austria.

Having fled Austria in 1938 and coincidentally finding himself in Greenville provided Heller, a victim of Nazism, with his first step to starting over and rebuilding his life. American business opportunities and the textile industry which so powerfully shaped Upstate South Carolina allowed this Jewish refugee the chance to make a fortune and then serve his new community. From his humble beginnings as a floor sweeper in a shirt factory in Greenville to the proprietor of his own garment factory, Heller experienced rapid upward mobility in the United States. All the while, his experiences as a victim of anti-Semitism in Hitler's Europe and his strong religious identity as a Jew informed his life and actions in America. Always cognizant of the teachings of Jewish ethics and morals that he learned from his Hebrew teacher, Heller tried "to live the way this man taught me" (Heller, Interview with US Holocaust Museum, 24 Sept. 1998, 1). Determined to give back to the country that gave him so much, Heller turned to politics where, as mayor of Greenville, he led a downtown renaissance, tackled difficult race issues and committed himself to the housing needs of the poor. Determined to make Greenville an economic powerhouse, Heller attracted foreign investors to the county and as Chairman of the State Development Board recruited major manufacturing companies to South Carolina.

Born in 1919, Max Heller grew up in an Orthodox home in Vienna where his Polish-born parents operated a dry goods business. He recalled his strict upbringing, observing kashrut and the Sabbath, and a father who instilled in his children a deep reverence for the scriptures.

At the age of fourteen, Heller finished high school and began attending business school at night. He went to work for his father in the bulk retail textile business but eventually left his father's business and was hired as an apprentice at the Kalmann Company, a chain of retail stores selling a variety of inexpensive household goods. He started at the bottom, sweeping floors, tending stoves, and pulling a delivery cart, but he advanced rapidly in the company and became head of the shipping department (Dunn, "Heller 1: 'If You Remember At Me'").

Heller recalled that Jews in Vienna grew up dealing with anti-Semitism; "it just wasn't state sponsored until after the Anschluss in March, 1938" (Heller, Interview with US Holocaust Museum, 24 Sept. 1998, 8). Heller dates his first personal encounter with anti-Semitism to 1935 when he was a wrestler in an amateur sport club. At one inter-club match in Vienna's tough 19th District, young thugs in the gallery shouted, "Kill the pig Jew!" The atmosphere worsened when Hitler's troops entered Austria in March 1938. Within hours, things changed dramatically. According to Heller, "every policeman pulled out a swastika [and] put it on his arm." That evening, as they were eating the Sabbath meal, the Heller family wondered what they would do. "We've got to get out of here," Max said. The family contacted an aunt in Newark but never got a response. Max decided to write to the American girl he had met in 1937 to see if she could help him get out of Europe (Heller, Interview by Rosengarten and Rosenblum).

Heller soon learned that in order to enter the United States he would need a guaranteed job. He told his girlfriend, Trude Schönthal, that he was contacting the American girl he had met the previous summer to see if she could help him. Trude was not hopeful: "Good luck and good weather," she said (Dunn, "Heller 2: "Luck and Good Weather").

Weeks later, Mary Mills received a letter written in broken English from the young man she had danced with in Vienna: "I don't know if you remember at me," he wrote. "I learnd know you, as you was in Vienna in sommer 1937 . . . Do you remember, you was dance, and I meet you a day later i your Hotel Imperial . . . Now I have a great beg to ou! I am here without position, and would be glade to drive to U.S.A., . . . If somebody guaranteed for me . . ." (Dunn, "Heller 1: 'If You Remember At Me'").

The Heller family's situation became more precarious each day as Max's parents' bank account was confiscated and Nazi harassment grew steadily worse. Meanwhile, his girlfriend Trude and her family were evicted with a mere six-hour notice from the apartment they had owned for years. Increasingly, anti-Semitism grew more pervasive, especially among the young Austrians that Heller had grown up with and had known for years. One day, he was walking down the street when he felt a tap on the shoulder. He looked around to see Hans, a longtime friend from his sport club. "Hans," he said. "How good to see you." Hans pointed to the Jews scrubbing the street; "Over there, pig Jew," he yelled at Heller, as he shoved him to the ground to scrub the streets (Dunn, "Heller 2: 'Luck and Good Weather'" 148).

In May 1938 Heller received a letter from the girl in South Carolina: "You probably think I have forgotten you," Mills wrote. "But I have been trying to work out something for you. A man here in Greenville named Mr. Saltzman is going to guarantee for you" (Dunn, "Heller 1: 'If You Remember at Me'").[1] Heller's gratitude to Mary Mills remained with him throughout his entire life and exposed him to his first favorable interaction with Southern Christians. "I cannot describe the feeling when I got that letter," he said. "My life was in her hands" ("Max Heller").

Shepard Saltzman was a Jewish manufacturer who had relocated to Greenville from New York City in 1928. As textile manufacturing expanded, Upstate cities grew, attracting Jewish businessmen and entrepreneurs to the region. Saltzman opened the Piedmont Shirt Company which produced men and boys' dress and work shirts and at its peak employed nearly seven hundred workers.

Mary Mills had contacted Saltzman and asked him to assist Heller in getting him out of Austria. Saltzman later said, "How can I not help? When she, a Christian, wants to help, [then] I, a Jew, must help" (Heller, Interview by Rosengarten and Rosenblum). Saltzman also cabled a job-guarantee for Heller's sister, Paula. After weeks of waiting in lines for passports, affidavits and police clearance, and enduring Nazi youths throwing garbage and picking fights with them and other Jews waiting in line, Max and Paula booked passage on the *Ile de France*, scheduled to leave Le Havre on July 20 (Dunn, "Heller 2: 'Luck and Good Weather'" 148).

A German officer who had originally told him it would take days to check his records, expedited his police clearance and said "Don't tell anyone. I am a German, only a political Nazi. I did not know it would be like this. I am ashamed . . ." (Dunn, "Heller 2: 'Luck and Good Weather'" 148).

Heller and his sister left Vienna on July 18, 1938. He carried his prayer book, a prayer shawl, and Star of David medallion given to him by his parents at his Bar Mitzvah. Their mother and father, who were surviving by selling their furniture and silver, wondered if they would ever see their children again as their train pulled out of the station.

Paula and Max Heller arrived in New York on July 26, 1938 and were met by their aunt in New Jersey. After spending a few days in Newark, Max's aunt bought him a ticket and he boarded a train for Greenville. There, he was greeted by Shepard Saltzman, Mary Mills and several girls from the European tour who welcomed him to Greenville.

At 1:30 that afternoon, the former junior wrestling champ of Austria (Francie Heller) started working at the Piedmont Shirt Company. His first job was what he had done when he started at the Kalmann Company in Vienna: sweeping floors (Dunn, *The Charlotte Observer*). Heller recalled the moment he entered the shirt company: "When I came into the factory everyone knew I was coming . . . I was probably the first refugee to come out of Europe, certainly after Hitler came to Austria. So, naturally, everyone was interested to meet me . . ." (Heller, Interview 21).

Heller left a country where Jews were physically segregated from "Aryans," and came to the South, where blacks were segregated from whites.

When he arrived in Greenville in 1938, "It was very segregated, as segregated as a community could be," he remarked. Greenville, similar to the rest of the South in the 1930s, strictly enforced Jim Crow segregation. Public schools, facilities and churches were all segregated. Railroads provided separate coaches for the two races; segregation was required on ferries and trolley cars, and later, buses, where whites were seated at the front, and blacks in the rear. When Heller entered the Piedmont Shirt Company, he found whites and blacks segregated in the jobs they did and the departments in which they worked: a consequence of the South Carolina Factory Law of 1915 which prohibited textile mills from employing people of different races in the same room.[2]

For a Jew who had been segregated from gentiles in Austria, this enforced segregation was more than unsettling. Heller was stunned. Whites held the better jobs. White women did the sewing and black women ironed and folded. White men did the cutting, while black men packed and shipped orders in the warehouse (Leffert).

The Piedmont Shirt Company, which employed around 250 people in the 1930s ("Piedmont Shirt Co. Ordered To Halt Employees' Union"), was one of many businesses founded as a result of the vast cotton production in Upstate South Carolina. Greenville's economy during much of the twentieth century was based on textile manufacturing, which had its roots in the antebellum period (Huff 185). Developing slowly through the panics of 1873 and 1893, Greenville's growth began to accelerate after 1894 as "textile entrepreneurs turned the industry into big business in South Carolina" (Huff 236). The historian, David Carlton, calls the rise of the textile industry in the South Carolina Piedmont "one of the more striking developments in postbellum southern social history" (6). By the early twentieth century, Greenville and nearby Spartanburg were the leading textile regions of the state (Edgar 456). By the 1920s, South Carolina was the third largest textile producing state in the United States. Its center was Greenville (Huff 305).

Max Heller had much to adjust to in South Carolina. In addition to racial segregation, he found himself living in the heart of the Bible Belt. Dominated by evangelical Protestantism, Greenville was to become home to Bob Jones University in 1947, an institution of higher education for Christians from around the world. Heller, however, did not find this off-putting. He adjusted to his new environment with an open mind and a great capacity for accepting people different from himself.

When he started work at the shirt factory, Heller became friends with several New York Jews who were employed in management. These were men who had been recruited by Saltzman through familial and social networking, a strategy commonly employed by Jews. The superintendent of the company, Harry Abrams, invited Max to stay in his home with his family. But Abrams wouldn't accept any money from Heller, who wanted to pay his own way. At the end of the week Heller moved out of the Abrams' home and rented from Saltzman's sister, who took in boarders and charged him $7.00 a week. Morris Leffert, a Polish Jew, and cousin of Shep Saltzman, had immigrated to New York City in his early twenties and came to work at the factory in 1928. Leffert, a foreman in the finishing department, also extended Heller a hand in friendship (Leffert).

The Abrams, Saltzman and Leffert families, were part of the small Jewish community that called Greenville home. A handful of Jews had settled in the city during the antebellum period, where they operated successful businesses, especially in clothing and dry goods. The Jewish presence in Greenville grew at the turn of the twentieth century as new businesses proliferated, particularly in clothing, tailoring, scrap-metal, shoes, and, later, auto-parts. There were also two congregations: Beth Israel, a conservative synagogue established in 1911, and Temple of Israel, a reform congregation, founded in 1916.

Heller worked hard and rose in the company, initially as head of the shipping department. He learned to write correct business letters by studying the company's past correspondence at night, which also helped him learn English. In addition, Saltzman himself spent many hours teaching Heller the English language. During this period of time, Saltzman helped other members of the Heller family escape Nazi Europe, including Max's parents. When his father, Israel, arrived in Greenville, he too, was given a job at the Piedmont Shirt Company and Max became his boss. Heller's sister, Paula, eventually came to Greenville as well where Saltzman gave her an office job in his company. Saltzman's generosity did not end there. He eventually provided employment to Heller's uncle as well as his future wife Trude and Trude's father. Like Heller, Saltzman's understanding of Jewish morals and ethics motivated him to perform many mitzvahs during his lifetime (Morrow).

Meanwhile, Heller's Austrian girlfriend, Trude and her family fled Austria for Belgium after the Anschluss and then made it to New York in 1940. Two years later, she came to Greenville and in August, 1942, Trude and Max were married by a rabbi at Temple Beth Israel.

Sadly, Max and Trude experienced their first brush with anti-Semitism in Greenville while they were looking for an apartment to rent. In one incident, the landlord refused to rent to them because they were Jews (Heller, Interview by Rosengarten and Rosenblum 26). Shocked and dejected, Max and Trude continued looking for an apartment. They found one in a "wonderful section of Greenville," according to Heller. However, it was too expensive. When Max told the landlady that he couldn't afford it, she said "pay me less. I want you to be here. I like you both." Heller retorted "we're Jewish," and Mrs. Keller said "that's wonderful" (Heller, Interview with US Holocaust Museum, 24 Sept. 1998, 40).

Several months after settling in Greenville, Heller was asked to speak to a Masonic group. At the end of his talk the members passed a hat and collected $30 to present him. He said he couldn't accept the money but would give it to a Jewish charity. The lodge members said that they would be honored if he did that (Heller, Interview with US Holocaust Museum, 24 Sept. 1998, 39). Rather than dwell on one hurtful experience, the Heller's chose to focus on the positive exchanges with gentiles.

Max and Trude settled into a happy marriage and Heller became increasingly proficient in English and knowledgeable about the shirt business. He was promoted to internal sales manager at Piedmont Shirts and at the age of twenty-six became the general manager of the company. In 1945, he was promoted to vice-president of the firm, which by that time had offices in New York and a new plant in Walterboro, South Carolina. Within seven years, by way of constant support from Saltzman, Heller had risen as high as he could at the Piedmont Shirt Company. He recalled the friendly relationships between employer and employees at the factory. "In Austria the boss was feared and workers were treated as inferiors. Here, I realized a man is respected for what he does, not for what he's called" (Stipp).

At the end of World War II, Max and Trude searched for displaced members of their families in Europe, but located only two cousins. All of the others had died at the hands of the Nazis. Heller never neglected his religion or his identity as a Jew and worked relentlessly trying to get a cousin out of Europe to no avail and felt despair over the plight of displaced persons and how they were being treated by the US government. In August 1947, Heller wrote a letter to Representative Brian Dorn (D-SC) in which he quoted a comment the congressman made about refugees: "I had a great deal of sympathy for them but on the whole I found them to be undesirable material for citizenship in America." Heller responded: "I am certain that amongst the hundreds and thousands of people who were unfortunate enough to be thrown into concentration camps, to be separated from their families, who have lost everything they ever possessed; there are a good percentage who are honorable, industrious, intelligent and worthy people . . . We should have more than sympathy for these people. We should have understanding and lend a helping hand to them." Heller then reminded Dorn that "had it not been for the fact that our Forefathers were willing to share this country and to open their arms to more newcomers, this would have never been the greatest Democracy the World has ever known" (Letter to The Honorable Bryan Dorn).

With a steadfast love for his new home, Heller wasted no time in becoming an American citizen. In June 1939, Max filed his declaration of intentions (*South Carolina Naturalization Records*). He became a citizen in 1941.

While Max was happy with his job at Piedmont Shirts, his aspiration to own and operate his own company eventually led to his resignation. Together with a business partner, he started the Williamston Shirt Company twenty-seven miles from Greenville. The business boomed. But in 1947 the partnership broke up and Heller sold out. In 1948, he achieved his dream: he established his own company, Maxon Shirts in Greenville, with forty employees in a 6,000 square foot plant. In 1952, increasing volume made larger quarters necessary, and the company moved into a building on Court Street in Greenville. In its tenth year, Maxon had 4,000 accounts and more than six hundred people on the payroll. Twenty-six salesmen covered the country while Max kept a finger on the pulse of public likes and dislikes. His Carnegie-brand shirts had a reputation for quality and good value ("Maxon Shirt: At 10-Year Mark").

By 1966, Heller's company, now a subsidiary of the Oxford Manufacturing Company, had relocated to a larger plant and employed seven hundred workers. Maxon Shirt Corporation had branch offices in New York, Chicago, San Francisco, Dallas, Baltimore and Los Angeles. Their products were sold in all fifty states as well as Puerto Rico, Nigeria, Rhodesia, Bermuda, and Canada (Steadman).

Heller's company provided employment to hundreds of single and married women in Greenville, mostly employed as machine operators. Like all manufacturing plants in South Carolina, the company was segregated into departments by race, a policy established by state law. Custom dictated that even Christmas parties be segregated. In 1960, a local newspaper article pictured Heller presenting awards to several black female employees. The caption noted that a company party was held "Tuesday night for its Negro employees . . . A similar party will be held for White employees Friday at the plant" ("Shirt Firm Honors Employees"). However, in the privacy of his own plant, Heller made some courageous moves regarding integration. One day he removed the signs that designated white/Negro drinking fountains and white/Negro bathrooms. White and black workers were forced to use the same facilities and according to Heller, "not a word was said" about it (Heller, Interview with US Holocaust Museum, 24 Sept. 1998, 41).

After a very successful and lucrative business career, Heller decided to sell his shirt company and pursue a new direction in life: public service. According to Ethel Steadman writing for *The Greenville News*, "Many of Maxon's first employees were still with the company when he sold it in 1971. Close business associates attribute this to Heller's personal interest in his workers and to his understanding from coming 'up the hard way'." A reporter for *The Greenville News* reassured the community that nearly five hundred jobs at Maxon Shirts would not be lost because Land and Sea, one of the nation's best-known manufacturer of women's apparel, had acquired the facilities ("Apparel Firm Buys Maxon Shirt Plant").

"I'M A BORN-AGAIN JEW . . . I WAS BORN AGAIN IN GREENVILLE." (MAX HELLER)

Having achieved great wealth in the garment business, Heller's decision to commit himself to public service was based in part on his conviction that he "had no desire to be the richest man in the cemetery" (Heller, Interview with US Holocaust Museum, 24 Sept. 1998, 35). Heller's desire to enter public service was motivated by much more, however. He truly believed that "It was my civic duty, as corny as it may sound. I feel that Greenville has been good to me and I've done well and I want to share what I have been able to get, so to speak, to give back" (Interview by Bass and De Vries [online p. 11]).

Heller's involvement in community activities began with his participation in the United Fund, Visiting Nurses, the Cerebral Palsy Foundation, Family Services and as Chairman of the Board of St. Francis Hospital. He was also involved with synagogue activities at Beth Israel and active on the Housing Foundation (Heller, Interview #A-0166 by Bass). Heller worked with a Christian woman who was interested in youthful, first offenders, a passion he would pursue during his years in public service. He was also driven by the housing needs of Greenville's poor. In one interview he stated:

> My political involvement came about because of my concern for housing. One time we went to a meeting (the Housing Foundation) and I gave a talk about the housing situation and I was very much annoyed that nothing was happening in Greenville. Somebody said to me "you ought to put your money where your mouth is." So I did. I ran for City Council and was elected. I advocated that we needed

to do something about the housing situation because it is part of a
community problem. It isn't just a problem of the individual who has
to live in a sub-standard home. This is how I really became involved.
(Interview by Bass 5–6)

Heller served on the Greenville City Council from 1969–1971, and continued working on local improvements that focused on keeping youthful offenders from becoming hardened criminals and addressing the lack of decent
housing for the poor (Stipp). Heller's work with underage crime and first-time
offenders resulted in the passage of a law in the legislature establishing a youthful offenders camp in Greenville County which improved treatment of youthful offenders by keeping them apart from hardened criminals (Chanes).

His work with the housing crisis began to reap benefits when he started a non-profit organization that was supported by the business community.
Heller initially raised about $200,000 that was used to buy property to build
new structures and sub-standard houses to fix and resell (Interview by Bass 6).
Working with black and white members of the Housing Commission, Heller
assisted in building houses for low-income people. Speaking to *The Greenville
Piedmont* newspaper in 1969, Heller stated, "Our aim is to remove the substan-
dard housing blight from the face of Greenville County, to replace it with low
or moderate priced housing available to everyone and to give this segment of
our population a pride of environment" (*Greenville Piedmont*).

Heller won many friends among the voters during his first and only term
as councilman. Greenville residents appreciated his businesslike approach to
city affairs and his work as Finance Committee chairman. His concern with
such issues as employee benefits, improving housing and race relations won him
the support of both white and black voters. At the same time Heller pursued his
policy goals through private foundations and community organizations.

His work on the city council gained the attention of many community
members impressed with his innovative ideas, good business sense, and commitment to the community. Numerous people, especially local business leaders, prevailed upon him to run for mayor (Steve Heller). Several of the most
prominent business leaders in Greenville, such as Buck Mickel, Thomas Wyche,
and Alester Furman, Jr., had been developing plans for a revived downtown as
a way to attract diverse industries to the Greenville area. They found an enthusiastic candidate in Max Heller, an individual who shared the same goals for
Greenville (Judith and Robert Bainbridge). Running as a Democrat, Heller was
elected mayor of Greenville in 1971 with a 70% majority (*Tampa Bay Times*).

The election of Heller as mayor of Greenville was not an anomaly in the South. As Jews settled in small towns and large cities throughout the southern states they began to play important roles in local government. According to the 2017 Goldring/Woldenberg Institute of Southern Jewish Life, there have been over two hundred Jewish mayors in the South since the late nineteenth century ("Jewish Mayors in the South"). Emanuel ("Mutt") Evans was perhaps the most prominent Jewish mayor in the South: an American businessman and progressive in Durham, North Carolina, his popularity and success were so great that he served six terms as mayor from 1951–1963 ("Emanuel J. 'Mutt' Evans").

In his inaugural address of July 21, 1971, Heller articulated his philosophy of government. In one comment, no doubt directed at the conservatives in the community, he noted, "If it is our responsibility to judge what is obscene to read, it is also our duty to say that it is immoral to sit by and let people live in slums, health hazards, and crime infested streets." Concerned for the environment and the aesthetics of the community, Heller stated: "Since it is our duty to plan orderly progress in our city, we must also say that progress means more than steel, brick and mortar—but it includes the preservation of the beauty of our trees, the cleanliness of our air, the clearness of our rivers." In an effort to create a city government that responds to the needs of all residents, he promised that his administration would establish "a direct line to a citizen's service desk where you can make known your suggestions or complaints; where you will be treated as promptly and courteously as possible, as you are entitled to." He pledged to rebuild the blighted areas of the city. He committed himself to "a total development plan including future land use in our entire city," and stressed the need to "take advantage of regional and federal programs to help with our future plans. We shall use urban renewal programs as a means of building—not tearing down." Deeply troubled by rising drug abuse and juvenile crime, Heller also focused on the youth of the community. "Good, wholesome recreation is the best preventive medicine against crime," he said, and vowed to listen to the youth by appointing a youth advisory committee consisting of young people only (Heller, Inaugural Speech).

Heller was elected mayor at a critical time in the city's history. Downtown Greenville and Main Street, in particular, had seriously declined since the late 1950s and early 1960s, as shopping malls on the outskirts of the city rendered downtown obsolete. Main Street stores closed and were boarded up, streets became deserted. Vagrants sought refuge in the abandoned Poinsett Hotel, once a downtown landmark. At a meeting of the Downtown Greenville Association, local business leader, Charles Daniel, told members that the city was "unclean and neither attractive nor competitive with comparable progressive cities" (Chanes).

Before Heller became mayor, city planners had been developing ideas to modernize downtown. Local businessman, Charles Daniel, a leading southern building contractor, had built the twenty-five-story Daniel Building. Roger Peace, who controlled a local media conglomerate including the *Greenville News*, along with other local publishing and broadcasting companies, erected a new building close to the Reedy River. They were admirable beginnings, but many people viewed them as mere window dressing of little consequence as the city continued to languish through the 1960s (Poland 19). "Downtown seemed incapable of rescuing itself until Max Heller developed a vision based on improving downtown's image through streetscape and traffic improvements" (Poland 19). With advice from Lawrence Halprin,[3] one of the most influential landscape architects of the twentieth century, Heller developed plans for altering Main Street, including downsizing its four lanes to two and adding angled parking. These plans were opposed by the few remaining downtown merchants who feared that reducing Main Street to two lanes, would totally destroy what little business they had. Heller, certain this was the right way to go, forged ahead. With the support of Buck Nickel and Tommy Wyche, Heller pushed the revitalization of downtown. Trees were planted on both sides of Main Street, decorative light fixtures installed, and parks and small plazas built. Main Street started to take the shape of a European village with green spaces, flower planters, and areas for outdoor dining, similar to what Heller experienced growing up in Europe. Thus, Mayor Heller was credited with "bringing a little bit of Europe to Greenville" (Poland 21).

Under the direction of Heller and the leadership of local businessmen, Mickel, Wyche and Furman, the Total Development Plan was initiated by the Chamber of Commerce in 1976.[4] The cornerstone of Main Street's renewal included plans for a $30 million downtown hotel, office building, convention center and city commons project, financed jointly by the city and private business. Knox White, elected mayor of Greenville in 1995 and still serving in 2018, credits Heller as the first person to truly promote public-private partnerships for downtown's benefit (Tollison, Personal Interview). Heller believed this would lead to an expanded economy which was "essential to building the city's tax base and stemming the flow of jobs and investment to the suburbs" (Max Heller Papers, Folder 1, Box 20).

In late 1978, Greenville received a federal Urban Development Action Grant for $7.4 million, one of the first in the nation ("It's Enough That I Can

Run for Congress"). With these funds, the city began to acquire land on North Main Street, and through the active involvement of Mickel and Wyche, the new hotel and convention center started to take shape. The Hyatt Hotel Corporation initially refused to build a hotel on Main Street, citing the size of Greenville as a reason not to invest. Not content with that answer, Heller did a little research and found out that the mother of Hyatt's CEO came from the same Polish town as his parents. He paid a visit to Jay Pritzker at Hyatt corporate headquarters in Chicago to inform him of that important "Old World" connection and that sealed the deal. Hyatt agreed to build the 330-room Regency Hotel and the city agreed to build a convention center atrium and a five-story office building (Marcus). The Convention Center was eventually named for Heller. When the Hyatt opened in 1982, the $34 million hotel signified a new era. A renaissance had begun in downtown Greenville (Chanes).

Working closely with the Greater Greenville Chamber of Commerce, Mayor Heller made plans for a new performing arts center, a school for the arts, a research park, and an upstate coliseum. With a $10 million pledge from the Peace family, community support was kindled for building a cultural center at the heart of the city. Another $42 million was raised by local donors and the Peace Center for the Performing Arts was built composed of a concert hall, theater and amphitheater located adjacent to Falls Park. It provided a countervailing anchor to the Hyatt Hotel, located on the other end of Main Street. When it opened in 1990, the Peace Center for the Performing Arts brought a little bit of New York to the community, ranging from world-class classical music to Broadway shows, popular musicians and dance. A number of local performing arts organizations eventually found performing homes at the Peace Center, including the Greenville Symphony Orchestra, South Carolina Children's Theater, Carolina Ballet Theatre and International Ballet.

Construction on "Liberty Square," was completed in 1986, creating an attractive entrance to the downtown area from Interstate 385. It consisted of two glass curtain towers with office space, outdoor courtyards, onsite dining and a parking garage. Thanks to an executive order by Governor Richard Riley, the South Carolina Governor's School for the Arts and Humanities opened in 1980. A residential school for artistically talented high school students, the school offered pre-professional arts curricula based on a classical, master-apprentice training model in creative writing, dance, drama, music and visual arts. The campus was built to model a Tuscan village and added a further touch of European elegance to downtown Greenville.

Tom Poland, in *Greenville's Grand Design*, notes: "Under Heller's watchful eye, a plan took shape that incorporated vision, resourcefulness, and public-private partnerships" (Poland 21). Greg Jensen, who worked as a producer and director at Greenville's television station, WFBC, maintains that "a huge advantage of working [there] during the late 1970s and early 1980s was meeting the movers and shakers of not just Main Street revitalization but the Upstate in general. Max *was* the leader. [His] vision and resulting revitalization was truly a culture-changing event" (Poland 21–22).

Local resident Lee Leslie believes that Heller gave the city momentum. "Max Heller started something that continued (into the 21st century) the Peace Center, the Bergamo, Italy sister-city development in the middle of downtown,[5] the festivals and the privately raised money for bridge removal revealing the Reedy River Falls, which led to Liberty Bridge[6] and a new baseball park."[7] Similar to his compatriot who served as mayor of Durham, Heller faced comparable challenges as Mutt Evans ("Emanuel J. 'Mutt' Evans"). Both of these progressive mayors dealt effectively with racial issues, juvenile delinquency, a deteriorating downtown and the needs of the poor.

BRINGING THE WORLD TO GREENVILLE

Perhaps the greatest crisis Heller faced as mayor was the decline of the textile industry and the loss of jobs in Greenville. During the 1970s, Greenville and other Upstate centers of the textile industry faced new challenges—environmental controls, world-wide inflation, and foreign imports. Local mills merged into larger companies and closures began. In the midst of the declining textile industry thousands of mill workers lost their jobs.

Heller tackled the economic downturn in the textile industry by enticing major businesses and industries to Greenville (Bainbridge, "Max Heller Considered"). Convinced that diversification was essential, he helped create the South Carolina Research Authority, an economic development program intended to help early stage companies to communicate innovations and create jobs.

According to Southern historian Lacy Ford, "from 1980 through the end of the century, state policy makers . . . and gubernatorial administrations . . . passed bipartisan legislative support to bring impressive levels of outside investment to the state" (19) continuing a pro-business tradition that evolved after World War II. South Carolina had passed a right-to-work law (1954), had a favorable tax and regulatory climate and a system of state financial incentives that included relatively cheap industrial sites developed largely at state expense (21). South Carolina experienced remarkable growth as new manufacturing jobs came from outside the original cotton-textile field in related industries like chemicals and synthetic fibers (30).

In 1973, Heller and five community leaders went to New York City to make a presentation to 225 Metropolitan Life Insurance Company employees and their families, urging them to move to Greenville with their company. Metropolitan Life had already agreed to locate a $12 million regional computer center in Greenville and the insurance company employees agreed to the move ("Greenville Presentation").

Heller's most significant achievement as mayor in terms of attracting investment occurred in 1975, when the French tire giant Michelin selected Greenville for its first American plant. Heller and the governor made several trips to France where they lauded the excellent training that Greenville Technical College could provide the local work force and as a crucial part of the deal, the state of South Carolina agreed to cover the cost of sending upper management to France for training (Max Heller Papers, Box 7, Folder 3).

During the early 1970s Michelin ultimately built plants in Greenville, Anderson, Lexington and Spartanburg. It also built a test facility for research and development in Laurens in the Upstate. To consolidate operations and manufacturing, Michelin made the decision to relocate its North American headquarters from New York to Greenville in 1988 (*Michelin*). A remarkable achievement for Heller and Greenville, Michelin became the cornerstone of manufacturing and business development along the I-85 corridor extending from Charlotte to Atlanta.

There were many city boosters in Upstate South Carolina who were courting international firms. Max Heller and the business leadership of Greenville were joined by business leaders in Spartanburg and the Spartanburg Chamber of Commerce, chaired by Richard Tukey. Spartanburg had already created economic ties to Europe, with German, Swiss and Italian manufacturers building in Spartanburg County. According to business professor Rosabeth Moss Kanter, in her 1995 study *World Class, Thriving Locally in the Global Economy*, "by systematically upgrading their ability to meet the needs of manufacturers," Greenville (and neighboring Spartanburg)[8] were becoming an important component of a global economy (242). Manufacturing and high-tech firms from Europe and Asia were investing in the Upstate. In 1977 Jain Chem, Ltd., a family-owned Indian company that designs chemical solutions for the textile, packaging and fiberglass industries opened in Greenville.

According to historian James Cobb, who examines the interaction between economy, society and culture, by the end of the 1970s South Carolina was the acknowledged pioneer in recruiting international business investment in the South. The state was drawing some 40% of its annual increase in investment capital from outside the country. According to Cobb, "only West Germany could claim more West German industrial capital than South Carolina" (Cobb 205). For the first time annual industrial recruitment reached the one billion dollar mark ("Under Heller's Leadership"). During Heller's term as mayor, more than 65,000 jobs were created in Greenville County.

CITY IMPROVEMENTS

The rapid growth occurring in foreign investments in Greenville County led to new industries and a growing population, nearing 250,000 by 1970. Letters to city and county council members reveal Heller's attempts to tackle the problems of a growing city, ranging from county landfill operations to modernizing the city government.

During his tenure as mayor, he not only improved the physical features of Main Street and downtown, "but reached into the old, and often ineffective ways of conducting local government. He consolidated city and county services, thus bringing more efficiency to local government, law enforcement, health services, record keeping and communication." He built five community centers and fifteen parks with educational and recreational facilities.

In January 1973, the *Greenville Piedmont* opined that 1972 had been a monumental year in the history of Greenville. It had been Heller's first year as mayor and according to him, "It was the year of self-analysis in City Hall." Heller implemented a self-analysis on a department-by-department basis, which resulted in a number of improvements and significant changes. Heller's administration completely restructured the fire department, separated the municipal court from the police department and appointed a full-time judge. They hired a full-time city attorney and a communications coordinator. The city manager revised the city code and updated the procedures for doing government business. A city-county landfill operation was implemented and a city-county transit authority was created to deal with the growing concern of transporting people in and around Greenville (Campbell). When Duke Power Company informed the city that it could no longer operate the municipal bus system, Heller created the Greenville Transit Authority. He asked the president of Greenville Technical College to start a program to train bus drivers and local churches volunteered the use of their buses to cover the transition (Chanes).

Because of Heller's passion for child welfare and the housing needs of the poor, Heller became president of the non-profit Greenville Housing Foundation, putting into action his ambitious plan to insure affordable housing for all (Stipp). He also served as a member of the Greenville County Health Policy and Planning Council and as a board member of the Children and Family Service Agency ("Meet the Mayor of Greenville"). His service extended to state and national organizations as well, including a stint as President of the South Carolina Municipal Association and a board member of the National League of Cities.

Heller was selected by the German Marshall and Kettering Foundation to travel to Great Britain, the Netherlands and Germany to meet with local and national government officials on an economic fact-finding mission. He represented the US Conference of Mayors on the Robert Wood Johnson Foundation Advisory Board, and also represented the organization and the National League of Cities in meetings with the secretaries of Housing and Urban Development, Health, Education and Welfare, Commerce, and others (Application for appointment).

Heller received hundreds of letters from Greenvillians who were grateful for the improvements he was making in the city. Public support was so great for Heller that the *Greenville News* endorsed a "Mayor Max Heller Day," stating:

> within the city of Greenville there is an underlying sense of confidence in the future . . . greatly dependent on City Hall and the elected officials who run it . . . caused by an informed policy of private-public cooperation. Add to this the dash of deep feeling, the abiding unselfish interest, dedication to the best interests of all the governed, that Mayor Heller's administration and supportive members of city council have apparently captured . . . It all adds to enlightened, efficient, positive government . . . and heralds even greater, more accelerated leadership in the vital metropolitan core city in the immediate future. ("Heller, Council Prod Leadership")

Race relations in Greenville were a greater challenge for Heller. One of the worst racial events in Greenville's history occurred nine years after Heller's arrival: the lynching of Willie Earle.[9] Heller recalled, "It was horrible. That was the only time I felt like I wanted to leave. How could I live here with a lynch-ing?" (Heller, "Max Heller Remembers").

Looking back on his decision to enter politics he remarked, "When I ran for public office, I was quite clear what I believed in. I believed that we needed to be integrated. I thought it was wrong [that] we—for instance, City Hall, was totally segregated. And I was very open. I said, "If I become mayor, this is one community. . . . I wanted to do something to pull the community together" (Heller, Interview by Rosengarten and Rosenblum). Francie Heller attests to her father's commitment to civil rights noting that he "successfully campaigned for civil rights when he became mayor" (Chanes). Holding office during the 1970s, Heller had an opportunity to make a strong statement about civil rights to the community. His first hire as mayor was an African American secretary, the first in City Hall (Moses). Heller desegregated all departments and com-missions in city government and, working with the police chief, made sure that new hires were based on the qualifications of the candidate and not the color of their skin (Heller, Interview by Rosengarten and Rosenblum). Heller's daugh-ter recalls that while he was mayor, the Country Club and the Poinsett Club, a private dining club, offered him honorary memberships even though they did not allow Jews. "But he would not join unless they opened the clubs up to other Jews as well as blacks" (Chanes).

In 1975, in a further attempt to bring people together, and foster a more cohesive city, Heller created the mayor's prayer breakfast, open to all denomi-nations and, all races. With the announcement of an interfaith dialogue, dem-onstrators from Bob Jones University marched with placards stating "How can you follow a man who doesn't believe in Christ," and "The mayor is a devil in sheep's clothes" (Nelson). Undaunted, Heller continued his mayor's prayer breakfasts year after year.

Jesse Jackson, Greenville born and raised, would become a well-known civil rights leader, but he got his start in activism in Greenville, when he and a group of black youths, known as "The Greenville Seven," led a movement to integrate the city library in 1960 (Jackson). While working for civil rights nationally, Jackson frequently returned to Greenville to visit his mother. On a visit to Greenville in 1973, Jackson met with Mayor Heller. He was impressed with the improvements that Greenville had made, but in a joint press confer-ence with Heller, Jackson did not hesitate to point out the ways that racism continued to plague the city:

> Greenville with its industrial base is uniquely situated in the state
> and the nation with a comprehensive economic plan. I am personally
> impressed with its potential. I am equally disturbed by the missed
> opportunities. Since I left home much has changed in Greenville. I
> am proud of that. But it is my observation today that while the social
> relationship between blacks and whites has changed, the economic
> relationship has not. (*FOCUS*)

Jackson pointed out that there were "no blacks on the city coun-
cil or county council. We have no blacks from Greenville to represent us in
Columbia or in Washington. If it is possible for Max Heller, a Jew, to be mayor
of Greenville, then it is possible for Greenville to have a black mayor" (*FOCUS*).
Three years later, the first black person was elected to serve on the city council
(Heller, Interview by Tollison).

There were black community members who appreciated the efforts
Heller had been making in the field of civil rights. In June, 1988, an African
American woman sent Heller a letter:

> I want you to know that I sincerely appreciate everything that you
> have done for black people in Greenville city/county and in the state
> of South Carolina. You are such an inspiration to so many people,
> especially me. I like the way you think . . . and your devotion to your
> religion. Above all, your love for people regardless of race. . . . God
> loves you and he has you here for a purpose. Namely, to inspire un-
> employed black people like me to never give up. I love you!! Mazel
> Tov!! (Butler)

"WOULD YOU VOTE FOR AN IMMIGRANT?": CAMPAIGN TO ELECT CARROLL CAMPBELL FOR CONGRESS

According to Charles Sowell, a local journalist, "It was his inherent humanity
that made Heller a favorite with Greenville's electorate, and to seek political office beyond the city of Greenville." After serving two terms as mayor, from 1971
to 1979 and a host of remarkable achievements, Heller was tapped to run for
the US House of Representatives on the Democratic ticket in 1978. He secured
the nomination beating out State Representative Nick Theodore but the race
that ensued was marked by bigotry and anti-Semitism.

Heller was well ahead of the Republican candidate, Carroll Campbell, 51% to 29% in October 1978 (Max Heller Papers, Box 1, Folder 1). But Campbell's campaign manager, Lee Atwater, crafted a strategy that relied on consistently reminding the electorate that Heller was an immigrant and a Jew. The Campbell campaign mailed a survey to potential voters, with loaded questions such as "Which phrase best describes Max Heller, and which best describes Carroll Campbell?" Among the available responses were "a Christian man," and "Jewish." Another question asked: "What personal qualities would make you more likely to vote for a candidate or less likely to vote for a candidate?" One of the possible selections was "a Jewish immigrant" ("Heller Questions Campbell's Tactics"). Meanwhile, Don Sprouse, an Independent candidate who petitioned his way onto the ballot, stated that "everyone who goes to Congress should be a Christian" (Dozier). Owner and operator of the City Wrecking Service, Sprouse asserted that based on his own "personal beliefs, he could be a better congressman because he is a Christian" (Saunders). He asked the voters, "can you vote for a foreign-born Jew who does not accept Jesus Christ as his personal savior?" Five days before the election Sprouse held a news conference at which he said the public had a right to know . . . [that] "he [Heller] had not made clear to the public that he's not a Christian" ("Heller Questions Campbell's Tactics").

Moreover, Heller even had to endure attacks from the Ku Klux Klan, who circulated a newsletter throughout the congressional district stating, "We must defeat Max Heller who is Jew Mayor of Greenville. If we allow him to become a Congressman it's another nail in America's coffin. Get out and shout against the anti-Christ rascal" ("Heller Says Klan Attack").

Heller's numbers started dropping. He lost the election by 6,000 votes but graciously stated "I don't think Campbell was anti-Semitic but he used whatever was available" (*Greenville Creative Loafing*). Politicians who knew Heller best said the race against Campbell hurt him deeply. Yet the former mayor never criticized Campbell and said in later years, after Campbell had become governor of South Carolina, that Campbell had made a good state chief executive. "For his part, Campbell consistently denied his campaign had anything to do with anti-Semitic rhetoric" (Sowell 8). But the *New York Times*, in September 1986, drew attention to the dirty politics going on in South Carolina when reporter Phil Gailey wrote that "Heller, who is Jewish, emigrated to the US from Austria in the Nazi era. Religion became an issue in the final week of the campaign after a third candidate, Don Spouse, an independent, asserted that Heller should not be elected to

Congress because he was not a Christian and did not 'believe Jesus Christ has come yet.'"

Heller received numerous letters from local residents who were sickened by the religious bigotry that was displayed in the campaign. One Greenvillian wrote to Sprouse and copied Heller saying, "I heard your comment concerning Mayor Heller's beliefs . . . and must say it is one of the lowest blows in the name of Christianity that I have heard recently. I too, am a Christian and would like to apologize to Mayor Heller on behalf of Christians, and Baptists in particular" (Glass). The vice president for student affairs at Furman University wrote Heller saying "I still have faith in the democratic way, but that doesn't keep one from being very disappointed now and then. I am so grateful for your leadership in Greenville, and sorry we didn't work hard enough to get your leadership expanded to Washington" (Chiles). Fourteen-year old, Trey Gowdy who was to become a US Representative from South Carolina representing the 4th District, wrote to Heller saying, "although I am normally a Republican, I must give credit where credit is due, and much credit is due to you for the way you conducted yourself regarding the remarks made by Independent candidate Don Sprouse. I know it must have been hard on you" (Gowdy).

BRINGING THE WORLD TO SOUTH CAROLINA

The day after Heller lost the election to Carroll Campbell, long-time friend Governor Dick Riley called him and asked him to be chairman of the State Development Board. According to Riley "the textile industry was down and we were wondering what was going to happen . . . I really needed a very good businessperson to head up the development of the state economy" (Riley, Personal Interview).

Riley would call this "the most important appointment I made as governor" (Riley, Personal Interview). Forerunner to today's South Carolina Department of Commerce, the board served as a major source for economic development. Heller went to Columbia and served as director from 1979 to 1983, traveling the world and meeting with heads of state, finance ministers and industrialists.

According to Riley, "Max and I knew we had to sell South Carolina and Greenville [and] the Upstate [to European and Asian manufacturers]. We had to show that we had large numbers of people who were good employees . . .

wonderful people who were loyal to their employer, who were loyal to their community, and good workers . . . we were going to make sure that they had the skills to do what was necessary" (Riley, Personal Interview).

Heller and his wife traveled with the governor and first lady to the United Kingdom, Germany, Italy, France, Japan, China, Taiwan and Russia. They went to Stuttgart several times and met with the leaders of the German automotive industry. The fact that Heller spoke fluent German was a great advantage. A business trip to Germany in November 1982 was punctuated with visits to companies such as Ernest Winter of Hamburg, Klingelburg and Sohne in Remscheid, Karo Werke in Troisdorf and S. W. E. Eurodrive in Bruchsal. These companies represented smaller, closely held enterprises, seeking to grow and diversify their risks through international investment ("Remarks by Mr. Max Heller").

One of the first companies they recruited to South Carolina was the German automotive supplier Bosch, which built a manufacturing plant in Charleston. The connections that Heller and Riley made with automotive engineers in Germany may have affected the decision by BMW to establish its North American headquarters in Spartanburg in 1992,[10] as well as hundreds of foreign plants that opened in South Carolina and became suppliers for Michelin, Bosch and BMW. They also recruited the Japanese company Fuji to Greenwood, another Upstate location, and 3-V, an Italian textile company to Georgetown, in the Lowcountry.

Heller was involved in the establishment of a new pulp and paper facility which became one of the most environmentally sensitive projects in the state's history ("Obstacles"). The new facility, operated by Union Camp Corporation, was located upstream from two of the state's most attractive recreational lakes and various interest groups perceived the proposed project as harmful to these lakes and to the environment. Heller carefully studied plans for the project and discovered that the proposed undertaking would not bring significant harm to the environment. In fact, the technology which Union Camp was incorporating into the project would be state-of-the-art and would make the facility one of the most environmentally sound projects of its kind. A committee was set up to study the environmental impact of the project.

Heller played a similar role in the retrofitting of the International Paper Company facility. With the encouragement of Heller and others whom he united to support the firm, International Paper decided to invest more than $500 million in reconstructing an outmoded, pre-World War II pulp and paper plant. This not only saved hundreds of jobs for South Carolinians in the midst of a recession, but also marked the largest single capital investment by a company in an existing industry in the history of the state.

Heller helped persuade the governor and the general assembly to establish the South Carolina Research Authority in 1982. The authority was charged with the development and management of three research parks in the state. He was also the major influence behind the passage of legislation to establish a new state-supported finance authority for economic development. The Economic Development Authority, established in 1983, promoted the business and economic welfare of South Carolina by assisting in financing public and private projects. Heller was influential is establishing the Rural Development Committee, a state program located in Columbia. The committee was designed to provide technical assistance and training leading to the development and expansion of small and emerging private businesses and economic development in distressed areas of the state.

In 1997, nearly one-half of the 5.5 billion dollars in capital investments in South Carolina came from international firms, with fifty-seven German companies leading the way. There were so many German suppliers in the state that I-85 was dubbed "the American Autobahn" (Murphy). Undoubtedly, Max Heller played a role in making that happen.

In her book, *World Class*, Rosabeth Moss Kanter devoted a chapter to the Spartanburg-Greenville region of South Carolina, which she characterized as "the site of the largest per capita diversified foreign investment in the United States."[11] Her surveys show how foreign investment has been a positive force, bringing benefits to local businesses, workers, and the community in Upstate South Carolina. Kanter explains that the area first attracted companies from Germany and German-speaking Switzerland and Austria, whose cultural style was to sink roots and assimilate. Often these expatriates became long-term residents and even citizens" (246). As time went on "selling the upstate became easier, because prospective investors could talk to people from their country already there. When one wave of immigration and foreign investment was exhausted, another formed" (246).

Today, the Upstate has a diversified economic base, consisting of high technology, computers, metalworking, plastics and automotive industries (Kanter 245). By 1994, it was home to over 215 international firms from eighteen countries, with fifty of the firms having their US headquarters in the Upstate. Today, Greenville County has the largest number of industrial jobs in the state (55,076) and the most manufacturing jobs (27,398) ("Greenville County, S.C.").

CONCLUSION

With all his public service, Heller never neglected his religion or his identity as a Jew. He and Trude raised their family of three children a block away
from the synagogue they attended. According to Rabbi Julie Anne Kozlow of
Congregation Beth Israel, Heller was a pillar of the synagogue. "That Heller
chose to live in the shadow of his temple speaks volumes about the man and
the family he raised," she commented (Sowell).

Heller's involvement with the temple dates back to his earliest days in
Greenville. He served as president of Beth Israel twice during the 1970s and
also chaired the building committee during the same period when the congregation was building a new synagogue. He led a Zionist organization as well as
the National Conference of Christians and Jews (Max and Trude Heller). His
son Steven noted that at home, Trude and Max often spoke to each other, and
always spoke to their parents in German and Yiddish. Heller loved the Yiddish
language and Yiddish theater, which he missed from his days as a young man
in Vienna. Writing for *The Greenville News*, Elizabeth Stipp commented that
Heller was known to "live his religion in everyday life." This was exhibited in
many ways: his commitment to social and civil equality, improving the living
conditions of Greenville's poor and making substantial contributions to charity. Heller gave one-third of his income to charity, including numerous Jewish
causes (Chanes, from his interview with Francie Heller).

The current mayor of Greenville, Knox White, who knew Heller since he
was eighteen years old and chair of the city's youth commission, remarked that
"Max was an inspiration to me and a wonderful teacher about the importance
of urban places" (Sowell). Heller felt fortunate that he had a chance to come to
America and grateful for the opportunities he had in Greenville. "I love living
here and consider this city my home," he said. According to Charles Sowell,
"his sense of humility, appreciation of liberty, an unparalleled compassion for
others, and love of his adopted country, compelled Heller to devote much of
his life to voluntary services to improve the general welfare of the people and
the state of South Carolina."

In 1975, Furman University awarded Heller an honorary Doctor of
Laws degree and in 1998 he received the Bell Tower Award for his exceptional
achievement and service to the school. The University also named its award-
winning student services program The Max and Trude Heller Services Corp
(Sowell). He was the first Jew to serve on the board of trustees at the university.
He was also awarded honorary degrees by two other South Carolina institutions, Winthrop University and Clemson University.

Heller received the "Man of the Year Award" from the National Council of Jewish Women in 1970; the Distinguished Service Award from Greater Greenville Ministerial Alliance; the Human Relations Award from Greenville Human Relations Committee and the Whitney Young Humanitarian Award from the Greenville Urban League. The Greenville Chamber of Commerce named its prestigious neighborhood improvement award for Heller.

Heller's service to the community reveals his commitment to diversity and civil rights, his compassion for people and his desire to make Greenville a better place. His service reflected his deeply held Jewish morals and ethics. He worked with the Visiting Nurse Association, the Community Council, United Fund, Phillis Wheatley Center, Greenville Symphony, served on the St. Francis Hospital Board of Trustees and was a volunteer for United Cerebral Palsy. In 1996, Heller had the honor of carrying the Olympic Torch down Main Street to the Peace Center, marking the route of his greatest achievements in redesigning Greenville's downtown ("Tracking the Olympic Torch").

On Heller's nintieth birthday, May 28, 2009, a bronze sculpture and storyboards were unveiled in his honor on Main Street. Known as the Max Heller Legacy Plaza, his life is memorialized with photographs and interpretive panels, from his escape to America, to his business life and public service.

Upon his death in 2011, at the age of ninety-two, US Senator Jim DeMint, a Greenville native and a Republican, eulogized the former mayor:

> Our state has lost a great leader with the passing of Max Heller. I will always remember Mayor Heller as a man with a generational vision for what Greenville could become. But, more than that, he was a man of action who rallied community leaders to make those ideas reality. His tenacity set downtown Greenville on its current path of success and spurred the economic investments that have brought jobs and tourism to the Upstate. The people of Greenville and the state owe him a debt of gratitude."

Heller once said "I've been fighting all my life because I am Jewish and I am so proud of it" ("Thoughts"). Max Heller fought for freedom and he fought for the integrity to live as a Jew in a free land. Moreover, he fought for the public good. He fervently believed that as a Jew you cannot walk away from injustices. You must speak up (Heller, Interview with US Holocaust Museum, 24 Sept. 1998, 2). But Heller was also eternally grateful, "grateful for his faith and grateful to God every day that we're here." He was also grateful to Mary

Mills, the young woman who made it possible for him to escape Nazi persecution and start a new life in America. A picture of Mary Mills remained on his bedroom dresser until the day he died (Heller, Interview with US Holocaust Museum, 24 Sept. 1998, 48).

His legacy in Greenville and the state of South Carolina is testimony to what community member Greg Jensen described as a "true visionary and an all-around good guy" (Poland 21).

Notes

1. The original letter from Mary Mills to Max Heller is at the Museum of Jewish Heritage, New York City.
2. The South Carolina Code of 1915, "prohibited textile factories from permitting laborers of different races from working together in the same room or using the same entrances, pay windows, exits, doorways, stairways, or windows at the same time or the same lavatories, toilets, drinking water buckets, pails, cups, dippers or glasses at any time." See Woodward 83.
3. Halprin's other accomplishments include Ghiardelli Square and the United Nations Plaza in San Francisco and the Franklin D. Roosevelt Memorial in Washington, D.C. See "The Landscape Architecture of Lawrence Halprin."
4. Buck Mickel, C. Thomas Wyche and Alester Furman, Jr. were business and community leaders in Greenville. With their support and backing they developed Heritage Green, created the financial plan for the Hyatt Regency, helped raise money for the Peace Center and backed the Governor's School for the Arts and Humanities.
5. Heller created a sister-city alliance with Bergamo, Italy, while courting an Italian firm for the Upstate.
6. The Liberty Bridge was constructed under the leadership of Mayor Knox White, who continued Heller's vision for Greenville. That vision culminated in a park on Main Street incorporating the Reedy River's forty-foot waterfall at Falls Park. In 2004, the renowned designer, Boston architect Miguel Rosales, designed a breathtaking bridge with a sweeping arc spanning the falls.
7. The baseball park was built in the historic West End heart of downtown. A replica of Fenway Park in Boston, the privately funded stadium is home to the Greenville Drive.
8. At the same time, Spartanburg leaders were also attracting foreign investments to the county including Hoechst Celanese, Menzel, Zima, Hobourn Aero Components, Rieter Machine Works, Sulzer-Ruti, and Symtech, to name a few.
9. Willie Earle was a twenty-four-year-old black man, charged with the murder of a white taxi driver in Greenville in February 1947. A mob of white men stormed the jail in Pickens where he was being held and lynched him. All thirty-one white men indicted in the murder were found not guilty.
10. Spartanburg business leaders and the Chamber of Commerce were instrumental in getting BMW to Spartanburg County.
11. Richard Tukey, Executive Director of the Chamber of Commerce from 1951 until his death in 1979, was the primary activist luring foreign investment to Spartanburg.

Works Cited

"Apparel Firm Buys Maxon Shirt Plant." *Greenville News*, 2 April 1971. Max Heller Papers, Mayoral Files, Box 4, Folder 2, Furman University Special Collections.

Application for appointment to the Federal Trade Commission, US Government during the Reagan Administration. Max Heller Papers, Box 10, Folder 1, Furman University Special Collections.

Bainbridge, Judith. "Max Heller Considered among Fathers of Today's Downtown." *Greenville News*, 13 Mar. 2017.

Bainbridge, Judith (Greenville historian) and Robert (Executive Director of the Greenville Central Area Partnership, 1981–1986). Personal interview. 14 Feb. 2018, Greenville, SC.

Butler, Miss Larnell C. Letter to Max Heller. Max Heller papers, Box 8, Folder 7, Furman University Special Collections.

Campbell, Stuart. "1972—It Was Year of Self-Analysis in Greenville City Hall." *Greenville Piedmont*, 8 Jan. 1973, p. 17. Max Heller papers, Box 4, Folder 4, Furman University Special Collections.

Carlton, David L. *Mill and Town in South Carolina, 1880–1920*. Louisiana State Univ., 1982.

Chanes, Adam. "When Greenville, South Carolina Had a Jewish Mayor." *Forward*, 25 Sept. 2014. Max Heller Papers, Box 4 Folder 2, Furman University Special Collections.

Chiles, Marguerite. Letter to Max Heller. 9 Nov. 1978. Max Heller Papers, Box 65, Furman University Special Collections.

Cobb, James C. *The South and America Since World War II*. Oxford Univ., 2011.

DeMint, Congressman Jim. Eulogy to Max Heller. *Greenville News*. Max Heller Papers, Scrapbooks, Box 17, Furman University Special Collections.

Dozier, Al. "Sprouse Attacks." *Greenville Piedmont*, 2 Nov. 1978. Max Heller Papers, Congressional/Gubernatorial Campaign Files, Box 1, Folder 1, Furman University Special Collections.

Dunn, J. A. C. *The Charlotte Observer*, Daily Magazine, 8 Sept 1966, p. 16D. Max Heller Papers, Box 4, Folder 1, Furman University Special Collections.

———. "Heller 1: 'If You Remember At Me.'" *The Charlotte Observer*, Daily Magazine, 6 Sept. 1966. Max Heller Papers, Box 4, Folder 1, Furman University Special Collections.

———. "Heller 2: 'Luck and Good Weather.'" *The Charlotte Observer*, Daily Magazine, 7 Sept. 1966, p. 148. Max Heller Papers, Box 4, Folder 1, Furman University Special Collections.

Edgar, Walter. *South Carolina: A History*. Univ. of South Carolina, 1998.

"Emanuel J. 'Mutt' Evans, First Jewish Mayor, 1951–1963." *And Justice For All*, 28 Jan. 2013, www.andjusticeforall.dconc.gov/gallery-images/Emanuel-j-mutt-evans-first-Jewish-mayor-1951-1963. Accessed 1 July 2018.

FOCUS, 12 Oct., pp. 3–4. Max Heller Papers, Box 21, Folder 8, Furman University Special Collections.

Ford, Lacy K., and R. Phillip Stone. "Economic Development and Globalization in South Carolina." *Southern Cultures*, vol. 13, 2007, pp. 18–50.

Gailey, Phil. "Bigotry Issue in Carolina Campaign." *New York Times*, 24 Sept. 1986.

Glass, J. L. Letter to Don Sprouse and Mayor Heller. Nov. 1978. Max Heller Papers, Box 65, Furman University Special Collections.

Gowdy, Trey. Letter Max Heller. 4 Nov. 1978. Max Heller Papers, Box 65, Furman University Special Collections.

"Greenville County, S.C." *Data USA*, datausa.io/profile/geo/greenville-county-sc/. Accessed 5 July 2018.

Greenville Creative Loafing, 6 Oct. 2001, p. 13. Max Heller Folder, Greenville County Library.

The Greenville Piedmont, 28 Mar. 1969.

"Greenville Presentation." *The Piedmont*, 11 Nov. 1973.

"Heller, Council Prod Leadership." *Greenville News*, 9 July 1975.

"Heller Questions Campbell's Tactics." *Columbia Record*, 1 Oct. 1986, p. 11. Max Heller Papers, Congressional/Gubernatorial Campaign Files, Box 65, Folder 1, Furman University Special Collections.

"Heller Says Klan Attack Shows 'Slimy Side of Campaign.'" *Greenville News and Piedmont*, 29 Oct. 1978. Max Heller Papers, Congressional/Gubernatorial Campaign Files, Box 65, Furman University Special Collections.

Heller, Francie. Presentation. The Jewish Historical Society of South Carolina Annual Conference, 23 Oct. 2016. Beth Israel Congregation, Greenville, SC.

Heller, Max. Inaugural Speech. 13 July 1971. Max Heller Papers, Box 1, Folder 8, Furman University Special Collections.

———. Interview. Max Heller Papers, Box 7, Folder 8, Furman University Special Collections.

———. Interview #A-0155 by Jack Bass and Walter De Vries. 3 Dec. 1974. The Southern Oral History Program Collection, #4007, The Southern Historical Collection, The Louis Round Wilson Special Collections Library, UNC Chapel Hill, cdr.lib.unc.edu/indexablecontent/uuid:e26cc345-3d40-46ca-b3ea-98a9ce5fd7d0. Accessed 21 Aug. 2018.

———. Interview #A-0166 by Jack Bass. The Southern Oral History Program Collection, #4007, The Southern Historical Collection, The Louis Round Wilson Special Collections Library, UNC Chapel Hill, https:cdr.lib.unc.eduindexableontent/uuid:e26cc345-3d40-46ca-b3ea-98a9ce5fd7do.

———. Interview by Dale Rosengarten and Sandra Lee Kahn Rosenblum. 28 Feb. 1997, Greenville, SC. College of Charleston Libraries, Jewish Heritage Project, libcat.cofc.edu/search/. Accessed 3 Mar. 2000.

———. Interview by Courtney Tollison, Professor of History, Furman University. Private papers.

———. Interview with the United States Holocaust Museum. 24 Sept. 1998, Accession #1998.A.0216, https://collections.ushmm.org/search/catalog/irn506450. Accessed 25 July 2018.

———. Letter to The Honorable Bryan Dorn, House of Representatives, Washington, DC. 18 Aug. 1947. Max Heller Papers, Box 4, Folder 1, Furman University Special Collections.

———. "Max Heller Remembers." Interview by James Shannon. *Creative Loafing*, 6 Oct. 2001, p. 11. Max Heller Papers, Box 22, Folder 6, Furman University Special Collections.

Heller, Steve. Interview with Ezra Hall. 29 Jan. 2018, Greenville, South Carolina.

Huff, Archie Vernon. *Greenville: The History of the City and County in the South Carolina Piedmont.* Univ. of South Carolina, 1995.

"It's Enough That I Can Run for Congress." *Baltimore Sun*, 10 April 1978. Max Heller Papers, A15, Folder 4, Box 4, Furman University Special Collections.

Jackson, Jesse. Personal interview. 14 Sept. 2013, Greenville Hyatt, Greenville, SC.

"Jewish Mayors in the South." *2017 Goldring/Woldenberg Institute of Southern Jewish Life*, www.isjl.org/jewish-mayors-in-the-south.html. Accessed 30 June 2018.

Kanter, Rosabeth Moss. *World Class: Thriving Locally in the Global Economy*. Simon & Schuster, 1995.

"The Landscape Architecture of Lawrence Halprin." *National Building Museum*, www.nbm.org/exhibition/Lawrence-Halprin. Accessed 15 Feb. 2018.

Leffert, Fred. Personal interview. 2 Oct. 2016, Greenville, SC.

Marcus, Ernest. "Max Heller: The Father of Modern Greenville." South Carolina Jewish Historical Society Annual Meeting, 23 Oct. 2016, Greenville, SC.

Max Heller Papers, Box 20, Folder 1, Furman University Special Collections.

Max Heller Papers, Box 7, Folder 3, Furman University Special Collections.

Max Heller Papers, Congressional Campaign, Box 1, Folder 1, Furman University Special Collections.

"Max Heller." *YouTube*, uploaded by ETVRoadShow, 6 Nov. 2007, https://www.youtube.com/watch?v=2jj3_61qncs.

"Maxon Shirt: At 10-Year Mark It's a Thriving Company." *Boys' Outfitter Newsletter*, Oct. 1957, p. 240. Max Heller Papers, Box 7, Folder 2, Furman University Special Collections.

"Meet the Mayor of Greenville, SC, Max Heller." *American Jewish Times-Outlook*, Nov. 1971, pp. 4–6. Max Heller Papers, Box 3, Folder 1, Furman University Special Collections.

Michelin. www.michelinman.com. Accessed 2 Feb. 2018.

Mills, Mary. Letter to Max Heller. Museum of Jewish Heritage, New York City.

Morrow, Victoria. Personal Interview. 10 Mar. 2018.

Moses, Susan Heller. "Max and Trude Heller: Giving Back to the Community." *The Jewish Historical Society of South Carolina*, vol. 21, no. 2, 2016, pp. 8–9.

Murphy, Tom. "'The American Autobahn': German and Other Suppliers Cruise into South Carolina." *WardsAuto*, 1 Jan. 1998, wardsauto.com. Accessed 2 Feb. 2018.

Nelson, Marilyn. "Max Heller Revisited." *Greenville Magazine*, April 1982, pp. 48–51. Max Heller Papers, Box 27, Furman University Special Collections.

"Obstacles." Max Heller Papers, Mayoral Files, Box 3, Folder 1, Furman University Special Collections.

"Piedmont Shirt Co. Ordered To Halt Employees' Union." *The Index-Journal* [Greenwood, SC], 3 June 1939, www.newspaper.com. Accessed 12 Feb. 2018.

Poland, Tom. *Greenville's Grand Design.* Publishing Resources Group, 2015.

"Remarks by Mr. Max Heller, Chairman, SC State Development Board, Management Symposium '82." Max Heller Papers, State Carolina Development Board, Box 14, Furman University Special Collections.

Riley, Richard. Personal interview. 8 Feb. 2018, Greenville, SC.

Saunders, Sally. "Sprouse Says Religion Makes Heller Unqualified." *Greenville News*, 3 Nov. 1978, pp. 1A–2A. Max Heller Papers, Congressional/Gubernatorial Campaign Files, Box 1, Folder 1, Furman University Special Collections.

"Shirt Firm Honors Employees." *Greenville Piedmont*, 22 Dec. 1960. Max Heller Papers, Box 7, Folder #2, Furman University Special Collections.

South Carolina Naturalization Records. Declaration of Intentions. June 1939. Max Heller Folder, Greenville County Public Library.

Sowell, Charles. "An Inspiration, a Teacher." *Greenville Journal*, 17 June 2011, p. 8.

Steadman, Ethel. "Heller: Man behind Maxon." *Greenville News*, 4 Mar. 1962, p. 1-D. Max Heller Papers, Box 7, Folder 2, Furman University Special Collections.

Stipp, Elizabeth. "Greenville, Heller Good for Each Other." Profiles, A Series. *Greenville News*, 21 April 1968, p. 3, sec. 4. Max Heller Papers, Box 4, Folder 2, Furman University Special Collections.

Tampa Bay Times [St. Petersburg, FL], 9 April 1978, p. 71.

"Thoughts." Max Heller Papers, Box 10, Folder 6, Furman University Special Collections.

Tollison, Courtney. Personal interview. 27 Feb. 2018, Greenville, SC.

"Tracking the Olympic Torch." *Greenville News*, 23 June 1996, p. 13.

"Under Heller's Leadership." Max Heller Papers, Box 11, Folder 2, Furman University Special Collections.

Woodward, C. Vann. *The Strange Career of Jim Crow.* Oxford Univ., 1955.

CHAPTER 8

"A Just and Righteous Man": Eli Black and the Transformation of United Fruit

by Matt Garcia

On September 3, 1973, *Time* magazine announced the transformation of United Fruit Company (UFCO) from an exploiter of Latin American plantation labor to a beacon of corporate responsibility ("Prettying up Chiquita" 76). The leading exporter of bananas from Central America entered its third year as the primary entity within United Brands, a food conglomerate led by 52-year-old CEO Eli Black. Black, a former rabbi and Polish immigrant, initiated a series of changes aimed at improving the conditions of labor and life on United Fruit's production sites. Honduras served as the locus of this conversion since the majority of United Brands' holdings resided in La Lima, a company town near the country's second largest city, San Pedro Sula. Within the first two years of Black's tenure, United Fruit had raised the salaries of its workers to six times the level of those of its competitor, Standard Fruit, provided free housing and electricity to employees, and offered workers the opportunity to purchase ranch houses below cost ("United Fruit Lives Down a 'Colonialist Past'" 1). Black also expedited the replacement of North American managers with those born in Honduras while ending the practice of hiring workers from Guatemala to break local strikes. Referred to locally as "Hondurization," labor leaders welcomed the transformation, creating an expectation that a new era had begun for a company once maligned as "El Pulpo" (the Octopus) for its influence over all aspects of Central American lives.

It therefore came as a shock to the world when, just seventeen months later, on February 3, 1975, Eli Black took his own life by jumping from the forty-fourth floor of the Pan American building in midtown Manhattan. Black left few clues as to what compelled this dramatic act, though newspapers were soon awash in scandal. He had paid the first half of a two-part bribe to the Honduran president, General Oswaldo López Arellano, in an effort to lower tariffs and break the back of a new cartel of banana-growing nations in Latin America. In the wake of Black's death, the Securities and Exchange Commission (SEC) opened a case against United Brands for failure to report the expenditure to shareholders. The investigation effectively cancelled the second $1.25 million payment to López Arellano and contributed to his ouster from office ("S.E.C. Suit"). For Black and United Brands approbation turned to post-mortem condemnation, confirming, it seemed, that Black had more in common with his predecessors than he wanted us to believe.

But, did he? My reconsideration of Black's legacy grows out of the discovery that Honduras was not the only front in which he committed to changing business as usual. He counted among the United Brands companies Inter-Harvest, the largest lettuce producer in California, operating in the irrigated Imperial Valley along the border with Mexico and in the "salad bowl" of the Salinas Valley just south of the Bay Area. When Cesar Chavez and the United Farm Workers (UFW) signed union contracts with grape growers in the San Joaquin Valley on July 29, 1970, most lettuce growers attempted to pre-empt the UFW arrival by signing with the grower-friendly Teamsters union. Black refused to participate in this scheme. His agreement to sign two-year contracts with the UFW made him the target of grower ire and lawsuits, and his lettuce the object of an ill-conceived and ineffectual Teamsters boycott. It also earned Black the friendship of Cesar Chavez. Chavez regarded Black as "a just and righteous man" and frequently visited him in New York and Connecticut to celebrate Jewish religious holidays.

Black's attempt to alter business practices to improve worker lives at two of the largest entities within United Brands should give us pause. Was this part of a grander scheme to integrate social justice into the business practices of his company? Black's efforts to address worker concerns were complemented by his personal decisions to distribute a greater portion of his wealth and time beyond the business world. He refused to sit on other corporate boards and restricted his service to philanthropic organizations. Black earned only $200,000 in salary, far below his CEO peers. In many ways, Black prided himself on doing things differently, signaling a willingness to be judged as much by his employees as by his shareholders.

Eli Black, I argue, is due for re-evaluation in light of the increasing narrative of "social responsibility" in the ads and the practices of corporations today (McCann). Companies such as Whole Foods, Ben & Jerry's Ice Cream, and even McDonald's have discovered that treating employees well can heighten the appeal of their stores, products, and restaurants to the buying public. Black's commitment to working with unions and governments to improve his company's image offers an early example of this phenomenon. That a Jewish American immigrant tried—and failed—to pursue such a business strategy makes the story both tragic and a harbinger of things to come.

*****

Eli Black arrived at Ellis Island, New York from Lublin, Poland on March 27, 1925, at an especially difficult time to be an immigrant in America. Over the previous decade, the United States Congress had debated legislation limiting the admission of immigrants who, critics of an open immigration policy alleged, had overwhelmed cities, taken jobs from native-born citizens, and fomented revolution in the streets. In 1921 Congress established a national origins formula that allocated admission quotas for each nation with the intent of reducing the flow of unskilled laborers and favoring a northern European ethnic composition. A full-throated movement against Asian and Southern and Eastern European immigrants by labor leaders and anti-immigrant legislators led to the Immigration Act of 1924, which lowered the percentage of immigrants allowed from any one European country, while fully barring immigration from Asia. Despite these restrictions, a provision supporting family unification and permitting non-quota status for wives and unmarried children under the age of eighteen allowed Black's mother, Chaje Blachowicz, two sisters, Goldie (twelve) and Sarah (ten), and Black (two) to legally enter the country and join Black's father, Benzion "Benjamin" Blachowicz, who had arrived on February 3, 1924.

Black's arrival as a child at a time when US laws sought to curb immigration provides important context for his extraordinary life that followed. As the object of scorn, Black and his family were acutely aware of anti-Semitism in America well before the events of World War II and the Holocaust discredited, if not eliminated, such blatant forms of discrimination. The Blachowicz family would have known a time when a good portion of society associated Jews with "Bolshevism" given that many Eastern European immigrants came from Russia, the first country to experience a Communist revolution in 1917.

After initially settling in the Bronx, the elder Blachowicz moved the family to the heart of the Jewish diaspora in America, the Lower East Side. On Stanton Street, one block south of Houston, young Eli thrived within a supportive Jewish community that encouraged him to seek meaning and value in the religious texts he studied. Black followed this impulse through his formal education, earning a degree, in 1940, from Yeshiva University, the only Jewish institution of higher education in the United States, located in Washington Heights.

Yet, if Black was a product of a deeply religious and supportive family and community, he was also a young man who came of age in New York City, the beating heart of American capitalism. At Yeshiva, his senior class peers voted him "most respected" and "handsomest," but also "most likely to succeed" ("Yeshiva Seniors" 38). And succeed he did. After graduating magna cum laude from Yeshiva, Black spent an additional year in its seminary, became an ordained rabbi, and served the Sons of Israel congregation in Woodmere, New York, from 1941 to 1945. The appeal of business and finance, however, compelled Black to take courses at Columbia University on the side, eventually persuading him to leave the rabbinate in 1946 for a position as a stock broker at Lehman Brothers investment firm. There he took on a challenge that others could not solve, convincing financier Robert Young to reorganize the Missouri Pacific Railroad in order to maximize profit. In a short period of time, he proved his business acumen and set his sights on moving from financial advising to actual management. The opportunity came after a move to American Securities Company, where he worked on the American Seal-Kap (AMK) account until he became AMK's chairman in 1954. Under Black, AMK went from making paper caps for milk bottles to producing various paper products that significantly increased the profitability of the company. From this modest perch, he surprised everyone by acquiring the Midwestern meat processor Morrell Meat Co. in 1967. In 1970 he shocked the business world by mounting the successful takeover of United Fruit, establishing United Brands.

*****

Black's background as a rabbi and his growing commitment to social responsibility made him an unlikely fit for the United Fruit Company. Although he left behind little written evidence of the influence of Judaism on his business practices, several friends and observers documented his life-long attempt to balance "two domains": finance and spirituality. His professor and mentor, Samuel Belkin, President of Yeshiva University, stayed in touch with Black throughout his life. Recalling Black's days as his *talmid* (student), he noted the "excitement and stimulation" their public debates often generated among the student body. "In a great sense at times," Belkin admitted, "I felt he was the teacher and I his student." He admired Black for his *"derek eretz"*—a concept that lacks an exact English translation, but can best be described as "respect for one's self and the dignity of man" ("Eulogy for Eli M. Black"). Bernard Fischman, longtime friend and confidant of Black, saw this attitude play out in his business ethics. "He felt deeply his responsibilities to his shareholders," Fischman acknowledged, "but he also believed that business was a human operation" ("Businessman with Social Conscience"). Black understood that the cost of doing business included addressing the needs of those who worked for the company—on and off the job. Such an approach stood in stark contrast to UFCO's historic treatment of its employees, especially in Latin America.

Prior to Black's arrival, the company's capacious appetite for land and its need to control every aspect of the banana business—from cultivation to transportation and marketing—contributed to a business model known as vertical integration: the ownership of all assets and industries to insure smooth operation and profits. United Fruit controlled the entire logistics operation for moving Chiquita bananas from plantation to tables abroad, including a sizable number of container vessels, known as the "White Fleet," and the national rail lines in Guatemala and Honduras. Often the company ran these businesses for the purpose of squeezing more profit from its holdings rather than meeting the needs of local populations. United Fruit's interference in the national sovereignty of its hosts reached its apex in 1954 when it inspired a CIA-led coup in Guatemala against the democratically elected government of Jacobo Árbenz Guzmán, after he expropriated unused UFCO land in exchange for its true value.

The United Fruit that Black sought to reform was also mired in the dirty politics of another "banana republic," Honduras. In 1910 Samuel Zemurray, an early banana entrepreneur, defended his investments in Honduran banana production by organizing a private military expedition to reinstall deposed president Manuel Bonilla for the purpose of canceling debts on his shipments north. Having sold his business to rival United Fruit in 1930, Zemurray bought up a majority share of the combined company during the Great Depression. The colorful life of "Sam the Banana Man" has provoked curiosity and a popular biography, largely inspired by his willful disregard for Honduran sovereignty and his business approach that contributed to the later subversion of Árbenz's government in Guatemala (Cohen).

Comparisons of Black and Zemurray, however, stop at their common origins in Eastern Europe and degree to which their Jewish faith shaped their decisions. Zemurray arrived in New Orleans in 1891 and came of age in Mobile, Alabama. The Mexican Gulf Coast served as the gateway to Latin America and the nexus of a burgeoning transcontinental banana industry. Beginning in 1895, Zemurray began his single-minded ascent to corner the banana market by imitating the practices of Gilded Age robber barons, seeking to usurp the declining influence of the Spanish Empire with American economic and political dominance.

Black's life in New York and his maturation as a businessman after World War II set him on a different course. He watched the fallout of the coup in Guatemala, which may have achieved US political goals but also cast American business as imperious and insensitive to local concerns. By the time Black acquired United Fruit in 1970, the civil rights and anti-war movements inspired a reconsideration of the role of the United States in the world. Black's takeover of United Fruit presented the opportunity to right the wrongs of the company's past and prove it could be a good steward of the land and industry for the benefit of both host and investor.

Black's approach reflected an appreciation of the counterculture's emerging critique of US foreign policy that agreed with the ethics inculcated in him during his early life. His exposure to the Judaic concept of Tikkun Olam—the belief that one can repair a broken world—at Yeshiva University manifest itself in the dignity he saw in his employees. Ironically perhaps, these ethics compelled Black to leave the rabbinate for a life of business. According to Fischman, Black lost faith in his role as a rabbi because "he didn't think sermons changed anyone's attitude about anything" ("Did Social Conscience Kill Businessman?"). Rather, he sought to restore trust between employer and employee by advocating for greater social responsibility on the part of business owners. Black believed "socially conscious, responsible corporate executives" should earn the "loyalty of employees" and the "esteem of the public" by being more invested in the well-being of society. While he worried about the growth of the welfare state and over-reliance on government, his impulse to invest in employee benefits came from a sincere desire to improve the quality of life for everyone (Black). Even his critics, like Thomas McCann who published two books about Black's United Fruit, admitted that "there is no doubt that [his] Talmudic training had a profound effect on his view of the world" (McCann

173). As CEO of United Brands, Black saw an opportunity to improve the lives of hard-working employees of United Fruit in Honduras who had suffered under generations of exploitation and expropriation at the hands of the company he now led.

For their part, Hondurans would not have it any other way. Honduran workers and small-scale farmers remained organized after the 1954 general strike that gave birth to the Tela Railroad Company Workers' Union (SITRATERCO) and the pro-labor Liberal Party. Since United Fruit owned the Tela Railroad Company, SITRATERCO became the voice of the company's employees—whether they worked on the railroad or banana plantations. Prior to Black's arrival, United Fruit had responded by expanding an "associate growers' program" that displaced the burden of planting, weeding, and harvesting bananas onto local growers who maintained exclusive contracts to sell their fruit to the company. Under this arrangement, United Fruit shifted their financial obligation from workers to irrigation, fertilization and disease control. In the 1960s, the Tela Railroad Company opposed a new land reform movement among local farmers in Honduras by suspending further investments in the country. These actions ran counter to the Kennedy administration's efforts to end poverty in Latin America through the Alliance for Progress, a program that encouraged private investment abroad.

Black embraced the associate growers' program but also worked to repair the reputation of United Fruit by instituting business practices that anticipated the rise of "socially conscious capitalism." During the takeover of United Fruit, he earned the respect of management by consulting with them throughout the process, winning their confidence by remaining respectful of those in charge. John Fox, chairman of United Fruit since 1965, initially felt threatened by Black's acquisition of significant portions of the company's stock but concluded that "Black never went back or changed a single thing he promised us" (Welles 28). That level of honesty paid dividends, as Black's company, AMK, beat out a wave of more established suitors to become United Brands.

*****

Black transformed United Fruit into United Brands on June 30, 1970, and took little time to implement his vision for a different company on both the domestic and international front. Less than one month later, on July 29, Cesar Chavez signed historic contracts with grape grower, John Guimarra in Delano, California, shifting the UFW's battle to lettuce. Black's decision to support

UFW and work with Chavez was a bold move, signaling his intention to build a company that respected the voice of its employees.

Agreeing to a contract with Chavez at the height of his popularity, however, took much less courage and vision than changing the trajectory of United Fruit abroad. The company was the most significant employer in Honduras, where it owned 200,000 acres of land. Although it controlled significant acreage in nearby Costa Rica, Guatemala, and Panama, Honduras constituted its most productive site and the greatest revenue producer across United Brands. In short, experimenting with La Lima meant that Black was tinkering with the company's foundation.

Yet, tinker he did, mostly to the approval of the Honduran government and unions. He rejected the usual piece-rate compensation by establishing a set rate of $95 per month for banana pickers based on a forty-four-hour week. Additionally, he made each employee a shareholder by including bank stocks as part of their wage structure. Such wages represented the best in the entire country, amounting to $22 million in salaries paid per year by United Fruit. For the first time in the company's history, compensation included ten paid vacation days. Whereas previously United Fruit would import managers from North America, the company now hired Honduran nationals for these positions. Of the 325 residential managers at La Lima, three hundred were Honduran and only five came from the United States by 1972. In another departure from previous practice, the company stopped bringing in workers from neighboring Central American countries: in total, Hondurans composed 99% of the workforce on the plantation. When asked how these conditions compared to previous ones, Alberto Reyes, a veteran picker at United Fruit shared: "I worked from 6am to 6pm. We never dared complain. They would bring in Guatemalans and others to pick the bananas. The Americans had all the good jobs then. All that is past." Oscar Gale Varela, president of SITRATERCO, confirmed these impressions, testifying, "The company respects us and we respect the company" ("United Fruit Lives Down a 'Colonialist Past'").

Black extended investments to Honduras' health and education infrastructure. La Lima maintained a 235-bed hospital with eleven full-time physicians and the capacity to perform major surgery. United Fruit workers and their families paid twenty-five cents to use the facility, while those not employed by the system also benefitted by an aggressive campaign against malaria and polio, which the hospital effectively eliminated within three years. The company also paid $500,000 per year to support the school system serving the United Fruit employees. The school employed 210 teachers who taught over 8,000 students up to sixth grade. The company provided $50,000 in scholarships for students to finish high school or college without any obligation to return to La Lima as employees of United Fruit ("United Fruit Lives Down a 'Colonialist Past'").

Black also increased the transfer of land ownership from the United Fruit Company to Honduran planters begun under the associate growers' program. United Fruit cast this initiative as an attempt to put Honduran land in the hands of Honduran farmers. While the program did return 135,000 acres to the Honduran government to be broken up into eighty-six fifty-acre groves for independent planters, it freed the company from much of the costs of farming. The company redirected a good share of its resources to controlling disease in the groves and building the Chiquita brand worldwide. At the same time, in the early 1970s, the program enjoyed popularity in Honduras and generated earnings of between $1,200 and $7,000 per year for participants. These investments also helped deter calls for the expropriation of unused United Fruit lands. When asked if Hondurans preferred the government to control land rather than United Fruit, Honduran labor leader Oscar Gale Varela said, "No, absolutely not." For him, government had a tradition of being "bad administrators" and lacked economic resources. He added, "The Honduran Government doesn't have these things; United Fruit does" ("United Fruit Lives Down a 'Colonialist Past'").

*****

Gale's impression that business could do what government could not confirmed that Black had achieved, at least for the moment, what he had aspired to when he became CEO of United Fruit. In an article celebrating Black's achievements, the author noted that "United Fruit, not only is not Chiquita, but is no longer United Fruit" ("United Fruit is Not Chiquita"). The author noted that, while Black exhibited incredible business acumen in wresting control of United Fruit from other, more seasoned suitors, his biggest challenge might be overcoming the company's past and expanding its future.

By the time of United Brands' birth, United Fruit had worn out its welcome in Latin America through its historically boorish behavior. The company's extraction of raw materials and wealth inspired countries to curtail its growth just as Black took ownership. In Honduras, for example, peasant farmer protests calling for agrarian reform throughout the 1960s led to President General López Arellano authorizing bond sales of $15 million in 1968 for projects on disputed land owned or rented by Black's predecessor, Samuel Zemurray. A year later, in response to land tenure pressure and union demands, López Arellano allowed an Honduran-Salvadoran immigration treaty to expire, which restricted workers arriving from Honduras' neighbor, creating more opportunity for locals to claim jobs and land in the Sula Valley. These developments signaled the empowerment of peasant organizations throughout Central America (Euraque 140–43).

Meanwhile, intense competition limited United Fruit's share of the North American market, going from 80% after World War II down to 39% in 1972. These decreasing profits required a pivot toward areas of growth, increasingly at the site of United Fruit's holdings: Central America. Although Black and his associates sought to cultivate new markets for bananas in Japan and Mexico, the company began to concentrate its efforts on the fifteen million potential Central American consumers of United Brands products. Paying employees a living wage not only made United Fruit a more socially responsible company, it also made for good business. And it wasn't just bananas; under Black, United Brands diversified to include a wider sector of the food business, including processed foods. They continued to grow bananas in Honduras and lettuce in California, but they added products such as meat, margarine, mayonnaise, salad oils, and shortening. Black had overseen the acquisition, in 1967, of Morrell Meats, produced in Iowa and South Dakota, while in 1965 United Fruit bought out Costa Rican company NUMAR S.A., the largest producer of processed foods in Central America. Both United Fruit and NUMAR, as Central American producers owned by a US multinational conglomerate, allowed United Brands to avoid costly tariffs under the Central American Common Market, established in the early 1960s ("United Fruit is Not Chiquita" 125).

Although some of the transformation began before 1970, Black clarified and amplified this strategy. His support of Honduran workers' welfare helped transform the reputation of the company and improved the potential for Central American consumers to see United Brands products as an investment in their future. Secondly, his pivot away from land ownership, towards processing, distribution, and marketing of food destined for the Latin American consumer, shifted the riskier parts of food production to local farmers. In good times, everyone—both company and planters—stood to gain. At the time Black began his work as CEO, the future looked relatively bright, and he, personally, was widely regarded as an up-and-coming mogul who came out of nowhere to create a business model Americans could be proud of in the age of civil rights and increasing ambivalence about America's role in the world— even if he did not share the motivations of those protesting in the streets or on campus. In an article for *Harvard Business Review*, Black advocated for "socially conscious programs" to "improve the quality of living of employees." His advocacy, however, stemmed from his concern over societies' overdependence on government welfare programs. For him, CEOs had an obligation to practice "business responsibility" so that "workers, in turn, will reciprocate by restoring their loyalties to the companies that employ them" (Black 2). Unlike some of his fellow executives, Black subscribed to the belief that a partnership between business and labor leaders could achieve this common goal.

Eli Black's decision to work with labor leaders in Honduras and California, then, came out of a commitment to recovering the reputation of his companies as much as his will to improve the lives of his employees. Given that so much of United Brands' profits remained contingent upon banana production in Honduras, this strategy would require time to mature.

*****

Black would not be afforded such time. The new economic and political realities of the seventies undid United Brands and drew Black to his tragic end. In 1971, US economic production had shrunk to such levels that Americans began importing more than they exported, causing the first trade deficit since the Great Depression. With unemployment on the rise and the cost of goods climbing, the era of stagflation—price inflation without economic growth— weakened the US dollar and forced President Nixon to desperate measures. These acts included the abandonment of the Bretton Woods accords, a change in policy that completely untethered the dollar's value from the price of gold. While the decision helped alleviate inflation, it also contributed to the depreciation of US currency—a condition that the Organization of Petroleum Exporting Countries (OPEC) countered by pegging the cost of oil to gold rather than a fluctuating dollar. When the United States sent arms and support to Israel during the Yom Kippur War, OPEC—which included Arab belligerents in the conflict—enacted an oil embargo on Israeli allies, including the United States. As a consequence, the price of gasoline shot from $3 to $12 per barrel in 1973. Fuel remained expensive and scarce through 1974.

Black felt the oil crisis deeply as he struggled to manage the cost of moving United Brands products across the Americas. In the case of bananas, United Fruit maintained an impressive fleet of cargo ships that tallied significant fuel costs each year even though Black worked to replace old container vessels with new, more efficient ones. Although United Brands depended on third parties to transport lettuce from rural California and meat from Iowa and South Dakota, the company bore increases in fuel costs through elevated freight charges. The oil crisis also drove up the price of fossil-fuel dependent

grains, triggering increases in the cost of cattle, and therefore, meat production at Morrell Meats, the third most profitable entity in the United Brands
family. When Hurricane Fifi came ashore in Honduras in September 1974,
United Fruit lost 70% of its plantations and $20 million dollars in crops and
facilities. To add to the strain, a cartel of banana producing countries—Costa
Rica, Honduras, Panama, Guatemala, El Salvador, and Columbia—modeling
themselves after OPEC, Unión de Países Exportadores de Banano (UPEB), demanded $11 million in new banana-export taxes. By year's end in 1974, United
Brands had lost more than $40 million in net income.

The unprecedented political and economic challenges of the 1970s
forced workers and business owners to seek their own solutions. For labor,
workers engaged in harrowing, often futile struggles to defend contracts and
maintain their unions. For business owners, the options ranged from reducing
investment in production to offsetting costs. Black's acceleration of the associate growers' program to displace the risks involved in farming had been an
attempt to insulate the company from such risks, but it came too little, too late,
especially after the convergence of the economic, political and natural disasters
of 1973 and 1974. These challenges forced Black to decide whether "socially
conscious programs" and the management of a modern multinational corporation could be compatible projects. In the end, his bribe of López Arellano
marked a breach in ethical standards—if not a violation of law—that drove
him to a final verdict.

In the wake of the scandal and Black's suicide, new questions arose about
the role governments should play in trade between nations. During the Cold
War, multinational corporations like United Fruit enjoyed the backing of the
US government, but often in a supporting role. After Black's death, the SEC
broke up United Brands but allowed Chiquita to continue. More telling, the
United States and its First World allies showed a greater propensity to set the
table for commerce between nations through free trade agreements and the
formation of world governing bodies to determine the rules of engagement.
Not surprisingly, the advantages enjoyed by US companies prior to the era of
coups and bribes continued, albeit with the legitimacy of a trade pact behind
it. Black's death would initiate a new way of doing business in Latin America,
but not a New Deal for Latin Americans.

The scandal also invited Black's critics to define him as an incompetent,
cold business executive. McCann, for example, reduced Black to "a failure" in
a book that does more to settle old grievances than render a complex man at
an ethical crossroad in his life (5). Undoubtedly, Black arrived at that place

because of his sincere and ever-present faith in Judaism. As he looked out over Manhattan just before jumping, he must have wondered whether his decision to trade the *kittel*, Jewish prayer vestments, for the three-piece suit in 1946 was the correct one for what he aimed to do: change the world. Asking a new generation to share that moment with him invites us to think about the intersection of religion and business, and to imagine a new, ethical role for the United States today.

Works Cited

Black, E. M. "Social Welfare Challenge for Business and Labor." *Harvard Business Review*, vol. 51, July–Aug. 1973, pp. 1–2 (6–7).

"Businessman with Social Conscience: Pulled Between 2 Worlds, Then He Came Apart." Beacon Journal Wire Services, date unknown.

Cohen, Rich. *The Fish That Ate the Whale: The Life and Times of America's Banana King*. Farrar, Straus, and Giroux, 2012.

"Did Social Conscience Kill Businessman?" *St. Louis Post-Dispatch*, Friday, 21 Feb. 1975.

"Eulogy for Eli M. Black." Delivered by Samuel Belkin, President, Yeshiva University, 5 Feb. 1975.

Euraque, Darío A. *Reinterpreting the Banana Republic: Region & State in Honduras, 1870-1972*. Univ. of North Carolina, 1996.

McCann, Thomas. *An American Company: The Tragedy of United Fruit*. Random House, 1976.

"Prettying up Chiquita." *Time*, 3 Sept. 1973, p. 76.

"S. E. C. Suit Links a Honduras Bribe to United Brands." *New York Times*, 10 April 1975, p. 81.

"United Fruit is Not Chiquita." Source and date unknown, p. 125. Columbia Univ. Archive. See also David. Tobis, "United Fruit is Not Chiquita." *NACLA Newsletter*, vol. 5, no. 6, 1971, pp. 7–15.

"United Fruit Lives Down a 'Colonialist Past.'" *New York Times*, 24 April 1972, p. 1.

Welles, Chris. "The Battle for United Fruit." *Investment Banking and Corporate Financing*, Spring 1969, pp. 26–33, 84–88.

"Yeshiva Seniors." *Masmid: Yeshiva University Yearbook*. Yeshiva Univ., 1940.

About the Contributors

ALLAN M. AMANIK is an assistant professor of American Jewish history at Brooklyn College of the City University of New York. His areas of interest include American and New York Jewish history, immigration, gender, history of the family, death and dying, and social welfare policy in the United States. He is author of the forthcoming book, *From Dust to Deeds: Family, Community, and New York Jewish Cemeteries, 1656–1965* (New York University) and he is also co-editor of a forthcoming volume *Till Death Do Us Part: American Ethnic Cemeteries as Borders Uncrossed* (University Press of Mississippi).

LISA ANSELL is Associate Director of the Casden Institute for the Study of the Jewish Role in American Life at the University of Southern California. She received her BA in French and Near East Studies from UCLA and her MA in Middle East Studies from Harvard University. She was the Chair of the World Language Department of New Community Jewish High School for five years before coming to USC in August, 2007. She currently teaches Hebrew language courses at the Hebrew Union College-Jewish Institute of Religion.

JULIA PHILLIPS COHEN is an Associate Professor in the Program in Jewish Studies and the Department of History at Vanderbilt University. She is the author of two award-winning books: *Becoming Ottomans: Sephardi Jews and Imperial Citizenship in the Modern Era* (Oxford University, 2014) and *Sephardi Lives: A Documentary History, 1700–1950* (Stanford University, 2014). Cohen's work has been supported by a number of grants, including fellowships from the National Endowment for the Humanities, the Stanford Humanities Center, the Foundation for Jewish Culture, the Memorial Foundation for Jewish Culture, the American Research Institute in Turkey, the Herbert D. Katz Center for Advanced Judaic Studies of the University of Pennsylvania, the Oxford Centre for Hebrew and Jewish Studies, and a Vanderbilt Chancellor's Award for Research. Her articles have appeared in a number of scholarly journals, including *American Historical Review, International Journal of Middle East Studies, Jewish Social Studies, Jewish Quarterly Review* and *AJS Perspectives*.

HASIA R. DINER is the Paul and Sylvia Steinberg Professor of American Jewish History and Professor of Hebrew in the Skirball Department of Hebrew and the Department of History at New York University. Her areas of research interest include American Jewish history, American immigration history, and women's history, and her honors have included the Guggenheim Fellowship and Fellow of the American Academy of Jewish Research. Dr. Diner's recent publications include *Roads Taken: The Great Jewish Migrations to the New World and the Peddlers Who Forged the Way* (Yale University, 2015) and *We Remember with Reverence and Love: American Jews and the Myth of Silence after the Holocaust, 1945–1962* (New York University, 2009), winner of the National Jewish Book Award and the Saul Viener Prize.

MATT GARCIA is Professor of Latin American, Latino & Caribbean Studies and History at Dartmouth College. He previously taught at Arizona State University, Brown University, University of Oregon, and the University of Illinois, Urbana-Champaign. He is the author of *A World of Its Own: Race, Labor and Citrus in the Making of Greater Los Angeles, 1900–1970* (University of North Carolina, 2001) that won the award for the best book from the Oral History Association in 2003. His book, *From the Jaws of Victory: The Triumph and Tragedy of Cesar Chavez and the Farm Worker Movement* (University of California, 2012), won the Philip Taft Award for the Best Book in Labor History, 2013. He is the co-editor of *Food Across Borders* with Melanie DuPuis and Don Mitchell published by Rutgers University Press in 2017. Garcia served as the outreach director and co-primary investigator for the Bracero Archive Project, which received a National Endowment for the Humanities Grant in 2008, and was the recipient of the Best Public History Award by the National Council for Public History in 2009–2010.

JONATHAN KARP is the author of *The Politics of Jewish Commerce: Economic Thought and Emancipation in Europe* (Cambridge University, 2008) and is completing a study of cultural and economic relations between American Jews and African Americans, entitled *Chosen Surrogates: How Blacks and Jews Transformed Modern American Culture.* He is also the editor of numerous volumes—most recently *The Cambridge History of Judaism: Volume 7, The Early Modern World, 1500–1815* (Cambridge University, 2017), with Adam Sutcliffe, and *World War I and the Jews* (Berghahn, 2017) with Marsha L. Rozenblit. From 2010–2013 he served as Executive Director of the American Jewish Historical Society.

REBECCA KOBRIN is the Russell and Bettina Knapp Associate Professor of American Jewish History at Columbia University. Her book *Jewish Bialystok and Its Diaspora:* (Indiana University, 2010), focuses on migrant Jews' relationship to their former homes in Eastern Europe and was awarded the Jordan Schnitzer prize in 2012. She is the editor of *Chosen Capital: The Jewish Encounter with American Capitalism* (Rutgers University, 2012), and is co-editor with Adam Teller of *Purchasing Power: The Economics of Jewish History* (University of Pennsylvania, 2015). Her forthcoming book, *A Credit to the Nation: Jewish Immigrant Bankers and American Finance, 1870–1930* (Harvard University, 2019), looks at East European Jews and the business of mass migration.

NIKI C. LEFEBVRE is currently Director of Natick Historical Society in Natick, Massachusetts. From 2017 to 2018 she held the Morton L. Mandel Presidential Fellowship at the American Academy of Arts and Sciences. Lefebvre's research considers the intersections of trade, politics, and the consumer sphere. She completed her dissertation, "Beyond the Flagship: Politics & Transatlantic Trade in American Department Stores, 1900–1945" under the direction of Professor Brooke Blower at Boston University. Lefebvre holds an MA in Public History from the University of Massachusetts Amherst and a PhD in American Studies from Boston University.

STEVEN J. ROSS is Professor of History at the University of Southern California, and Myron and Marian Director of the Casden Institute for the Study of the Jewish Role in American Life. He is the author of *Working-Class Hollywood: Silent Film and the Shaping of Class in America* (Princeton University, 1998), *Movies and American Society* (Blackwell, 2002), and *Hollywood Left and Right: How Movie Stars Shaped American Politics* (Oxford University, 2013), which received a Film Scholars Award from the Academy of Motion Picture Arts and Sciences. The *New York Times Book Review* selected *Hollywood Left and Right* as one of its "Recommended Summer Readings" for 2012. His recently published book, *Hitler in Los Angeles: How Jews and Their Spies Foiled Nazi Plots Against Hollywood and America* (Bloomsbury Press, 2017) was a 2018 finalist for the Pulitzer Prize in History. Ross's Op-Ed pieces have appeared in the *Los Angeles Times, Wall Street Journal, Washington Post, Politico.com*, and the *Huffington Post*.

DIANE VECCHIO is Professor and Chair of the History Department at Furman University in Greenville, SC. Her research interests include immigration history and the history of Upcountry South Carolina. Her recent publications include "The Scourge of the South: Pellagra and Poverty in Spartanburg's Mill Villages" (*Recovering the Piedmont Past*, edited by Paul Grady, vol. 2, University of South Carolina, 2018). She is also writing an economic history of the impact of textile manufacturing on Jewish migration to the Upcountry.

The USC Casden Institute for the Study of the Jewish Role in American Life

The American Jewish community has played a vital role in shaping the politics, culture, commerce and multiethnic character of Southern California and the American West. Beginning in the mid-nineteenth century, when entrepreneurs like Isaias Hellman, Levi Strauss and Adolph Sutro first ventured out West, American Jews became a major force in the establishment and development of the budding Western territories. Since 1970, the number of Jews in the West has more than tripled. This dramatic demographic shift has made California—specifically, Los Angeles—home to the second largest Jewish population in the United States. Paralleling this shifting pattern of migration, Jewish voices in the West are today among the most prominent anywhere in the United States. Largely migrating from Eastern Europe, the Middle East and the East Coast of the United States, Jews have invigorated the West, where they exert a considerable presence in every sector of the economy—most notably in the media and the arts. With the emergence of Los Angeles as a world capital in entertainment and communications, the Jewish perspective and experience in the region are being amplified further. From artists and activists to scholars and professionals, Jews are significantly influencing the shape of things to come in the West and across the United States. In recognition of these important demographic and societal changes, in 1998 the University of Southern California established a scholarly institute dedicated to studying contemporary Jewish life in America with special emphasis on the western United States. The Casden Institute explores issues related to the interface between the Jewish community and the broader, multifaceted cultures that form the nation—issues of relationship as much as of Jewishness itself. It is also enhancing the educational experience for students at USC and elsewhere by exposing them to the problems—and promise—of life in Los Angeles' ethnically, socially, culturally and economically diverse community. Scholars, students and community leaders examine the ongoing contributions of American Jews in the arts, business, media, literature, education, politics, law and social relations, as well as the relationships between Jewish Americans and other groups, including African Americans,

Latinos, Asian Americans and Arab Americans. The Casden Institute's scholarly orientation and contemporary focus, combined with its location on the West Coast, set it apart from—and makes it an important complement to—the many excellent Jewish Studies programs across the nation that center on Judaism from an historical or religious perspective.

For more information about the USC Casden Institute,
visit www.usc.edu/casdeninstitute, e-mail casden@usc.edu,
or call (213) 740-3405.